JOHN HUME
in
AMERICA

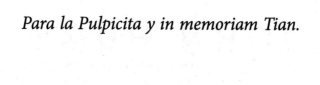

Para la Pulpicita y in memoriam Tian.

JOHN HUME
in
AMERICA

FROM DERRY TO DC

Maurice Fitzpatrick

IRISH ACADEMIC PRESS

First published in 2017 by
Irish Academic Press
10 George's Street
Newbridge
Co. Kildare
Ireland
www.iap.ie

ISBN 9781911024958 (Cloth)
ISBN 9781911024972 (Kindle)
ISBN 9781911024989 (Epub)
ISBN 9781911024996 (PDF)

British Library Cataloguing in Publication Data
An entry can be found on request

Library of Congress Cataloging in Publication Data
An entry can be found on request

Interior design by www.jminfotechindia.com
Typeset in Minion Pro 11/14 pt

Jacket design by www.phoenix-graphicdesign.com
Front jacket centre: Left to right: Tip O'Neill, Ronald Reagan, John Hume, Ted Kennedy and Peter Barry, St Patrick's Day, 1983. (Courtesy of the Seán Donlon Collection)
Top left: John Hume and Speaker Tip O'Neill, at O'Neill's ancestral home place in Drumfries, Co. Donegal, 1979. (Courtesy of *The Derry Journal*)
Top middle: John Hume and President Clinton in the Oval Office, 1990s. (Courtesy of the Hume Family Collection)
Top right: John Hume confronts a British army soldier at Magilligan Strand on 23 January 1972 during a protest against Internment Without Trial. (Courtesy of *The Derry Journal*)
Jacket back: President Bill Clinton, Pat Hume and John Hume, 1990s. (Courtesy of the Hume Family Collection).

CONTENTS

ACKNOWLEDGEMENTS

Michael Lillis has provided unremitting support for the book and was at all times unintrusive in offering his perspectives for which I am most grateful. I am also grateful to Frank Sheridan and Tom Fleming for their huge help in research; to Pat Hume, John Hume Jr and Aidan Hume and the Hume family for their comments and help; to Sean O'hUiginn for reading the book in an early draft. Responsibility for any mistakes is mine.

Infinite thanks to Marina for her endless patience with my absences and to Seamus and Bernadette Fitzpatrick, and Orla and Natasha Fitzpatrick. Thanks to Eoin Brophy, Josephine Farrelly and Hume Brophy.

I am grateful to the interviewees who include (in alphabetical order) Gerry Adams TD, Bertie Ahern, Tony Blair, Bono, President Jimmy Carter, President Bill Clinton, Senator Chris Dodd, Sir Jeffrey Donaldson, Ambassador Seán Donlon, Congressman Charles Dougherty, John A. Farrell, Robert Fisk, Mayor Ray Flynn, Loretta Brennan Glucksman, Pat Hume, Ambassador Robert Hunter, Taoiseach Enda Kenny, Senator Paul Kirk, Ambassador Michael Lillis, Sir John Major, Seamus Mallon, Eamonn McCann, Karl E. Meyer, Senator George Mitchell, Congressman Bruce Morrison, Matthew Murray, Congressman Richie Neal, Prof. Brendan O'Leary, Tom O'Neill, Ambassador Sean O'hUiginn, Paul Quinn, Ambassador Jean Kennedy Smith, Ted Smyth, Nancy Soderberg and Lord David Trimble.

Thanks also to Richard Ryan, Dr P.J. McLoughlin, Mark Durkan, Jim King, Prof. Ronan Fanning, Dr. Martin Mansergh, Phil Coulter, Austin Currie, Hugh Logue, Brian Barrington, Chuck Daly, Christine Daly, Ivan Cooper, Frank Costello, David McKittrick, Martin McGuinness, Ambassador Peter Jay, Jimmy Neary, Tom Melia and Kevin Cullen.

And thanks to Ciaran Murray, Tom Arnold, Paul Duane, Eugene and Adele Hutchinson, The American Ireland Funds, *The Derry Journal*, Sean McLaughlin, Dr. Niall Ó Dochartaigh, Donal Donovan, Mike Connolly and Becky Hitchcock, Tom O'Grady and Katie Conboy, Prof. Mike Cronin, Prof. Crawford Gribben, Jack Roney, Charles H. Dolan, Aideen Kane, Bill McNally, Francis and Gena McGrath, Joseph and Sabryna Reciniello. I am grateful for the institutional support of the Moore Institute NUI Galway, the Cavan Arts Council, Boston College Dublin and Queen's University Belfast.

He looked at this as a political process that was going to be
built upon different traditions and mutual respect. It was
going to be resolved in a political evolution ... A process was
going to be established that he believed could move the whole
debate and discussion within a non-violent framework and
could result eventually in some settlement ... It was important
to listen to someone who had suffered the way he had, and
had shown the courage and determination he had shown,
living on the ground as he was and experiencing the harshness
he was experiencing. I believe it's important to listen to the
ones who are risking their lives and are attempting to do it
in a non-violent way.

Ted Kennedy on his first meeting with John Hume in 1972
(interview with Edward M. Kennedy, 27 February 2006)

FOREWORD

John Hume: Founding Father

The all-party peace talks that began in Northern Ireland in June 1996 were the product of an effort that spanned decades and involved the British and Irish governments and political leaders from Ireland and Northern Ireland. The talks were cumbersome: two governments, ten political parties and the independent chairmen. The issues were complex and overlapping.

Many people contributed to that effort. But the primary architect, the person who conceived the manner in which all of the disparate parties and issues could be brought together, in a process that had some chance of success, was John Hume.

He understood the full dimensions of the conflict, especially that it was not just between Unionists and nationalists in Northern Ireland, but also included the relationships between Ireland and Northern Ireland and between Ireland and the United Kingdom. When the talks finally began, they were organized in three 'strands', in almost precisely the manner suggested by Hume years earlier. Twenty-two months later, when agreement was reached, it was in that same format.

Throughout human history, great leaders have emerged to lead their societies into and out of conflict. The successful leaders were those who had a large and positive vision, and the courage and stamina to lift themselves and their followers to a higher level of expectation and performance.

In Northern Ireland John Hume was that leader. His vision of Northern Ireland was acquired over the years of his immersion in the difficult and dangerous life of a society in conflict; a society torn by anger, hostility, fear and anxiety. It is hard to have a grand vision when bullets are flying. But John Hume was unique, an extraordinary leader who was able to offer, in his personal courage and his sharp and incisive mind and rhetoric, a new way. In the United States we would call him a 'Founding Father'.

Politically, the nationalists were divided between the Social Democratic and Labour Party, led by Hume, and Sinn Féin, led by Gerry Adams. They had taken different paths toward their common goal. Hume insisted that the nationalists be reconciled to a single approach, and that the only way forward was through the political process. With Adams and the Prime Minister of Ireland, Albert Reynolds, a unified approach was agreed.

A ceasefire was declared in the summer of 1994 by the IRA; it led to a reciprocal ceasefire by the Loyalist paramilitaries. That laid the foundation. Then, many others joined in building the edifice of peace.

David Trimble and Reg Empey, leaders of the Ulster Unionist Party, were essential to the Agreement; David Ervine and Gary McMichael were the leaders of small but important Loyalist parties; also small but influential were the women of Northern Ireland, led at the talks by Monica McWilliams and Pearl Sagar. Adams's colleague Martin McGuinness, and Hume's colleagues, Seamus Mallon and Mark Durkan, were major contributors, as were John Alderdice and his colleagues in the Alliance Party. Later, at St Andrews, in a critical turning point, Ian Paisley and Peter Robinson led the Democratic Unionist Party to take a major step forward. A succession of Prime Ministers created and maintained the momentum for peace: John Major and Tony Blair in the UK, and Albert Reynolds, John Bruton and Bertie Ahern in Ireland. Bill Clinton was the first American president to become fully engaged in the effort to end the conflict in Northern Ireland.

The negotiating process, which I chaired with my colleagues, General John de Chastelain and Prime Minister Harri Holkeri, was slow and difficult; it was, as I have previously noted, the product of decades of effort. Among the earlier major steps was the Anglo-Irish Agreement (1985); it committed the two governments to work together to bring the conflict to an end. The Downing Street Declaration (1993) built on that; in it the British Government made clear that it had no strategic or long-term interest in controlling Northern Ireland. A series of Prime Ministers reaffirmed that policy.

Another major factor was the creation of the European Union. There the United Kingdom and the Republic of Ireland worked together, along with two dozen other European countries, for a common and great objective: a peaceful and a prosperous Europe. Perhaps without even recognising it, British and Irish leaders became acclimated to dealing with each other; gradually the cold hostility that had marked their relationship dissipated.

John Hume was full of life and energy, a natural leader, a man who took courageous and personally dangerous positions all his life, in an effort to find a way forward in Northern Ireland. I am deeply gratified that a history of his work with American leaders has now been written.

Senator George J. Mitchell
October 2017

PREFACE

This book is a companion to a film I made on the same subject, *In the Name of Peace: John Hume in America,* which was funded by the Irish Film Board, the BAI, RTÉ and the DFAT and has already been released. Where quotations have not been cited, the reader may assume that they derive from interviews conducted in the course of making the film.

A common assumption when a book and film on the same subject co-exist is that the book brought the film forth. My experience has been rather the opposite. In an earlier book/film, *The Boys of St. Columb's,* I discovered very late in the day that I was writing a book as well making a film. It was during that production that I interviewed John Hume and discovered the breadth of his connections with US politicians. I heard about the Four Horsemen straight from the Fifth Horseman's mouth and, in time, I grew determined to tell the story of Hume in America both in book and film form.

While elected and re-elected to the parliaments of Northern Ireland, Britain and Europe over a timespan of thirty-five years, this book asserts that John Hume's role as a political strategist and touchstone of credibility in the eyes of politicians in the United States Congress and in the White House from 1972 to 1998 was the most decisive and far-reaching dimension of his political life. Hume has won the Nobel Prize for Peace, the Martin Luther King Peace Award, and the International Gandhi Peace Prize – the only person ever to win all three. His distinction is widely, though not uncritically, accepted yet the full significance of what he achieved is not so often fully understood or documented. For instance, Hume's work in the US has not even received book-length treatment. This study attempts to do that.

Maurice Fitzpatrick, 2017

1

The Journey towards Politics, 1964–74

John Hume, the man who did more than anyone else to break one of Europe's most bitter and intractable stalemates by creating a constituency of support for peace at the highest levels of the United States, made his first major political statement at a national level in May 1964. The editor of *The Irish Times*, Douglas Gageby, asked him – then an unknown school teacher from Derry – to write two articles to illustrate for the *Irish Times* readership in the South of Ireland the political dilemmas faced by the Catholic minority in the North. Hume's arguments in those articles were every bit as revelatory as Gageby had hoped, and they underlay much of Hume's political thinking since that time.

In 1964, Northern Ireland was conspicuously absent from print reportage in the South, and consciously avoided by the national broadcaster. *Radharc in Derry*, a documentary film made in August 1964, a few months after the appearance of Hume's *Irish Times* articles, only aired on RTÉ twenty-five years later, and was introduced thus: 'In an act of self-censorship the then controller of RTÉ, Gunnar Rugheimer, decided that this material was too sensitive for transmission and the programme was shelved.' The sensitive aspects of the material meant the way division and discrimination were highlighted. The plight of the Northern Ireland Catholic was met with official indifference in Dublin.

Yet the articles Gageby commissioned were novel. They argued that the question of Northern Ireland was neither resolvable through the irredentist claims of the Irish Constitution, nor was it a matter which Dublin could properly ignore and the Irish government, led by Seán Lemass, was beginning to acknowledge that fact. A few months after the articles were published, a tentative detente began between Dublin and Belfast: Taoiseach Seán Lemass and Prime Minister Terence O'Neill met at Stormont in January 1965 and in Dublin in February 1965, the first time that the Taoiseach and Prime Minister of Northern Ireland had met since partition.

In the 1960s, Hume was beginning to gain prominence in Derry – as a public debater and as a businessman in an initiative to smoke the salmon catch in Derry and export it. He had written an MA thesis focusing on the North-West region, which later led to his making a documentary about Derry, *A City Solitary*. It was on the basis of *A City Solitary* that Hume was asked to write the articles for *The Irish Times*. Entitled 'The Northern Catholic', Hume addressed the complete disaffection and disenfranchisement felt by the Catholic population who lived in Northern Ireland. Equally, though, Hume expressed the inadequacy of the response of the Nationalist Party to these dilemmas. In the minds of young people in the Catholic minority, he wrote, there was a 'struggle for priority' between the realities of social problems – unavailability of housing, unemployment, the push to emigration – and the hackneyed slogans championing a United Ireland.

Hume was anxious to highlight the faults of Nationalism in Northern Ireland for holding up the ideals of a United Ireland as a panacea to cure profound underlying problems, which would endure irrespective of any alteration to the constitutional arrangements. The magical thinking of Nationalism was, he argued, an excuse for having failed to deliver any real political gains to its electorate:

> In forty years of opposition [the Nationalist Party] have not produced one constructive contribution on either the social or economics plane to the development of Northern Ireland which is, after all, a substantial part of the United Ireland for which they strive. Leadership has been the comfortable leadership of flags and slogans … It is this lack of positive contribution and the apparent lack of interest in the general welfare of Northern Ireland that has led many Protestants to believe that the Northern Catholic is politically irresponsible and immature and therefore unfit to rule.[1]

Having stated the negative perception of the Northern Catholic, Hume then proposed a new approach which would enable an exit from the futile bind that the Nationalist Party represented:

The position should be immediately clarified by an acceptance of the Constitutional position. There is nothing inconsistent with such acceptance and a belief that a thirty-two county republic is best for Ireland. Such a change would remove what has been a great stumbling block to the development of normal politics in the North. Catholics could then throw themselves fully into the solution of Northern problems without fear of recrimination.

Hume acknowledged the blatant discrimination in the North, but also called for the minority to address the apparatus of exclusion in the State through constructive politics, modernisation from within rather than boycott. Accepting this premise, Hume suggested that the initiative lay with the 'Northern Catholic' to create a politics of change by evolution:

> The necessity for a fully organised democratic party which can freely attract and draw upon the talents of the nationally-minded community is obvious. It is to be hoped that the new Nationalist Political Front will create such an organisation so that we shall never in future be embarrassed by one of our political representatives declaring on television that he was not an encyclopedia when asked to produce figures to substantiate his charges of discrimination.

Finally, throwing down the gauntlet to would-be political activists, Hume asserted the centrality of an inclusive economic programme to transcend the division: 'Community activity, in which all sections play their part can do nothing but create mutual respect and, above all, build the country with our own hands.'[2] Read more than a half century after their publication, Hume's articles were extraordinarily prescient. In his insistence that the mode of change needed to be gradualist, participatory and inclusive; in his identifying the endgame for the divided people in Northern Ireland, Hume identified the Northern problem correctly. Even before the eruption of the Troubles, Hume was a diagnostician of the core principles required to heal the society's ills.

Since the remit of the articles is an examination of the 'Northern Catholic', there is perhaps a disproportionate emphasis on the Catholic role as an agent of change in the political landscape of Northern Ireland. It is important to remember that other political reforms intrinsic to the

Protestant community were also necessary. As Seamus Deane has written: 'As soon as sectarianism is seen to be the basis upon which many Protestants accept unnecessary poverty (and thereby uphold the grotesquely large property holdings of this small group of [wealthy Unionist] families) then the feudal basis of Unionism will have vanished.'[3] Even if the articles appear to ask a lot of the minority and not enough of the majority, they are outstanding in identifying the essential elements required of the minority to achieve an equitable settlement in the North. Remembering that the embrace of violent methods to advance political aims was at that time dormant in Northern politics, Hume's constructive vision was a necessary antidote.

The softness of tone in Hume's articles hardly matched the desperate circumstances in which Northern Catholics found themselves, nor did it match the fervid tone which John Hume would later, as a practising politician, often take in criticising the intransigence of Unionism and the British government which validated it. In protests such as the one to establish the second university of Northern Ireland in Derry, the 'University for Derry' campaign, fought throughout the 1960s, the doctrinaire indifference to the minority's plea for justice hardened Hume's stance. By the time he became an elected representative of the Foyle constituency in February 1969, Hume was firmly of the view that well-intentioned cross community cooperation alone would not move the Unionist government to concede basic civil rights demands.

The Early Years

John Hume was born in Derry in 1937 and was the beneficiary of radical educational reform (the 1947 Education Act) which enabled children from working-class backgrounds to access free education. Hume's secondary education took place in St Columb's College in Derry and he attended university at Maynooth where he specialised in French and History. He was, as his wife Pat Hume recounts, 'the eldest of seven children, born in very poor circumstances in the gerrymandered city. So he was very conscious of politics, not the tribal politics but practical politics'.[4] Practical politics for Hume took the form of a variety of jobs, roles and initiatives when he was in his twenties: he was a key member of the Irish League of Credit Unions and became its president at the age of 27; he taught full-time at St

Columb's College in Derry; he was a member of the Housing Association of Derry; he was a leader of the University for Derry campaign. Pat Hume remembers that he was 'always very conscious of restoring dignity to the Catholic people of the North'.

James Sharkey, a teaching colleague at St Columb's and later Irish ambassador, recalls that Hume was deeply rooted in history, which also informed his political views: 'I used to drop in at the back of his modern history class. It was clear that the great constitutionalists – Grattan, O'Connell and Parnell – for Hume were not simply admirable historical figures, but they were also exemplars on whom you could base political judgements and political approaches.' Through Hume's reading of the ways in which Irish constitutional leaders in the eighteenth and nineteenth centuries had used the political process to advance their aims, he arrived at a firm conclusion about his own tactical approach: to move away from the traditional Northern Nationalists' self-definition as Anti-Partitionists. As Phil Coulter, a school friend of Hume's, observed, 'any party defining itself under an anti-anything rubric, does not speak volumes about what are they for'.

Thus, one of the things that Hume managed to do from the very beginning of his public life in the sixties was to work from within the political structure of Northern Ireland to benefit the Catholic minority, deploying the logic that if there is a one-man, one-vote system in England, then why not the same in the Northern Irish State? What rankled the Nationalist minority in the North of Ireland more than the fact that they lived in a State into which they had been corralled without their democratic consent, was the way in which the administration of that State had from the point of its foundation systematically excluded them from participation and stymied their prosperity. As former Irish Ambassador Sean O'hUiginn has noted:

Hume is a conservative in an Edmund Burke sense, in that he has a keen sense that a community that rejects the framework in which they operate, that they do not have any sense of identity with institutions governing them, is an unstable community. When you, as it were, superimposed the red lines of the different forces that play in Northern Ireland, you got quite a small area where a compromise might be found. Hume focused on that with great persistence.

After the publication of the *Irish Times* articles, Hume was encouraged by some friends and supporters to run for election, but he declined. He instead acted as election agent for Claude Wilton ('Vote for Claude the Catholic Prod') in 1965, while Hume retained his job as a teacher. However, the latter part of the 1960s was a period of a rapidly rising political temperature in Derry, with several aspects of governmental callousness converging to prompt Hume's decision to become prominently active in public affairs.

The first augury of the Civil Rights Movement was the University for Derry protest in February 1965, which was remarkable in that it represented the entire community of Derry. Hume fronted this cross-community rally and motorcade to Stormont Parliament in February 1965 to establish the 'second university' in Derry, the 'second city' of the Northern Irish State. This 25,000-strong motorcade was one of the earliest and strongest expressions of non-violent protest in Northern Ireland, and was comparable in intent and conviction to the Selma to Montgomery march, led by Martin Luther King the following month, March 1965.

The campaign to establish a university in Derry failed when, on the basis of the Lockwood Report (1965), the second university was established in Coleraine, a predominately Protestant market town, rather than in largely Catholic Derry City. This decision was entirely in line with other bigoted policies emanating from Stormont: the Benson Report (1963) cut rail infrastructure to the western part of the North dramatically; the Matthew Report (1963) situated Northern Ireland's 'new city' at Craigavon and consequently the infrastructure in the North orientated still more on the eastern and predominantly Protestant part of the State. Moreover, economic woes attended these political injustices: the shipping line between Derry and Glasgow was closed and the Birmingham Sound Reproducers (BSR) factory, which had employed 1,700 people, closed in 1967. Poverty in Derry City had noticeably worsened just as the political grievances accumulated.

Above all, the rigged system of allocating houses embittered the predominately Nationalist electoral ward of Derry. As journalist and activist Eamonn McCann observed: 'We had thousands of people on a housing list and everybody in Derry knew that one of the reasons that more houses were not being built was that … to give a person a house was to give them a vote: only householders could vote and the Unionist Party in Derry had to be very circumspect about to whom it handed a vote.'

Unsurprisingly, then, it was more than anything else the housing situation that made it inevitable for John Hume to enter parliamentary politics. The property qualification for franchise in Derry meant that unequal housing allocation (in addition to being a source of misery in itself) produced a concomitant political injustice – it deprived Catholics of the vote. Having been corralled into confined and overcrowded areas, like the working-class Bogside, their surroundings continually reminded them of the inequality of the State. A visitor to Derry at the time, who viewed the Bogside from the higher grounds of St Columb's College, commented on the rising chimney smoke of the area and remarked on 'the smouldering fires of Derry'.[5]

In 1968, Paddy 'Bogside' Doherty, an influential community activist, asked Hume to consider running for election. Hume judged, based on the five years of activism leading up to the 1969 election, that to effect decisive political change required becoming an elected representative. It was both the next logical and necessary step: community activism, documentary film-making, publishing journalistic articles, becoming the President of the Irish Credit Union and taking business initiatives was still not enough.

The Catholic minority, and Hume too, had lost patience with the putatively reformist Terence O'Neill (Prime Minister of Northern Ireland, 1963–9). O'Neill's persona, in stark contrast to his predecessors, was relatively ecumenical and open to interaction with Catholics. He exuded a fresh, well-meaning approach to including the Catholic minority in the affairs of Northern Ireland, to make them stakeholders. Yet, as a reformist he was ineffective. In his *Autobiography*, O'Neill expressed disappointment that the Catholics of Northern Ireland did not support him enough to pass 'liberalising' legislation.

His disappointment was naïve. Despite his well-meaning rhetoric, O'Neill's tenure as Prime Minister was characterised by retrograde steps to marginalise and to alienate the minority, which even the more reasonable strands of the Catholic minority perceived as a provocation. O'Neill faced decisive opposition to his tentative reform from the ranks of his own Unionist Party (which ultimately conspired to remove him from office) and he was unable to carry his reform measures. Hume was later to say:

> I cannot forget that the administration which is about to go out of office is the administration which created Craigavon [the Matthew Report] as a second city, instead of Derry. I cannot forget that it

produced development plans for Ballymena, Bangor, Antrim, Larne, et cetera, before one was forced out of it for Derry. I cannot forget that it is the administration of Benson and the closure of the railways ... it was also the administration of Lockwood and the creation of the second university in a market town ... No economic risks were taken to develop the Indian territory that lies on the other side of the Sperrins. What we have received we have received because it has been forced.[6]

Having been cut off from its natural hinterland of Donegal/Inishowen by partition, Hume believed that only cross border cooperation consolidated by governmental support would help to develop the North-West. Yet, given how Stormont was constituted, such cooperation was very remote. Remembering Frederick Douglass's dictum that 'power concedes nothing without a demand', the move towards politics on the part of Hume was animated by a profound sense of alienation from the political structures that existed. The 'awakening of conscience' (as Hume had called the University for Derry campaign) was not followed by the requisite recognition of the Catholic minority, especially in the western part of the State, nor any acknowledgement that it was being deliberately immiserated by its government.

A fundamental aspect of Hume's political life was to reimagine a politics capable of transcending ancient historical constraints and to envisage Ireland benefiting from wider international partnerships; his will to seek and ability to find support for his reconciliation agenda in broader spheres – Europe and America. In the case of the latter, when he went to America and read, on the memorial to Abraham Lincoln, *E pluribus unum* 'Out of many, we are one', he believed that Northern Ireland's divided people also had much to learn from such a cultivation of diversity. As his wife Pat explained: 'He felt that here were people who had had to leave the place of their birth because of conflict, because of intolerance and they went to the United States and they were able to come together under the one constitution. He felt that this was the model, why can we not get over our differences?' Eamonn McCann elaborates:

John saw things, unlike the old Nationalist Party, in a European context. Even before he became a Member of the European Parliament he would talk about the resolution of conflicts within Europe after World War Two. He also was very acutely aware of the American dimension, right from the very beginning and, from the beginning, he was relating to US power. It did not make sense to him to talk in Harlem to Black Panthers. He wanted to talk to the White House.

A more extensive analysis of the wider circles of Hume's influences will come in subsequent chapters. However, before Hume formally entered parliamentary politics, he became engaged in the most dramatic and far-reaching shift in the political landscape of Northern Ireland since its foundation: the Civil Rights Movement.

The Civil Rights Movement

One of the defining moments of modern Irish history was the first civil rights march in Derry on 5 October 1968: due both to the march itself and the RUC violence that repelled it. The civil rights campaign was a radical new direction in a society that very badly needed it. From the first it was an inclusive movement, open to everyone who wished to establish civil rights in Northern Ireland. Even so, the difficulties of creating a broad-based political movement in a society where politics had resolutely broken down on sectarian lines persisted. As James Sharkey, who was there, recalls:

> On the fifth of October I remember having a debate with someone and I said, 'I wonder how many unionists, how many working class Protestants are here today?' I felt that maybe things were just a little bit too early, because if you got off on the wrong foot you could be seen as sectarian. The great success of John Hume, I would argue, has been his persistent focus on the concept of reconciliation.[7]

Whatever is said about its necessity, inevitability or desirability, the efficacy of the Civil Rights Movement in Northern Ireland is undeniable: it gained many of its core demands almost immediately on the basis that it remained non-violent and determined. Even in his earliest awakening as a civil rights campaigner in the streets of Derry, it was always clear that it simply did not occur to Hume to resort to throwing stones at the police. Much as that temptation was prevalent in the community, and the provocation was strong, Hume did not believe in the efficacy of violence. Film footage exists of Hume lecturing Derry teenagers to 'have a bit of sense' rather than to fight back physically against the Unionist government's security forces. Hume's Social Democratic and Labour Party (SDLP) colleague, Denis Haughey, remembers that the importance of that stance was to 'preserve the integrity' of the moral case that a rights-based reform programme sought. Another of Hume's colleagues, Seamus Mallon, elaborates:

> Hume had the vision to see that violence wasn't going to solve the problem, that the British Government was never going to really tackle the problem, that the Irish Government had just wakened up to the fact that there was a Northern Ireland. The Civil Rights Movement in America inspired John. It started with this very simple phrase: 'things can be done, if we do them the right way'.

Mallon remembers a defining moment of the type that led both he and Hume to fully embrace politics:

> One day somebody who I had gone to school with came to me. He lived in a hovel and had no running water, no toilet facilities. He said, 'Seamus, I went to George Woods [the local Unionist councillor] and I asked for a house. He told me "no Catholic pig or his litter would get a house in Markethill" as long as he was there'. I could not get that out of my mind.

Mallon, like Hume and many others, was a beneficiary of the 1947 Education Act and had obtained a university degree. As a teacher he was, like Hume, economically comfortable. He also had, like Hume, a strong sense of responsibility for those of his own community who did not have the education to adequately defend themselves against such institutional prejudice and contempt. Mallon elaborates:

> The Civil Rights Movement was beginning to expand and I knew it was the way to go. I could not have walked away from it without trying to do something. There was a man selected to become a councillor in the first council election: I got home from school, and my wife said to me, 'that guy has pulled out'. Between four o'clock and five I had

to get a candidate. There came a crucial point where I had to accept that I was not going to get one. Were we going to give this seat to the Unionists and let them do what they were doing? Going into politics was no decision of mine.

The Unionist Reaction

The intensity of the depravations suffered by the Northern minority had crystallised in the Civil Rights Movement's protests. However, rather than having the emancipatory effect of bringing both sides closer together to create an equitable political structure, the movement exposed demons within Unionism and the bias of the British parliament which supported it. This combination eventually fuelled the rationale for an alternative response to the injustice of Northern Ireland, the armed guerrilla struggle launched by the Irish Republican Army (IRA). In the following, James Sharkey gives a comprehensive sweep of the declension of Unionist responses to the changes demanded in Northern Ireland in 1968–72:

> Equality for all was the determining motif of the civil rights campaign. Unionism could not accommodate this demand; it imploded, it factionalised, it fragmented. Unionists eventually found solidarity in a sort of sectarian intransigence and they operated with very severe policing. They saw IRA conspiracies everywhere at a time when the IRA barely existed in Northern Ireland. Through their inflexibility, their heavy-handedness, their discrimination, they provoked the revival and recruitment of the IRA, the force in history which they hated and feared most. The two of them became locked in a sort of lethal, cadaverous embrace and that set the scene for the early 1970's: spirals of violence and counter-violence, the British got drawn into it in a one-sided way. And it fell to people like Hume and other leaders to point the way forward, to look for political structures that could accommodate all these different tensions, including a role for the Irish government – and that was broadly the message that Hume carried to the United States.

The reaction within Unionism to reasonable demands on the part of the minority in Northern Ireland was extreme: the security forces of the State countered non-violent protest with violence; Unionism also spawned the illegal UVF in 1966 and later popular movements such as Vanguard, which had David Trimble as its legal advisor and whose leader, Bill Craig, said in a famous speech in Belfast's Ormeau Park: 'we'll liquidate the enemy'. Was such language, and the position he was taking, unsettling to adherents of the movement? David Trimble recalls: 'Bill was using that language in the hope that it would make London stop and think. Unfortunately, they didn't.' Even so, as a matter of principle or morality, and recalling twentieth-century history, was the language 'to liquidate the enemy' not disturbing? 'No, look, I don't think one should pay too much attention to those words and what was said,' recalls David Trimble. 'The substance of the matter was that at the time, governments were driving towards what became the Sunningdale Agreement [in 1973]. The Sunningdale Agreement was a mistake.'

Hume was representative of a generation of young Catholic graduates who used politics and the legal apparatus to take cases and adopt a civilised approach to resolving this – is that fair to say? David Trimble: 'I don't find it particularly helpful to be going back over that. If we take the issue of housing, it was suggested that local councils were discriminatory in housing and that is acknowledged. You can point to the fact that there was some inventive boundary drawing.' Trimble acknowledged that the Unionist point of view 'would have regarded the Civil Rights Movement as being unnecessary and as being something that opened the door to violence. In the early days, the Unionist man in the street, I'm afraid, would have lumped all the Catholic political leadership together as being the people who effectively created the violence. Not a particularly fair judgement but that was the general view'.

Trimble's reflection, that Unionism viewed the Civil Rights Movement as unnecessary, is correct in the sense that it was unnecessary for the perpetuation of the Unionist monolith. His second point, that it opened the door to violence, was given amplification in the South by writer and former Irish Labour Party politician, Conor Cruise O'Brien: 'Would the removal of the disabilities of Catholics in the Northern Ireland electorate be worth taking at the risk of precipitating riots, explosions, pograms, murders?'[8] The argument propounded by Conor Cruise O'Brien was that a Civil Rights Movement could easily beget a violent movement and that such a movement could be hijacked. How can such risks be weighed against the injustices that the Civil Rights Movement sought to remedy? Austin Currie, John Hume's close political colleague and co-founder of the SDLP, recalls: 'It was John Hume who said that when you throw a rock into a lake it will cause ripples but you [weren't] quite sure where the ripples would continue. You do something that you see as being an objective which will be successful and useful and there can be other consequences. It's always the danger to any agitation.'

As David Trimble has indicated, there were a variety of Unionist perspectives about this new rights-demanding movement. The more hardline people were in denial that the rights demanded were ever withheld. There was also a perception that the Civil Rights Movement was merely a vehicle for the IRA to generate enough chaos to gather itself into an armed struggle for a United Ireland. It was never going to be ecumenical, even though it might have started with that ideal. As Irish political and constitutional expert, Brendan O'Leary, says: 'The truth is that the Civil Rights Movement was a coalition. It contained communists, it contained socialists, it contained Republicans disillusioned with previous IRA and Sinn Féin activity. It included Northern Nationalists unhappy with the Nationalist Party.'

It also contained Protestants, particularly those who had been to Queen's University Belfast in the 1960s and who were willing to discuss options for building a new society together. There was a pervasive view that when people from a Unionist background made any form of coalition with those from a Nationalist background it was tantamount to ceding political ground. When Ivan Cooper, for example, a liberal from a Church of Ireland background, became a civil rights activist and formed a political alliance with John Hume, friends and neighbours from his village, Killaloo in County Derry, were openly contemptuous of his 'betrayal'. Even among younger and educated Unionists, there came to be a clash between conscience and tribal instincts; typically, the latter won out. Brendan O'Leary relates: 'We know from the archives that the O'Neill cabinet, right up to 1968, knows that it's wrong not to have universal suffrage in local government but it's obsessed by the fact that if they apply universal local government suffrage, Nationalists are going to gain twice as many votes as Unionists and they're going to lose all of the west.' As previously noted, the legacy of the O'Neill cabinet was not only a failure to reform the rigged franchise, making mass protest and civil disobedience to force them to do so practically inevitable, for good measure it also disinvested the west.

Parallels between the Irish and American Civil Rights Movements

A future US leader from the American South, Bill Clinton, who in 1968 was a Rhodes Scholar at Oxford University, observed:

> I first became aware of John Hume when he became widely written about in the news and the SDLP was attempting to do the most difficult of all things, which is to be an inclusive political party in a polarising time. We know what works in the world is inclusive politics, inclusive economics, [and] inclusive social policies, but the more people are polarised and distrusting – and particularly if they're shooting guns – the more difficult it is to say, 'I'm for inclusive cooperation, I'm for peace', and John just held the line. He wanted an inclusive peace and he thought that non-violence was the best way to pursue it. He was the Irish conflict's Martin Luther King or Gandhi and I thought as a tactical matter he was right.

Informed by the American Civil Rights Movement, the leaders of the Northern Ireland Civil Rights Movement saw that rights could be very rapidly obtained through non-violent mass protest. In the United States, the events from Bloody Sunday in Selma on 7 March 1965, to the successful march in Selma under federal protection on 21 March 1965, to the passage of the federal Voting Rights Act on 6 August 1965, showed that enormous strides towards full participation in society could be achieved, and quickly. In the view of Brendan O'Leary, 'by adopting the methods of the American Civil Rights Movement, what Hume and a range of others did, particularly Austin Currie inside the Nationalist Party, was to reorient the strategy, both as a strategy of protest against the Belfast government and to be heard by the London government in insisting on British rights for British citizens'.

This strategy put the British government in an untenable moral position. As Gandhi had done in the 1940s, the Civil Rights Movement used the principles that the British government purported to uphold against them by demonstrating that they were being honoured in the breach. Similarly, in the United States, the appeal to sacred ideals of the founding documents by the Civil Rights Movement also eventually turned the tide in American public opinion. At all times Hume, despite the escalation of violence, nevertheless continually looked to the model of Martin Luther King, and his insistence, especially when circumstances became very intense in the US, that the movement must remain non-violent. Other parallels with the American Civil Rights Movement abound, as Brendan O'Leary elucidates:

> In both the American and Northern Irish contexts, communities were subject to local control, and in both cases a local majority discriminated against a local minority. The local majorities organised themselves, sought exclusive patronage over public appointments, they monopolised the local policing, the local security forces, the local judiciary, and in some jurisdictions they disenfranchised the minority. In both cases, the local majority also discriminated against the local minority. The discrimination extended to both public employment and private employment – members of the minority community were not hired or, if hired, were not promoted. As African-Americans mobilised behind the banner of their constitutional rights as American citizens, Northern Nationalists in the Civil Rights Movement mobilised behind the demand for equal rights as British citizens.

The February 1969 Election

In a State which had raised parliamentary elections to a high level of irrelevancy, the February 1969 election was a dramatic break with tradition, a crucible in which radically differing goals and aspirations and methods for achieving them were, for the first time in the history of the Northern Irish State, exposed to the reality of the ballot sheet. Eamonn McCann, a candidate in that election in the Derry (Foyle) constituency, describes the principles defining that election, in its Derry context, as follows:

> People like John were looking for what was called British rights for British citizens. It seemed a rather modest ambition. I had a more

radical agenda, a socialist agenda. The election in February 1969 was called with the prime minister of the day, Terence O'Neill, and a famous broadcast said: 'What kind of Ulster do you want, Ulster is at the crossroads'. It was a crossroads election. John won the election beating the old Nationalist Party leader Eddie McAteer and myself. That signalled and demonstrated that John's style of looking for … not a United Ireland, but looking for equal rights within Northern Ireland and advocating a strong but moderate way of pursuing that, matched the mood of the people to a greater extent … than Eddie McAteer or myself.

McCann's socialist approach failed to command broad appeal and the Nationalist Party, with its age-old strains of indignation and abstentionism, was effectively wiped away. Throughout its decades of existence, it had achieved nothing other than managing to speak to the Nationalists' sense of being a minority, of being deprived. The party that effectively swept it away, though still in formation in 1969, was the SDLP.

Hume's approach spoke to the electorate and it was to continue to do so for the next three decades, as Hume topped the poll again and again. In 1969, he had stood for the principles of inclusion and justice. Neither socialism nor nationalism had appealed to the Derry electorate as much. The words 'justice' and 'inclusion' may well resemble the pat words of many politicians at the hustings, yet the degree of injustice and exclusion that the Catholic electorate in Derry faced meant that the mandate Hume sought went to the core of their dilemmas. It also had resonance beyond Northern Ireland, first in Britain where the media attempted to convey the causes of the Northern problem, which helps to explain why, that same year, Hume's profile was noticed by Senator Ted Kennedy.

Terence O'Neill was later to say that he called what he termed the 'crossroads' election to give the people of Northern Ireland the chance to break the mould of sectarian politics.[9] In electing a candidate such as Hume, the electorate had availed of that chance, since one of the four basic principles Hume articulated in seeking a mandate to form a social democratic movement was that it 'must be completely non-sectarian and must root out a fundamental evil in our society, sectarian division'.[10] But the tragedy was that the Unionists did not perceive it so.

Hume the Parliamentarian

The newly minted MP, elected to represent the Foyle constituency at the Parliament of Northern Ireland, had never before held political office. Nevertheless, he gave the impression of one who had considerably more experience than his thirty-two years and novice status might indicate. He had already represented Ireland in the United States during his presidency of the Irish Credit Union, and he was alert to the wider movements of the world, which were gathering pace: from Prague to Memphis equality movements were challenging traditions and demanding new approaches to politics. Such changes were the nub of what the Parliament of Northern Ireland in Stormont had stood against. Even so, Hume had considerable confidence in himself and in his approach to politics. The least parliamentary of parliaments, the atmosphere in Stormont towards the new, articulate generation hungry to establish themselves in Northern Ireland could hardly have been less welcoming. Yet, in spite of such intolerance, the sclerotic and self-perpetuating cycle of the rigged parliament was about to be unsettled by a parliamentarian of uncommon ability.

As Parnell and his party had done in Westminster in the 1880s, Hume and others managed to use the parliamentary process to shame Stormont into facing up to the injustices of the State. Those injustices included gerrymander, sectarian housing allocation and hiring policies. Increasingly, those injustices – when challenged by public protests – had in turn spawned further injustices: in the judiciary, in policing and in legislation to give validation to them. On 3 April 1969, for instance, on the floor of parliament Hume spoke of the nexus between housing allocation and political patronage: 'Each petty potentate in each little rural electoral division allocates all the houses in that division and perpetuates himself in power. That is part of the housing policy ... the political jobbery which has been a root cause of the social injustices.'[11] In so doing, Hume challenged politicians for lacking the communal instincts which would have tended to the needs of all of the people they represented: 'If the Government were to take a referendum they would find that the people would be in favour of reform. The people who would resist it would be the local Caesars who would lose their power and would not be able to shove their cronies and party hacks into jobs.'

Another consequence of this, for Hume, was that the Unionist government, by abdicating from its responsibilities to govern fairly, invalidated both its own authority and made it harder for anyone in the parliament to assert the need for democratic processes. By energetically hacking away at the root of sustainable government – respect for authority – Unionists were, Hume argued, destroying the possibility of people having faith in the State itself:

> One fine day some students in this community announced that they were going to hold sit-downs and occupy public buildings. The Government react immediately like frightened rabbits and decide to make them illegal without giving any real or due consideration to what they are doing. What they have done is that they have refused to listen to grievances aired in Parliament and have left a large section of the community with very little faith in Parliament or in parliamentary democracy by refusing to listen to grievances.[12]

Fearing the growth of the IRA, Hume urged Unionist MPs to understand that, when the rule of law falls into disrepute, then people will feel that 'they have a duty to break that law'.[13] How, when such pleas were consistently ignored, did Hume respond? When rational argument failed, Hume, along with Ivan Cooper and Paddy Devlin – future co-founders of the Social Democratic and Labour Party – and others, would occasionally take over the floor in the middle of the House and sing 'We Shall Overcome', thereby replicating in parliament the modality of protest that existed on the street. In addition, this ongoing dialogue of the deaf in Stormont naturally elicited from Hume and his colleagues the obstructionism tactic that Parnell and his party had practised in Westminster a century earlier. (Parnell remained a central influence on Hume throughout his political life: shortly after being elected to Westminster, when he discovered that there was no recognition of Charles Stewart Parnell in the Houses of Parliament, he sought donations from MPs to ensure that a bust of Parnell was sculpted, which was placed close to Committee Room 15, where Parnell's party had split.) Throughout his time in Stormont, Hume's unqualified belief in parliamentary politics remained steadfast: his eagerness to put an argument on the record in *Hansard*, even when its practical impact seemed elusive, indicates not only a respect for parliamentary politics, but also a sharp sense of history.

Hume was later to say in Westminster that the central problem of the British having created in Northern Ireland a system based on a sectarian headcount was that 'When one tells the majority that it can protect itself only by remaining in majority, one invites it to maintain sectarian solidarity as the only means of protection. Therefore, one makes sectarianism the motive force of politics.'[14]

That deeply rooted fault line of the Northern Irish State, since it was created through partition, vitiated any realistic prospect of reform from within: a perception that Hume was to reluctantly accept after the possibilities of reform from within had been exhausted. Power in Northern Ireland was so perniciously enmeshed with religious justifications for its possession that its holders had comprehensively absorbed the myth of their own entitlement. From the opposition benches Hume faced not merely political intransigence but a deeply tribal confederacy whose identity depended on not admitting any modification to the Orange State.

Membership of the Orange Order (and of the Freemasons) was almost a prerequisite for Unionist MPs. Therefore, for Unionist MPs the breaking with the orthodoxy of banning civil rights marches would have had the consequence of losing caste within their own community. If their pretext for banning civil rights marches was that they posed a risk to public security, Hume asked how (given that they identified as Orangemen) those MPs could possibly be called on to ban an Orange march, when there were grounds to believe it would equally threaten the peace? He put it to them that when members 'have so much regalia around their necks the flow of blood to the brain is affected'.[15] Under threat of a form of excommunication, the Orangemen and Masons who ran the Unionist parliament sustained its sectarian character. The effect of this tribal clustering was to block the possibility of compromise; it was a design which ensured sufficient Unionist solidarity in parliament so the majority could always prevail, but at the cost of perpetuating division within the society at large. The Ulster Unionist Party's operation at the Parliament of Northern Ireland was like a wall prescribing clear positions: those hidden behind the wall were unable and unwilling to hear any form of opposition; those who were banished to live outside the wall, and who launched attempts to be included, were all but foredoomed.

In contrast to the bowler-hatted insularity of Unionist MPs, Hume continued to add growth rings of internationalism to his perspectives. In the following quotation (ironic given the support he later received from President Reagan), Hume traces a repressive measure in then Governor Reagan's California through to Stormont's legislative measures intended to contain non-violent protest. The connection between the Sacramento and Belfast administrations reveals the power of mass media as well as the butterfly effect of both civil disobedience and measures to contain it:

> At the end of November last a local newspaper contained an article indicating that Governor Ronald Reagan intended that it should be an offence in California to sit, kneel or lie down on a road. The wording of this provision is rather peculiar. Who dreamt it up? It does not exist in many laws elsewhere. We must assume that someone read this newspaper report. The paper went further and referred to one of its favourite themes, the rebelliousness of modern youth, particularly the grant-aided miscreants of Queen's University, and commended the proposed Californian measure to this Parliament.[16]

Yet the Unionist Party continued to ban marches and stymie reform. In one instance, when Prime Minister Brian Faulkner removed protesters' barricades, Hume said angrily in an improvised interview in Derry: 'If Faulkner thinks that the taking down of the barricades here today means that the people of this area have withdrawn their opposition to the regime, then of course he is being very deluded.' When hope of effecting change through their political representatives, through demonstrations or sit-in protests diminished, Hume warned that then some people would embrace hopeless methods out of frustration. Hume was to give this message to senior American politicians when he began his process of educating them about the origins of the IRA, and as an MP in the Parliament of Northern Ireland he conveyed the same point. In one of the great counterfactual propositions of twentieth-century Irish history, the question raised by Hume – how could political leadership have contained the anger of the minority by making basic concessions and allowing their voice to be heard – still rings down the years:

> A large section of this community are a permanent political minority and over a long period of time they have felt that they have no part in the decision-making process. This causes frustration and the frustration is all the greater when those same people know that

their elected representatives are not being listened to ... What does a person do then? He turns to another method of drawing attention to grievances, and in any democratic society these methods should be left open. The people then go on to the streets in the mass demonstration ... It has been quite clear that this is a method of protest which is not permitted for long in this community ... The third or final method of protest is the protest whereby a person draws attention to his problems by sitting or kneeling down in a public place. Now that is to be wiped out. Surely any intelligent person judging this situation would see that, when one systematically removes all means whereby people can air their grievances democratically, one thereby creates an explosive situation ... militancy can only be strengthened by such intransigence.[17]

Here, Hume attempts to expose the connection between incitement to hatred and acts of violence on the street and, as a corollary, to impugn the actions of Ian Paisley, who was to cloak himself in violent rhetoric for the duration of his political career until the peace process in the 1990s. Hume identifies the ways in which extreme Loyalists and Republicans became objective allies in word and deed:

Nothing at all is to be gained from extreme speeches. It is worth pointing out that when one takes up an extreme position in politics one depends upon extreme opponents, on the development of extremism for one's survival ... The victory of the policies and politics of people like the hon. Member for Bann Side [Ian Paisley] depend on a breakdown of law and order. If law and order do not break down they are defeated and shown to be wrong.[18]

As both a preacher and politician, Paisley had, even in the 1960s, perfected the dual approach of rallying people by infusing theology in politics, which meant that when he had a political setback, he could always retreat to the comfort of theological justifications.

The political process that Hume and his colleagues from the minority sought to promote was animated more and more by a belief that power-sharing in the divided community was the precondition for any sustainable political change in Northern Ireland. Embracing violence to force their objectives upon others, he argued, 'may appear at one time or another to achieve short-term objectives, but in society as it exists here violence inevitably leads to polarisation and civil war between Catholic and Protestant ... We are going nowhere unless there is a breaking down of the barriers between the religious divide'.[19]

Getting Organised: The Formation of the SDLP

The Social Democratic and Labour Party was formed in August 1970, and its foundation was a fulfilment of one of Hume's election campaign pledges the previous year. The SDLP was one of several parties to emerge in the two years following the start of the Troubles. Hume understood the weakness of a fragmented opposition in such a recalcitrant administration as Stormont Parliament. Therefore a central motivation for forming the SDLP was to organise against the Unionist bloc, which went hand-in-hand with another core objective: the establishment of Proportional Representation in Northern Irish elections to replace the first-past-the-post Westminster model of elections, which had been so schismatic in the North and which the SDLP believed would enable fairer representation. Beyond that, the SDLP wanted to establish a Bill of Rights and a Council of Ireland to replace the outmoded (and entirely theoretical) territorial claims to the North in the Irish Constitution of 1937.

The SDLP was determined to break with tribal politics and to plot a third way through the vehicle of social democracy around which, it was hoped, diverse elements of Northern Ireland could rally. In its earliest composition, the SDLP was an umbrella organisation in that it gathered together Belfast Socialists, Derry and Mid-Tyrone Nationalists, and liberal Protestants all under the banner of social democracy. From the outset, it was a party of leaders, of strong personalities and of sharp regional cleavages which led in time to conflicts as well as common cause among its members. As a sitting MP in London, Gerry Fitt had the highest political standing of the founding members and was appointed party leader. While not the party leader until 1979, many people saw Hume as the de facto leader, the person whose capacity for strategic thinking and planning was clearly the best. Ivan Cooper remembers that Hume had a particular talent for forming policy and remembers 'one occasion that he dictated policy for a period of three hours and that became the SDLP policy'.

Parliament and the Street: Civil Disobedience

Hume married his activities as a leader of street protests with his parliamentary life. It was not atypical that he would attend Stormont throughout a given a week and on Saturday or Sunday participate in street demonstrations. This became a form of double duty whereby one role reinforced the other. Hume combined his considerable skill in stewarding marches with his authority as an MP: men, women and children understood that, with Hume in the lead, a march was much more likely to pass off safely; they knew, too, that the objective of the march was more likely to succeed. The often suggested parallel between Hume and Martin Luther King was particularly apt for the ways in which he channelled the power of street demonstrations into a parliamentary campaign for justice.

Hume's participation in protest events in Derry City has been captured in iconic photographs which includes images of Hume, Hugh Logue and Ivan Cooper being arrested, put up against the wall, and doused with water cannon. Hugh Logue recalls one such incident:

> John went forward – he was the MP for the area and had the authority – and spoke to the officer in charge of the operation and said: 'If you guys move back and withdraw, I'll get the people to go home and there won't be any more trouble'. My recollection is that the officer on the ground agreed, and went through to headquarters, and told them what he was doing. He was countermanded and told by his commanding officer in Derry that they were not going to have a precedent of people sitting in the street and that they were going to drive through, at which point Hume said: 'Well if you're going to go through, you're going to drive over all of us, we'll be in your way'. The people, I think, expected him to lead them. The people would not have expected him to step aside for the British army.

Logue explains how the face-off progressed:

> They [the British Army] charged, firing rubber bullets, and dousing us at that stage with purple dye – and to this day I still admire the courage of the people who still sat their ground and did not move.

Then the army charged [again]. I got hit with a rubber bullet, was dragged out of a garden by the hair that I once had. We got arrested. We were paraded up and put against a wall, frisked, searched. But we did not give up, and that was as much John's leadership as anything else. We took the case with a very good lawyer, Charlie Hill, and we appealed it. We proved that the British Army did not have the right in Northern Ireland to arrest anyone under Northern Irish law. For the first time in British parliamentary history they sat up all night and legislated retrospectively to allow that.

The tactic of civil disobedience took various forms aside from sit-ins. The rate and rents strikes in Fermanagh (1970) and Derry (1971) constituted a peak of the civil disobedience tactic in Northern Ireland, and Hume was deeply involved with both strikes. Speaking in parliament of the case of Fermanagh, he defended his course of action thus:

In the course of his speech the right hon. Member for Enniskillen (Mr. West) referred to a speech made by me at the Diamond in Enniskillen on Saturday, 10th October [1970]. He wondered whether the police had given the Attorney-General a full report of my speech. Lest the police did not give a full report to the Attorney-General I shall tell him exactly what I said. I make no apology for opposing tooth and nail by every peaceful means at my disposal Fermanagh County Council in the same way as I opposed Derry Corporation. I shall continue to oppose it until we have done to Fermanagh County Council what we did to Derry Corporation. On that day I advised the people of Fermanagh to withhold their rents and rates. I advised them to elect local committees and to pay their rents and rates to those committees until such time as there was a democratic council. I advised them that if the county council retaliated by withdrawing its services they should organise lorries, collect the refuse and then go and empty it into the garden of the chairman of Fermanagh County Council. Dr. Paisley [Bann Side]: Shame. Mr. Hume: Or the garden of the nearest Unionist councillor.[20]

By 1971, however, Hume was beginning to believe that prioritising the political process over civil disobedience would ultimately be necessary to counter the IRA; that he needed to create a system of authority that could be acceptable to all communities in Northern Ireland. The idea of electing a local committee to usurp the authority of Fermanagh County Council was an intelligent tactic to force the State into exhibiting some modicum of accountability. However, it was also potentially dangerous because leading a programme of civil disobedience was riddled with risks: how to measure the exact length to which civil disobedience could go? How to ensure that the inevitable retaliation would not lead to lethal consequences for its practitioners? How to ensure that extremists did not exploit it to their own ends?

Moreover, civil disobedience also begged an important strategic question. The more civil rights privations were highlighted, the more the state was undermined; the effect of this process, which to an extent was redemptive, also reinforced a perception that the State was irredeemable through politics alone. When the balance tipped towards such a conclusion, a peculiar genie emerged from the bottle. The tactic of civil disobedience presupposes a way back to the normality of civil obedience once certain concessions are won. If the belief in society erodes sufficiently through the acts (and brutal reactions to) civil disobedience, how can civil society prevail? As David Trimble conceded, 'we Unionists built effectively Northern Ireland, and we built it a good house there, but it was a cold house for Catholics'. In the hope of replacing the cold house with another more inclusive one, civil disobedience nevertheless ran the risk of eroding the foundation upon which such a house could stand.

Background to Bloody Sunday

Since 1968, for three and half years the people in Northern Ireland had demonstrated by turns in organised and in ad hoc ways to establish their rights. There had been immediate gains in 1968, but significant losses as well, through repressive legislation and in particular with the introduction of internment without trial. Codenamed Operation Demetrius, internment without trial was introduced in Northern Ireland on 9 August 1971, and oversaw the 'lifting' of Catholics by the security forces and their imprisonment in internment camps (such as Magilligan) where they were unaccountably held and, in many cases, tortured. Catholic victims of these practices were interned on the slightest pretence – membership of an Irish language club or of the Gaelic Athletic Association, for instance.

Internment without trial discredited Stormont's already diminished reputation in the eyes of the Catholic population still further: while the British army was directly responsible for interning, it was the Prime Minister of Northern Ireland, Brian Faulkner, who had introduced the measure. The fact that he and his cabinet could preside over such outrages made Stormont's claims to be a government of law and order risible. For all the evidence of brutality within the walls of the internment camps, the nadir of the army's misconduct was still to come in its reaction to the protest marches first at Magilligan on 23 January 1972 and then in Derry on 30 January 1972.

On 23 January 1972 (one Sunday before Bloody Sunday), Hume led a protest on Magilligan beach to demonstrate the anger in the Catholic community about internment. In response to the peaceful demonstration, the British Army's Parachute Regiment fired plastic bullets at point-blank range at men, women and children, all of which was recorded by film cameras. The following exchange between Hume and the British army official responsible for the firing, likened by James Sharkey to the 'encounter between Hugh O'Neill and the Earl of Essex four centuries earlier',[21] does indeed suggest a face-off not only between protesters and security forces, but a collision of civilisations:

Hume: Could you tell me on what authority that you're holding us back from walking in there?

Soldier: This is a prohibited area. You are not allowed into a prohibited area.

Hume: Under what law – would you ask those men to stop firing rubber bullets at men and women please?

Soldier: They will not. They will stop it provided you keep away from the wire and don't try to enter this prohibited area.

Hume: Under what law is it prohibited, or under what authority is it prohibited? Can you tell me?

Soldier: It has been prohibited by the police and by the government.

Hume: The police tell me that it is you who is in charge here, not them … Are you proud of the way your men have treated this crowd today?

Soldier: This crowd has tried to come into a prohibited area. You as a Member of Parliament could try to stop them.

Hume: You shot them with rubber bullets and gas. The crowd was marching over there. The leaders were going to speak to you. Before we even got here you opened fire … I wouldn't be very proud of the conduct of your men today. They opened fire on a crowd of people and they were totally unarmed people …

Soldier: You are not allowed to march in there.

Hume: Why not? It does not belong to you.

Soldier: It is prohibited.

Hume: It does not belong to you. You cannot prohibit it …

Soldier: It has been prohibited by your government.

Hume: [shouts] Who's government?

Soldier: The government of Northern Ireland.

Hume: Not our government. And that's why you're here – because it is not our government.[22]

In his final response, John Hume MP had come to the point of repudiating the Northern Irish government. After years of commercial initiatives, of civil rights demonstrations or raising awareness through teaching, campaigns and journalistic articles and three years as an elected representative, Hume's conclusion was simply that a government which would sanction such actions was not his. Now, Hume intimated, there was a palpable risk that people could be shot dead for simply expressing themselves through marches, and Magilligan was the moment when Hume ultimately rejected the tactic of civil disobedience. Hume later explained that he realised something new was happening, that the power of decision-making now lay with the military and there was no negotiating with the Parachute Regiment. Hume realised at Magilligan beach that something terrible could happen. Robert Fisk, who at that time covered Northern Ireland for the *Times* in London, remembers:

I realised there was something wrong with the Parachute Regiment. I do not know if it was a Parachute Regiment decision or whether the politicians and military people in Lisburn knew what the Parachute Regiment would do. But John was right. He spotted right at the start something had changed. I mean, when you looked at the soldiers of the Parachute Regiment – they were trained to fight and kill and beat.

The Parachute Regminent solider who Hume was remonstrating with in the iconic footage maintains that the British government had legitimised their presence, and that they could open fire with plastic bullets if people insisted on marching beyond the barbed wire boundary. Hume disputed his authority entirely and demanded to know the law that permitted his Regiment to act as it did. So wherein did authority lie for what happened at Magilligan? In Robert Fisk's opinion:

> For a long period in Northern Ireland, there was clearly among most Brits, however well educated [and] whatever their roles, politicians (not Whitelaw but beneath him) and certainly army officers, there was a very colonial mentality. Remember most of the senior officers in the British Army at that time had taken part in the retreat from Empire. They had been in Aden or they had been in Cyprus or they had been in some cases in Kenya. So they had seen the withdrawal of the Brits, the weakening power of Britain. As the years moved on, the army officers became slightly less colonial in their minds but the politicians became more so (Roy Mason is a classic example).

Hume's view was that if the Parachute Regiment was willing to open fire with plastic bullets on the beach, they would do that and worse on the streets of Derry. Three days later, he spoke at a meeting at the Ardowen Hotel in Derry and made it clear that he would not participate in the march scheduled in Derry on 30 January. Not unlike Martin Luther King's decision on 'Turn Back Tuesday', Hume urged people to regroup in the new political context engendered by the Magilligan attacks. Was Hume vindicated in urging people not to proceed with a march on the streets of Derry the following Sunday? Eamonn McCann, who was not present at the Magilligan Beach march on 23 January 1972, but did participate in the Bloody Sunday march the following Sunday in Derry, remembers:

There was a number of possible reactions to what had happened at Magilligan. One was John's reaction to say well if that's the way it is going to be, we want to draw back from it, that these people are going to kill us. The other reaction was we are not going to be intimidated, we are not going to be driven off the streets by these people. I thought myself at the time that the bigger the crowd we had, the less likely it was that there was going to be violence from the State. Nobody could foresee the future. Nobody knew how things were going to unfold. After half a century of stasis, events were moving very quickly in the North. We were hurtling into the future, and I think that people did not have time to stand back and try to work out what exactly was happening. John did not seem to grasp that what had happened at Magilligan made a big march in Derry the following week absolutely inevitable.

Like the march at Magilligan beach the weekend before, the march scheduled for 30 January 1972 in Derry City was an anti-internment march. However, the brutality exhibited by the Parachute Regiment at Magilligan had to a considerable degree reconfigured the march as a contest; it was the people's defiance of the Parachute Regiment, which had been called in to 'police' the Derry demonstration. The presence of a multitude of television cameras and journalists was also certain to make the Derry march an even higher-profile event.

Of all the acts of terror and aggression that were to follow over the course of over twenty years of war, the Parachute Regiment's firing of live rounds against innocent demonstrators in Derry on 30 January 1972 remains the most transformative act of the Troubles because it was perpetuated by a 'professional' army which instantly lost any integrity it had left in the eyes of the Catholic minority. In the aftermath of 30 January 1972, as Eamonn McCann put it: 'to suggest to people after that that they should seek redress for their problems through constitutional means was just laughable … Bloody Sunday was the definitive moment when the real trouble started'.[23] Hume's position of holding the constitutional line became exceptionally difficult after Bloody Sunday. Eamonn McCann further elaborates:

> One of the big mistakes made by the State in relation to the early civil rights marches was to attack them. Had they not attacked them,

had they just allowed these marches to proceed peacefully and a few people make their speeches and everybody go home ... It was no longer possible after Bloody Sunday for John or anybody else to say what we are looking for are British rights for British citizens. That slogan was gone. That perspective was shot off the streets on Bloody Sunday.

Embarrassed by international outrage and protest, within two months of Bloody Sunday, British Prime Minister Ted Heath summoned Northern Ireland Prime Minister Brian Faulkner to London and peremptorily informed him that he was proroguing the Parliament of Northern Ireland. Without any further discussion, Northern Ireland would be ruled directly from London. The first phase of Northern Irish history (1920–72) was over. The parliament which had symbolised a half century of injustice towards the minority was finished. Its demise represented the failure of any form of self-government in Northern Ireland without substantial oversight from London and Dublin. While the removal of its powers gave the minority occasion for relief, the fall of Stormont also left a political vacuum – 1972 was one of the bloodiest years of the Troubles – with an attendant sense of hopelessness. For Hume, while a solution within Northern Ireland had been unworkable, there was still one more option to work towards and it involved winning support for his strategy from Dublin and London.

The American Dimension Unleashed

John Hume had first travelled to the US to represent the Irish League of Credit Unions in the 1960s. Hume brought to the US a fascination for the republican model of government and an admiration for those who challenged the government to live up to the ideal of equality expressed at the founding of the United States. Mayor Ray Flynn of Boston walked John Hume through the city's streets and recalls that Hume was:

> Fascinated with Martin Luther King [who] was a strong presence in Boston since the days when he went to Boston University. I would tell John stories about how I saw Martin Luther King out in the Roxbury neighbourhood marching into downtown Boston. John would want to know the whole background. I would take him to different locations where Martin Luther King lived. I realised that John really looked up to Martin Luther King, probably more so than any political leader or personality in the world.

By the late 60s and the eruption of the Troubles, Hume, by then a prominent politician, was sought out for his views on the unfolding situation by concerned Irish-America. That began a series of false starts before an effective coterie of supporters could form.

As early as the autumn of 1969, when Hume was invited to address the Donegal Men's Association in Boston, he had a realisation about where his political activities in the US would centre – it was to be at the treetop level rather than at the grassroots. As Seán Donlon, who was Irish Consul General in Boston from 1969–71, remembers:

In those days Ted Kennedy, as far as I recall, had no presence in Boston. He didn't live there. John began to form the view that organised as it was, Irish-America was not the route to power. Organized Irish-America was extraordinary in the sense that there were maybe 500 different groupings – whether it was the Donegal men, Cork men, the Éire Society of Boston, the Irish Cultural Centre – you had lots and lots of organisations dealing with specific issues, for example, immigration or dealing with social matters. But John quickly came to the view, and he was absolutely right, that these are not the route to power; these people are not into the American political scene. If I want to influence American policy somehow or other, I'm going to have to break into the Washington scene … I think very quickly John began to focus on: Where is the power? Who has the power? How can I enter that zone of power?

Hume found that America was receptive to the Irish Question, but only on preconceived grounds and through the filter of their own experience, and that a good deal of education would be required to elucidate the complexity of the Northern Irish conflict for American audiences. Again, Seán Donlon explains:

The American media could easily relate to what was happening in Northern Ireland, particularly in 1968–69 because it was almost a copy of the Civil Rights Movement in their own country. The complexities were not easily understood in the United States; people understood civil rights, housing, electoral reform, discrimination, all of these things were understood. What was not easily understood was: Where was Northern Ireland? Why was it a part of the United Kingdom? What was the background? Why did people want a United Ireland, and of course in the Irish-American community, why don't we achieve it by violence? In 1969, even people who subsequently became phenomenal supporters – Tip O'Neill, Ted Kennedy, and Hugh Carey – were inclined to look towards what became the Provisional IRA. That was their first instinct.

In time these supporters – Hugh Carey, then in the US Congress and later Governor of New York, Ted Kennedy who was a senator from Massachusetts and Tip O'Neill who was a rising star in the Democratic party – were to join with Daniel Patrick Moynihan, senator for New York, and form very powerful grouping concerned to support Ireland's search for peace and justice. Thus, as American politicians became more involved, the need for an effective communicator, who combined a deep understanding of the historical evolution of the political problems in Northern Ireland with a vision of their solution, became even more necessary. Bloody Sunday, and the broader disintegration of the North of Ireland in 1972, focused the attention of Washington on the Irish Question as perhaps never before. The massacre in Derry that day made the need for a touchstone on the Irish Question all the more necessary for US politicians wishing to engage on Irish matters.

Bloody Sunday and its Repercussions

From any point of view, Bloody Sunday was a diplomatic disaster for British policy makers. After the massacre of innocent, non-violent protesters on their own streets, Britain's moral case to act as an 'honest broker' among a divided people instantly proved risible. To exacerbate the sense of injustice in Derry, and to completely extinguish Britain's integrity, Lord Chief Justice Widgery, who presided over a Tribunal on Bloody Sunday, exculpated the Parachute Regiment – which was guilty of the murders – and instead blamed the marchers. The international community's sympathy for the Catholic victims of the massacre in Derry was apparent no less in Washington. Senator Ted Kennedy, who had called for a British withdrawal from Northern Ireland in 1971, stated in Congressional Hearings on Northern Ireland: 'Just as Ulster is Britain's Vietnam, so Bloody Sunday is Britain's My Lai.' Tip O'Neill, by now House Majority Whip, was similarly exercised, if less outspoken in public. As Seán Donlon remembers:

> When Bloody Sunday happened there was a huge reaction and enormous criticism of the British military, of the British political system. At that stage, Tip O'Neill got together with some of his colleagues in the House of Representatives and arranged to hold hearings on the Northern Ireland situation; technically, he did that through a subcommittee of the House Committee on Foreign Affairs.

When Tip O'Neill invited a delegation from Derry to Washington to give evidence Hume declined the invitation, judging that at such a fraught time his focus needed to be squarely on the domestic situation at hand. As a result of those hearings, O'Neill sponsored a petition signed by 102 House members in response to the Northern Irish crisis. At the same time, a perception was growing in the US Congress that Hume would be central to any effort to address the crisis.

The need for a new voice on the Northern Ireland Question, someone who could show a way forward, was also shared by visiting American media reporters, and early on it was recognised that Hume could be that voice. As *The New York Times* reported in August 1972:

> The Social Democratic and Labor party, a disparate grouping of Opposition politicians, sometimes is described as 'six men and one mind'. The mind belongs to Mr. Hume, who at 35, is generally held to be the deepest thinker and most able tactician in the group. It is not just intellect that accounts for his importance in efforts to break the impasse here. Mr. Hume is also believed to have won, in part through frequent television appearances, more prestige in Dublin than any other politician in Northern Ireland. But his strongest claim to influence is his ability to speak for Derry ... That ability has been somewhat eroded by the successive waves of violence, for Mr. Hume has consistently condemned the terrorism of the Irish Republican Army, even when much of his natural constituency was ready to condone it. But he retains strong support and is respected enough to get a hearing where he can no longer count on automatic allegiance. 'I can't influence the I.R.A.', he says, 'but I can influence the people'.[1]

The American Dimension: An Irreversible Shift in Perspective

The background to the first substantive encounter between Ted Kennedy and John Hume is somewhat protracted. Hume and Kennedy had briefly met at Trinity College Dublin in March 1970, not long after the Chappaquiddick incident. Kennedy had also sent a supportive telegram to Hume in 1969, stating that the Catholic minority did not struggle alone and that 'the reforms you seek are basic to all democracies worthy of the name'.[2] Meanwhile, in Derry, street violence began to escalate. However, it was not until a visit to London in 1971, after an encounter with an Irish woman, that Kennedy committed himself fully to working with Hume. The woman challenged Kennedy for having criticised the Kent State Massacre and yet having done, in practice, nothing to assist the Catholic minority in the North of Ireland. Kennedy's Chief of Staff, Carey Parker recalls:

> The Senator felt she was right, and in October 1971, a month after his return from Europe, he signed on to a resolution that Senator Abe Ribicoff and Congressman Hugh Carey, who was a member of the House at the time, introduced in Congress calling for immediate British withdrawal from Northern Ireland and the reunification of Ireland. That was what the American Irish wanted to hear, but as John Hume indicated to some friends of ours in Ireland, 'We can understand your frustration, but that's not the way the crisis in Northern Ireland will be resolved'. He wanted to talk to the Senator, and the Senator said, I have to go see John Hume.[3]

The Meeting

After Bloody Sunday, the smouldering conflict in Northern Ireland 'became a war', in the words of Eamonn McCann. Non-identification with the State on the part of the Catholic minority continued – civil servants and Catholic police resigned, public spaces became more clearly identified as 'Catholic' or 'Protestant' – and against that backdrop, forging an inclusive approach to politics became considerably more difficult. The deepening divide fed absolutist and paramilitary 'solutions'. With politics in Derry deteriorating, the timing for a determined American engagement on the Irish Question was right.

John Hume, unemployed since the Stormont Parliament had been prorogued by Prime Minister Ted Heath, was sitting in his kitchen at West End Park in Derry when he received an unanticipated telephone call from Senator Ted Kennedy. Hume was initially disbelieving, thinking the call a hoax, but the caller assured him that he was indeed Ted Kennedy and that he wanted to meet. Kennedy was scheduled to travel to Bonn for a NATO meeting and he asked Hume to come to Bonn to see him. As Hume's wife, Pat, remembers: 'I was teaching. I was the bread winner. We had five small children. But he realised that this was very important.' Hume borrowed money from the Credit Union (of which he had been president) and bought a flight to Bonn. That meeting took place at the residence of the then Irish Ambassador to West Germany, Sean G. Ronan, at 65 Rolandstraße, Bad Godesberg, and as Senator Ted Kennedy himself put it:

> He came to Bonn, and I spent a couple of hours with him in the residence of the Ambassador … that's where John began the great education of Edward Kennedy about Northern Ireland and planted the seeds that grew and grew and grew into a wonderful relationship … Hume was pointing out to me, certainly, that if we were going to have any success with a political process, we had to stop the flow of arms and funds for arms to the IRA from the U.S.[4]

Seán Donlon recalls: 'The ambassador had set up the meeting, arranged dinner, but the meeting was just between John Hume and Ted Kennedy. Nobody knows exactly what happened, but I do know that immediately afterwards Kennedy said to Ambassador Sean Ronan, "that's the man … that's the man I will listen to".' The first horseman was in the saddle.

The other aspect of Kennedy's education was the clear-headed perspective and constant stream of solid information provided by his exceptionally talented Chief of Staff, Carey Parker. Parker worked the phones on the Irish Question like nobody in the US. In the early phase of the conflict, Parker found that the British effort was 'not so much to try to reach reconciliation between the two sides as it was to end the violence, and they treated it as a war that they had to win, not as a peace they could negotiate'.[5] That a United States senator consciously sought out Hume was indicative of a rapidly sharpening view of Northern Ireland among senior US politicians. Kennedy wished to identify a trusted partner through whom he could channel what would become enormous US influence on Anglo-Irish relations. Hume had appeared to be that man and the meeting in Bonn confirmed Kennedy's belief that Hume was. Carey Parker corroborates:

> That meeting began a decades-long relationship, during which we didn't do anything on Northern Ireland without first talking with John Hume … We felt that the Irish issue needed a voice in Congress that was clearly for reconciliation and peace, so it was the only voice in

Congress that wasn't being heard via the IRA. ... It was largely a way of showing that Republicans and Democrats could work together on the Irish issue and that we were all in favor of the John Hume initiative.[6]

But the question remained: why did US politicians feel moved to become involved at all?

Background to Tip O'Neill's Involvement

Something in Tip O'Neill's background helps to explain the emotional centre of gravity for many Irish-American politicians. O'Neill's son, Tom O'Neill, relates:

My father's mother's family came from Buncrana in Donegal – the Drumfries area of Buncrana, a farm area – and both sides of her family worked in the soil. His father's father had worked in brickyards in Ireland and when he came to America he landed naturally enough in Cambridge, because there were brickyards in North Cambridge.

He certainly knew the history of the Irish and what the Irish-American condition was, not only in North Cambridge but in Dorchester, South Boston, and other enclaves where the Irish lived. He was old enough and early enough in American history to understand the British and what they felt about the Irish coming to America. I'm talking about the Brahmins and the Patrician Yankees here in New England and how they treated the Irish, and others frankly, coming in from other European nations, and how they were not welcomed.

There was a bank run by the Yankees in North Cambridge which bypassed all the ethnics, all the Irish and Italians, and never gave them loans. So my father went to the bank president and said: 'You know, you've got on deposit all the Irish money and all the French Canadian money from our neighbourhoods. There'll be a run on your bank if you don't start loaning the money out'. And so the next day the bank started loaning the money out.

Tip O'Neill brought his inherited grasp of the Anglo-Irish imbroglio with him to the House of Representatives. O'Neill's first Congressional speech, given on 5 March 1952, was 'a five-minute address on a bill he had sponsored to improve working conditions and salaries for longshoremen. With an eye toward his new constituency, he spoke out on behalf of foreign aid to Israel and Italy – and for Irish reunification.[7] Even so, without a coherent framework rooted in the realities of the North of Ireland, any effort by a would-be supporter such as O'Neill in favour of Irish reunification or any aspect of policy relating to Ireland, was destined to fail.

Resolutions introduced in the US Congress on Ireland – given that Congress was becoming more Irish as decades passed – were a source of anxiety for the British. This became apparent when sixteen anti-partition resolutions were proposed in the US Congress between 1948 and 1951. These were substantially driven by Congressman John Fogarty of Rhode Island, who also tried to leverage US Marshall Aid to the UK by linking it to a push to end the partition of Ireland. As James Sharkey relates:

> This was strongly opposed by the State Department by Secretary of State Dean Acheson. The State Department secured a major abstention in the vote and, as a consequence of that, the resolution failed. The British Embassy, reporting back to London at that time, spoke not just about the defeat of the Irish lobby in Washington, but the defeat of any ethnic lobby which came forward to divert American policy from its mainstream intent.

A tight alliance of the US State Department, the British Embassy and the White House was able to forestall any effort to reassess the US relationship with Ireland. But that coalition was about to be challenged by a concerted movement of influential figures in the US Senate and the House of Representatives.

Ted Kennedy, like Tip O'Neill, had imbibed Irish nationalism from an early age, through his maternal grandfather, John 'Honey Fitz' Fitzgerald, who had been Mayor of Boston. This included walks through Irish parts of the city where the NINA (No Irish Need Apply) culture that had prevailed excluded the Irish from circles of power in both politics and commerce. The core lesson Honey Fitz imparted to JFK when he ran for election was: 'He said: "The only thing you have to know about foreign policy is that Trieste belongs to Italy, and all of Ireland will be united and free", and with those two things, you could get elected in Boston.'[8] While that simplistic view may have worked for the ethnic politics of Boston, and indeed coloured Kennedy's earliest pronouncements on Ireland, Hume disabused him of the validity of such simple views when applied to the contemporary Irish reality.

Yet even before Hume fully embarked on his partnership with US politicians, the establishment of a power-sharing government in Northern Ireland in 1973 had emerged from talks between the Irish and British governments at the Prime Ministerial level (Liam Cosgrave on the Irish side and Ted Heath on the British side). Hume, who had long identified power-sharing as a key element to solving the problem of Northern Ireland's divided people, immediately and wholly committed himself to the power-sharing arrangement contained in the Executive agreed at the Sunningdale Conference, in Berkshire, England.

The Sunningdale Agreement

In the preliminary talks leading to the Sunningdale Agreement in December 1973, it was clear that any discussion on a settlement in Northern Ireland would involve a recognition in London and Dublin that the conflict could not be defined solely within the Northern Irish State; rather, the Irish and British governments would have a considerable role to play in the creation of any new structure for Northern Ireland. That was an analysis that Unionists largely rejected. Similarly, the Hume/SDLP concept of a 'New Ireland' which provided for territorial unity by consent was assailed by the Unionist population on the grounds that a New Ireland was a Trojan Horse for a United Ireland by stealth. 'Dublin is just a Sunningdale away' ran a contemporary Unionist slogan. Undeniably, however, the Irish dimension to the Northern Irish crisis needed to be recognised: the Irish and British governments were expected in any authentic reassessment of the Northern Irish State to construct institutions that would reflect all of the strands of Northern Irish political identity.

At Sunningdale, the Irish delegation insisted that everything be recorded in writing. There were six meeting rooms at Sunningdale to accommodate the talks, though in practice a great deal of the negotiations actually took place in the corridors. The British representative was James Allen, who reported directly to the British government, and he was assisted by Philip Woodfield, Deputy Head of the Northern Ireland Office. Their counterparts from Dublin were Declan Costello and Garret FitzGerald, both of whom were immersed in the details. William Whitelaw, Secretary for State for Northern Ireland, put his political career at risk to guarantee Sunningdale's success and at key moments in the negotiations he would speak at length with John Hume and the SDLP *in camera* to ensure their views were accommodated. Eventually, on 9 December 1973, a deal was agreed which provided for a power-sharing Executive in Belfast and a North–South Council of Ireland, in the form of a Consultative Assembly made up of thirty members from the Northern Ireland Assembly and thirty members from Dáil Éireann.

The Guarantee

A recurring bugbear for Hume and other Constitutional Nationalists was London's guarantee to Unionists that no constitutional change would ever occur without their consent. That guarantee had the appearance of properly taking account of Unionists' constitutional rights. However, in doing so it took absolutely no account of Nationalists' legislative rights. Hume even made the blunt argument that such an unspoken guarantee to Unionists had been the cornerstone of the intransigent one-party government that ran Northern Ireland for sixty years and was the root cause of the Troubles.[9] The fact that Britain had given a legislative guarantee of no constitutional change to Unionists strengthened their hand immensely. In negotiations, not just about constitutional change, but on any agenda for reform, it served Unionists to simply retreat to their constitutional guarantee position, which tended to be enough to foil any initiative for change. Therefore Hume and others railed against it and attempted to rethink and reconfigure the political landscape outside it, based on the fact that Northern Ireland was an artificial jurisdiction from its foundation and that the consent of all its people was never sought. For as long as the guarantee obtained in Northern Ireland existed, democracy could only exist in a vitiated form.

Sunningdale was a fundamental break with London's position that no new political structures were required to achieve stability for Northern Ireland. Today the agreement reads as both a reasonable and a prescient document. For example, both the Irish and British governments accept (in paragraph five) that there could be no change in the constitutional status of Northern Ireland without the consent of a majority. This was an unprecedented recognition for the Irish government. At the same time, the British prime minister signed up to a clause providing that 'if in the future the majority of the people of Northern Ireland should indicate a wish to become part of a united Ireland, the British Government would support that wish'; and (in paragraph thirteen) that it 'was broadly accepted that the two parts of Ireland are to a considerable extent inter-dependent in the whole field of law and order'.[10]

In 1973, the slightest hint of a United Ireland in the future and the acknowledgement of an existing symbiotic relationship between Ireland North and South seemed to enrage Unionism. The structure of the Council of Ireland, designed to reflect the interdependence of the two states in Ireland, became a source of contempt for hardline Unionism. Conor Cruise O'Brien, then Minister for Posts and Telegraphs, argued that the Council of Ireland was asking Unionism to concede too much, while Republicans recoiled from the Council of Ireland because they saw it as an implicitly partitionist institution.

Besides the philosophical misgivings of both the nationalist right-wing and the Unionist right-wing, the practical task of sustaining Sunningdale's institutions represented an enormous undertaking. Dermot Nally, a senior official of the Irish government, estimated at the time that sustaining the Council of Ireland alone would require 2,000 civil servants to maximise its functions. Sunningdale required for its success a huge degree of good will and determined commitment.

Sunningdale

The civil rights protests had been a necessary step, but only a first step, toward recasting politics in Northern Ireland. Hume's attempts to awaken the conscience of Stormont were met by an almost preternatural unwillingness. With the signing of the Sunningdale Agreement, however, Hume realised that Northern Ireland now had a reasonable framework within which the diverse facets of Northern identity could be recognised. The Sunningdale Executive contained within it the strands – centrist Nationalist and Unionist parties in the North, along with Southern Irish and British participation – that together would form the basis for a workable political process in Northern Ireland *provided that* Britain and Ireland would stand by the newly minted Executive.

However, it was going to take enormous political will to prop up the Sunningdale arrangements and within weeks of the signing of the Agreement signs of serious tension were already evident. In a December 1973 report to the Department of Foreign Affairs Headquarters, Seán Donlon, then head of Northern Irish policy for the Irish Department of Foreign Affairs, expressed doubt that Sunningdale could last because Faulkner had lost too much Unionist support. Getting on the ground and exercising 'shoe-leather diplomacy', Donlon had spoken to people who held the keys of Orange Halls in Newry, Dungannon and Omagh and the isolation of the Executive was becoming clear to him.

The murder by the Provisional IRA of Thomas Niedermayer, general manager in Northern Ireland of the German company, Grundig, and honorary consul for West Germany, was devastating. Niedermayer was murdered on 27 December 1973 (subsequently his wife and both his daughters committed suicide), and his abduction and murder happened against the backdrop of Hume, as Minister for Commerce in the Sunningdale Executive, attempting to promote Northern Ireland as a location for foreign investment by multinationals. In a broader context, it also occurred at a time when Ireland and the UK had just joined the EEC, and the possibility of new investment from Europe and from the US were opening up.

For all the hostile reception and the variety of opposition Sunningdale provoked among disparate political groups, North and South, it marked a glimpse of a new political era. The Catholic minority, which had been dispossessed for half a century since the foundation of the State, finally had achieved parity of esteem in a power-sharing Executive. The degree of the shift which occurred could be seen in this succinct summation by Austin Currie: 'I became the Minister for Housing and Planning. The person who had been squatting in a discrimination case in a house in Caledon in 1968 was, by 1974, in charge of housing and planning. It was quite a remarkable achievement and it was done by non-violent political activity.' Hume's wife, Pat, remembers that Hume, as Minister for Commerce in the power-sharing Executive, had scarcely ever worked so hard in his life: he was convinced that the path to securing political stability lay through economic growth.

In advance of a trip to the US by Hume in April 1974, to promote industrial investment in Northern Ireland, an official of the Foreign and Commonwealth Office forearmed himself with briefing material for Hume, but decided that given Hume's experience in the US, his command of

Irish history, and the historic significance of the power-sharing Executive, it would have been 'otiose' to hand Hume the briefing material. In the US, Hume spoke to the media regarding Northern Ireland as a prime destination for investment. Hume was due to meet Senator Ted Kennedy, which he had confided to the FCO in strict confidence (as he was already conscious of the SDLP members' sensitivities that the media was putting a preponderant emphasis on Hume's personality). Nevertheless, there was wide coverage of his visit in print and television media in Washington, New York, Boston, Philadelphia and Chicago. The US State Department report of his visit in print and television media in Washington, New York, and Boston, asserts:

> Hume proved to be effective spokesperson for moderates in Northern Ireland before key Congressmen who until hearing Hume had evidently had more exposure to IRA views than those of hitherto unknown SDLP. SDLP case, however, proved convincing and further visits to Washington by Catholic leaders like Hume could very well result in recognition of SDLP as legitimate spokesman for Catholic minority in Northern Ireland.[11]

Hume's visit resulted in a letter of thanks and encouragement from the Secretary of State for Foreign and Commonwealth Affairs, James Callaghan, on 13 May 1974.

The Collapse of Sunningdale

The Executive's problems continued to multiply exponentially, primarily because it was built on unstable foundations. The Sunningdale Agreement was technically a Joint Communiqué, intended as a prelude to an international agreement to be registered at the United Nations for full ratification. However, animosity to it from all sides intensified. In the South, Kevin Boland, who led a splinter from the Fianna Fáil party and held extreme nationalist views, challenged Sunningdale's constitutionality but failed; during his challenge, Southern politicians were prohibited *sub judice* from defending it. Yet while the Council of Ireland is often cited as the determinative element that finally brought Sunningdale down, there were other factors that weighed heavily in its demise.

The Heath government faced an election in February 1974, and so the UK had to pass a judgement on Sunningdale almost immediately after it came into existence. If the Council of Ireland were to have already been in existence for a year, it might have gained more traction, but Kevin Boland's constitutional challenge meant that the Irish government was obliged to sell the Agreement merely as a Joint Communiqué (it was in limbo until the Irish judiciary declared on its status). It may have been legally expedient, but it was politically unwise, to undersell the Agreement. When Harold Wilson succeeded Ted Heath as British Prime Minister, neither he nor Merlyn Rees, whom Wilson appointed as Secretary of State for Northern Ireland (1974–6), were genuinely committed to the Agreement. Thus when a general strike was called by the Ulster Workers' Council (UWC) it posed an existential risk for the Agreement.

The Ulster Workers' Council Strike

The UWC strike, supported by the wider Unionist community, had the sole objective of sabotaging the Sunningdale Executive. Countering Unionist opposition would have required an enormous feat of courage and dedication by Unionist politicians, and that was lacking. To counter the strike, the British had to deploy the army to man the electric and sewage works as described in Robert Fisk's book, *Point of No Return: The Strike Which Broke the British in Ulster*.[12] On 23 May 1974, Gerry Fitt urged the British army to deploy men to the power stations; by 27 May, the army was running petrol stations across the North to combat the UWC's shadow government coup. The British government did not immediately surrender to the mob; it did so after thirteen days. That capitulation was fatal to the prospects of a functioning democratic Assembly in Northern Ireland for another generation. As Seamus Heaney stated in his Nobel Lecture, 'until the British government caved in to the strong-arm tactics of the Ulster loyalist workers after the Sunningdale Conference in 1974, a well-disposed mind could still hope to make sense of the circumstances ... After 1974, however, for the twenty long years between then and the ceasefires of August 1994, such a hope proved impossible'.[13]

Continuing Republican paramilitary activity throughout the time of the Sunningdale Executive provided Unionists with the argument that any form of diminution of the British administration in Northern Ireland (which they believed was implicit within a full power-sharing arrangement) would result in a state of anarchy. Briefly, both hardline Unionists and Republicans rallied to the same cause, albeit spurred on by opposing political motives. Fear of any encroachment by Dublin on Northern Irish affairs convinced Unionists that negotiations involving the Southern government, of which they were instinctively suspicious, would not serve their interests. So they sabotaged the Sunningdale Agreement and its institutions, which did not sustain their majority prerogatives. The Provisional IRA portrayed the UWC strike, which brought the Sunningdale Executive down, as a fascist victory: an irony of ironies, since the IRA intensified its terror campaign for the same purpose, hastening the collapse of the Executive. Republicans believed that by continuing to destabilise the state they could legitimise their claim that only a United Ireland was a viable resolution. As Brendan O'Leary observes:

> [Sunningdale was] rejected by the Unionist community, and they came to the negotiation table in the 90s partly because they believed that things would only get worse for them. It is true that Republicans also rejected the settlement of 1973–74. They had just got rid of the Stormont Parliament, so they believed it would be easy to pursue getting the British out of Ireland completely, which turned out to be a fantasy.

The hue and cry unleashed by Unionist leaders over the Council of Ireland proposal served to cloak the more fundamental point: their unwillingness to concede to any power-sharing arrangement. Brian Faulkner's admission that the Council of Ireland controversy was a useful diversion says a great deal: 'Certainly I was convinced all along that the outcry against Council of Ireland was only a *useful* [author's emphasis] red herring – the real opposition was to sharing of power.'[14] Unionist opposition was bolstered by a small but growing constituency in Dublin that sympathised with the Unionist paranoia of being encircled, and in some cases that support was animated by historical naiveté and an intellectually capricious espousal of 'liberalism'. In the case of Conor Cruise O'Brien, it was a convenient argument to covertly advance the cause of Unionism in the South, a cause which in later life he openly embraced by running as a UK Unionist candidate in the 1996 Forum Elections.

There was certainly a depressing aspect to the failure of Sunningdale, and as Seamus Deane, responding to the unwillingness of the British Government to face down Unionist resistance in 1974, put it:

> The failure of Sunningdale was sinister because it showed that a certain kind of refusal, a certain kind of recalcitrance, was very much political war. It was partly the lack of backbone that [British Prime Minister] Harold Wilson displayed, but it was also a sinister indication that you could be rewarded for bigotry. I'm not really sure if the British government formed a policy in relation to Northern Ireland until about ten years after that, a policy that it felt it could actually pursue without being pulled to the side by its own army or its own officer corps. The Sunningdale Agreement was a very clever agreement, very cleverly designed. What we have been seeing is a version of Sunningdale, and a series of extensions from Sunningdale, actually becoming part of an agreed policy between Dublin and London, which is the crucial thing: the Dublin and London axis. That that has been formed and that that's well greased.[15]

The enormous opposition Prime Minister Harold Wilson faced to his predecessor's Agreement undermined, in his eyes, the case for continued commitment. Merlyn Rees, Secretary of State for Northern Ireland, intimated that Wilson was even considering a full British withdrawal from Northern Ireland, including the cutting off of the financial subvention which effectively sustained Northern Ireland, in the hope that that would encourage Unionists to be more conciliatory with Dublin. However, John Hume believed that the Sunningdale provisions – all parties working together across the divide, cross-border political and economic cooperation, including the British and Irish governments – had great validity. Gerry Adams disagreed:

> I see a validity. But I see the Sunningdale Agreement as a bad deal. It was not a good deal. It did not get to the root of the problems. We did not get to the root until we got round to the Good Friday Agreement negotiations. Whether it was the Anglo-Irish Agreement, whether it was Sunningdale or the Downing Street Declaration; all of them improved as things went on.

When the Good Friday Agreement was signed in 1998, Seamus Mallon, ever ready with a stinging formulation, stated that it was 'Sunningdale for slow learners'. How so?

> The Good Friday Agreement in my view (and I was one of the people very much involved in creating it) was not as good a deal [for Nationalists] in many ways as the Sunningdale Agreement, which had much stronger North-South structures. The irony of it all is that those who claimed to be defending the Nationalist community in the North of Ireland in 1974 – the IRA and Sinn Féin – were the very same people who bombed the Sunningdale Agreement out of existence.

That campaign, in combination with the withdrawal of support by some Unionists and the British government's failure to stand up to the striking Loyalist organisations, preventing travel and the delivery of food and other basic services, spelled the end of the Executive. In Seamus Mallon's opinion:

> They buckled. It is the most you can say about it. That opportunity, had it been taken, would have saved many lives. The tragedy was Unionism did not see the opportunity for a revitalisation within their community; Sinn Féin–IRA made the destruction of Sunningdale their priority. How contradictory can you get? The Good Friday Agreement is Sunningdale for slow learners. That is how I described it at the time.

Seán Donlon corroborates: 'The subsequent agreements, whether the Anglo-Irish agreement of 1985, [or] the Good Friday agreement of 1998, are all based on the Sunningdale principles, or the John Hume principles: unite the two communities in Northern Ireland; create North–South structures for cooperation. Essentially what we have today is what was agreed at Sunningdale.' What effect did the collapse of the Sunningdale Executive – that represented so much of Hume's thinking – have on him? In Seán Donlon's opinion: 'Once the Sunningdale agreement had collapsed, Hume felt that he must now focus on getting support for his position particularly in the United States. So it was after Sunningdale's collapse that Hume began what I call his American chapter.'

The demise of power-sharing drove Hume to seek the support of the most powerful government in the world, and to bring its influence to bear on Northern Irish politics. Simply put, Hume's analysis, post-Sunningdale, was that the two communities could not do it on their own; the British government had failed to stand by power-sharing in Northern Ireland and gave in to its traditional allies, the Unionists. The Irish government had proved unable to dissuade the British government from abandoning the Joint Agreement. It was now clear to Hume that bringing the support of the US to bear would help to balance the equation enough for a return to constitutionality and the establishment of a lasting power-sharing arrangement based on Anglo-Irish consensus.

Hume's US strategy

Building firm and sustained relations on Capitol Hill and, eventually, in the White House was without precedent in Irish-American relations. Senator Ted Kennedy was later to remark:

> It was rather interesting why the leaders of Ireland had not [engaged America meaningfully on policy matters]. De Valera was certainly alive when my brother visited Ireland but there was no real kind of a play towards involving, interesting, and engaging ... I don't think there's any question that the dramatic shift and change are really attributed to Hume and the confluence of events that took place at this time.[16]

In a speech entitled 'Ireland in the Atlantic Community', Hume stated: 'The great tides of Irish emigration began to flow to America in the 19th century ... The Irish in America tried without success to interest the Washington administration in the Irish question.'[17] Hume fully understood that by focusing on Washington and not on grassroots Irish-American organisations that he was breaking with the precedent of Irish leaders. Partly due to a lack of focus on federal power, but in large part due to vigorous resistance by the British to Irish involvement in political Washington, the Irish in America were contained. As former Irish diplomat Michael Lillis argued:

> Irish leaders in the nineteenth century and in the twentieth century before Independence – Charles Parnell, Padraig Pearse and De Valera – responded to the enormous Irish-American interest in Anglo-Irish

relations and in the cause of Irish freedom. The difficulty was that although Dev and Parnell and Pearse, and all such notable leaders, were greeted by huge crowds of thousands at public meetings and in City Halls in New York, Boston, Philadelphia, San Francisco, they never had the slightest effect on British policy. What they wanted of course was to get the United States to pressure the British to be flexible, or even to give in to Irish demands, which would have to involve the President of the United States, the Secretary of State and the State Department. But those three offices of the United States, which actually make up the foreign policy of America, were completely controlled by the British. The British had enormous influence in Washington, more than any other country in the world.

Breaking the British government's exclusive hold on US foreign policy vis-à-vis Northern Ireland was completely removed from the honest outrage expressed on St Patrick's Day in Shamrock Clubs throughout the US. Hume's approach was measured and it consisted of clear-headed historical analysis fortified with the credibility of a moderate practicing politician in Northern Ireland who faced risks to himself and his family (Hume and his colleagues sometimes had to exit the SDLP office in Derry under armed guard). These aspects in Hume, compounded with sound judgement, had great resonance with US politicians; enough to persuade senior figures in the US Congress and, in turn through their leverage on the White House, to persuade successive US presidents to become engaged in the Irish Question. These senior politicians resolved to channel their activity through the politics of John Hume. As Senator Paul Kirk recalls:

My first recollection of John Hume took place sometime in the early 1970s in Washington DC, when I was invited to an event at a home in Georgetown. He described the situation in Derry, that the unemployment was at 47%, it was a staggering figure to absorb and he described in eloquent detail that one of the issues was that 47% of the people, being unemployed, had time on their hands and had really nothing to do but engage in this violent situation that existed there. And he made the point that for Americans of Irish heritage who loved the island, and loved its people, and loved all the lineage, that we were on a misguided course by providing funds for armament to the IRA.

And that's what [John Hume] advocated, and this was why I describe him as a transformative thought leader.

For those reasons, Hume began to be seen as the touchstone. Senator Kennedy referred to Hume as the '101st Senator of the United States', and Senator Kennedy's sister, Ambassador Jean Kennedy Smith, recalls:

> I think his relationship was very close. I think he trusted him absolutely. I think he realised he didn't want a victory, that he wanted peace. And that he always saw that possibility. He saw both sides and understood both sides very completely. He realised that the American connection was important, which it was, because a lot of people in Congress have Irish roots and they also feel strongly about the problem. He was always very clear and he was very measured and sensible and direct about everything. The sentence that everybody always knew was 'what does John Hume think?'

Hume saw in a motto etched on the Lincoln Memorial a model for the divided people of Northern Ireland. As Tom Melia, a senior staffer for Senator Daniel Patrick Moynihan, remembered, Hume would say:

> You Americans probably take this for granted, there's a commonplace saying, a famous saying that's so famous in America you've probably forgotten about it – *E pluribus unum* – 'From many, one'. And he said, 'It's so commonplace in America that you have it on your smallest coin, here on the back of a penny'. And he said, 'That's what we're striving for in Northern Ireland, from our diversity to create one nation, *E pluribus unum*, which has long been the American national slogan and something we're striving towards even today to create one nation of equal citizenship among all our diverse constituent communities'.

What finally proved to be the requisite glue to bind together the embryonic political involvement on the American side, with Hume's will to lead a new agenda on Ireland in Washington, was an extended period of living in the United States, which afforded Hume the possibility of following through with several initiatives in the US. This was afforded by a fellowship awarded to Hume by Harvard University in autumn 1976.

The Growth of the Irish Machine in Washington

The Monster of Irish Nationalism

The degree of unsettlement that the British were to experience as Hume and his American friends began to exert pressure in Washington can hardly be overestimated. The paranoia over heightened Irish political awareness in the US had existed in the British ruling class for over a century. In 1887 a British peer, Lord Spenser, argued that because the Irish were in communication with America and were inspired by its republican model of government, their 'social condition at home is a hundred years behind their state of mental and political culture'.[1] Furthermore, the new potentiality of the Irish in America represented a pernicious force that could in time be let loose upon the cosy relationship between Britain and the US. Sean O'hUiginn suggested: 'As the Victorians saw it, the monster of Irish nationalism had escaped the confines of the island and was now frolicking in the United States, and being a spoiler to what they saw as being the relationship between the … two Anglo-Saxon sister democracies.'

Congressman Richard Neal of Massachusetts is familiar with the accounts by earlier British political leaders commenting on the moral strength of the argument for a more equitable settlement in Northern Ireland. He notes the statement by William Gladstone, four times British prime minister in the nineteenth century, 'forewarned what was to happen, he said, "you cannot win the argument in America on the Home Rule Question". And Churchill, you could see in his memoirs, warns as well, "you can't win the argument in America". True, the *argument* was increasingly difficult to win in the US, particularly in Congress, which in the late 1970s housed over one hundred Congressmen of various hues of 'green' Irish nationalism. In 1948, the defeat in Congress of the Fogarty Resolution (on re-uniting Ireland) severely damaged the credibility of the Irish-American cause for a generation. However, the outbreak of the Troubles in 1968, dovetailing as it did with the presence in Congress of newly elected politicians of Irish lineage, inadvertently re-established the Irish Question in a prominent position.

Irish-America had been, for all British fears, woefully ineffective. Irish-American engagement with Ireland, North or South, before the 1970s is routinely overestimated. The theory that the US government was dedicated to overseeing the interests of Ireland is pervasive. Yet an examination of the evidence shows an unimpressive record. Instinctive resistance to a pro-Irish line in Washington can be traced from Franklin D. Roosevelt, who came from an Anglophile background. However, his special advisor and campaign manager, James Farley (the Chairman of Coca Cola who lived in the Waldorf Astoria and a man of immense political influence), managed to sensitise him somewhat on the Irish Question. Still, Ireland never used its contacts to influence the US to balance out the Anglo-Irish relationship. The arms of government in Washington – The White House, the State Department, Congress, and later, founded in 1947, the National Security Council – ignored Northern Ireland. Partition remained no concern of US foreign policy and Dublin did nothing to attempt to change that.

From 1922 onwards, the 'Special Relationship' kept the agents of Irish nationalism shut out of American politics. Despite timid initiatives, nothing emerged and nothing took America off the fence. It was clear to the British government that it could run the North without external interference. For John Hume, it was clear that the British retention of a monopoly on Washington meant that their interests and their perspective on Northern Ireland would continue to be furthered, to the detriment of a fair solution. Somehow, a channel needed to be created to access the White House (which had been markedly unused during the JFK presidency), to break the indifference in Washington towards Ireland, an intransigence which was replicated in British policy towards the Northern minority.

The Four Horsemen

In the autumn of 1976, the Director of the Harvard Negotiation Project, Roger Fisher, author of *Getting to Yes*, invited Hume to spend a semester at Harvard University (Fisher wanted to professionalise the art of negotiation). Hume accepted the fellowship at Harvard University's Center for International Relations, which positioned him on the East coast and enabled him to liaise with Ted Kennedy. With Hume in situ in Cambridge/Boston, Ted Kennedy arranged for him to meet influential congressmen, especially Tip O'Neill, who hailed from Cambridge and travelled there every weekend. As Ted Kennedy put it, reflecting on Hume's transformative period in the US in 1976:

> John Hume was at Harvard and was my contact. He was clearly the most persuasive and the most articulate, passionate, knowledgeable person about all of this situation. I worked with Tip [O'Neill] and Hugh Carey, both of whom had a long – traditional position on the Irish issue, which was to support unification and fudge the question on violence. By showing that there was another way, which John Hume was able to do – these were enormously important meetings that he had with them to convince them of the appeal to non-violence.[2]

In the same interview, Kennedy spoke of the logistics of arranging those meetings: 'There were several [in Washington] but the most important ones were in Boston … I guess we had Hugh Carey come down to Washington another time and John couldn't make it. These were meetings that took place by and large in Boston with John Hume.'

On one occasion, Senator Kennedy took Hume on one of his midnight monument tours around Washington in his limo. Kennedy was a huge admirer of Hume and it was clear that Kennedy had more than just a sentimental attachment to Ireland. He would continually say to Hume, 'what can I help you with?' On this particular night, having nearly completed the monument tour, he brought Hume to the Lincoln Memorial and there Hume first read the inscription *E pluribus unum*, 'Out of many, one', which was to feature so much in his speeches in the future: the ideal of diversity in society.

Just at this time, in 1976, a hugely able and energetic Irish diplomat named Michael Lillis was posted to the US, initially to New York. Lillis combined political nous with a personal dimension – a love of Irish music and Irish culture – which appealed to O'Neill in particular. The man who would later become Irish ambassador to the US, Seán Donlon, related:

> Michael used to meet Governor Hugh Carey in a pub, Neary's, on 2nd Avenue, New York. As with most of Michael's meetings with contacts, they were never in an office setting, usually they were in what euphemistically could be called a social setting. Michael had the diplomatic standing, he represented the Irish government, but the real voice of Northern Ireland was that of John Hume.

Through working together, Hume, Lillis and the senior politicians who readily met to discuss Northern Ireland (Kennedy, O'Neill, Carey and a fourth, Senator Daniel Patrick Moynihan from New York) formed a pressure group, which became known as 'the Four Horsemen'. As Michael Lillis put it, Hume was 'using them with their full agreement and awareness, to create a system of power politics in which the United States would put pressure on Britain to help to solve a problem which they had neglected for so long'. Hume had twin objectives in his campaign to generate political support for the Irish Question in the US: to subject British policy in Northern Ireland to critical scrutiny, while simultaneously persuading Irish-America against supporting the IRA, which was associated with the Green Army rhetoric of yore, and to push for a peaceful settlement. In line with political scientist Joseph Nye's concept of soft power, 'the ability to set the agenda in ways that shape the preferences of others',[3] Hume set about creating a network to alter perceptions of Ireland in the US.

Why were the Four Horsemen happy to freely lend their political capital? The respect that Hume inspired in them partly explains it; Hume became the person through whom they could effect a political objective of their own. Tip O'Neill's eldest son, Tom O'Neill, explains: 'When something as important as a peace process or a leader for peace was being introduced, that held great sway and they wanted to leave their mark and their fingerprint on that process.' In addition to the careful political construction with the Four Horsemen, Hume, during his time at Harvard, was also active in other arenas, particularly in New York City. On one visit to New York he had, thanks to the Irish Consulate, lunch with politicians, members of the press and senior Wall Street figures. He also gave a talk at Fordham University. What was most striking about all his interactions was the way in which he communicated the endgame of the Northern Ireland crisis – what was necessary to end the strife. He took pains to caution the media against lending any credence to the legitimacy of the IRA's campaign. Asked his views on the 'Peace People', a grassroots movement that sought to end the conflict, he said that they were well-meaning but that the politicians would ultimately need to negotiate a settlement for the divided community, with proper representation of all sides. Separately, Hume also visited UN Secretary-General Kurt Waldheim to ensure continued interest there.

It was on Washington, however, that Hume concentrated most of his energy. Hume saw Washington as the key element in creating a new political equation that would lead to stability. Paul Quinn, a Washington attorney, relates that Hume said to him:

> You must understand the problems in Northern Ireland were not created by the people in Northern Ireland. They were created in London and in Dublin. And the problems of Northern Ireland were not resolved by the people of Northern Ireland. We need the cooperation and the help of London, Dublin and Washington. It is only you in Washington that can make the difference and it can really pull this together.

(On this theme, former Irish ambassador the US Sean O'hUiginn likened Hume's approach to politics to that of a mathematician 'who solves an equation by bringing in extraneous elements to get a solution'.) Hume put the issue very succinctly to Quinn that no easy solution to the Northern Ireland problem was possible from within the Dublin–London–Northern Ireland triangle. Hume had absorbed in his bones how difficult it was to attempt to broker an equitable settlement within that triangle of political pressure points – for him, the fall of Sunningdale had amply demonstrated that unless bigger pressures were exerted, the political will to create a new political structure for the North of Ireland within a New Ireland would falter. Quinn remembers that Hume, always given to extemporisation in his scheduling, would abruptly arrive in Washington and his friends had to 'pull together at short notice receptions and briefings and hold seminars, inviting people from the Hill, occasionally members of Congress. Ted Kennedy was very helpful and he would be there'.

Despite the palpable enthusiasm from US politicians of Irish extraction, the climate in political Washington remained anything but hospitable to the agenda of reconfiguring US policy on the Irish Question. Paul Quinn elaborates:

> The United States State Department was effectively a puppet of the British government when it came to Northern Ireland. So, any attempt during that period, of the mid-to-late 1970s, to get any encouragement or help from the US State Department for what John Hume was trying to accomplish was resisted very strongly. The Irish Department of Foreign Affairs encouraged us to get involved, and they did so somewhat cautiously. They did not want to get too far in front because that would antagonise the British and lead to other problems.

Hume, his American supporters and Michael Lillis as Irish Political Officer in the US set themselves to cracking the code of how to exploit Washington's power. What they did could serve as a textbook case for how a foreign government and a foreign politician might gain influence in the United States government. Seán Donlon relates:

> Washington is a one-industry city: politics. And Washington is a city of lobbyists. Not everyone calls him or herself a lobbyist, but most of the law firms in Washington are registered as lobbyists because most of the work they do brings them into contact with government. So Hume saw the advantage in cultivating prominent lobbyists in Washington because he knew that if a small group could be persuaded of the correctness of his approach then the lobbyists would spread the word.
>
> There were many Irish-American lobbyists in Washington. It seems to be a well-established pattern: the first generation laboured; the second generation became policemen; the third generation became lawyers. So there were a lot of people with Irish connections and many of them – people like Paul Quinn – were interested in Ireland but they had to be persuaded and converted. It was natural enough for people like Paul Quinn, going to see US Senators or members of the House

of Representatives, that Ireland would come up; when it did, it was critical that the line was John Hume and the Irish government's line.

Ironically, the IRA campaign had made many senior Irish-Americans cautious of openly exploring the Irish cause. It was important that the approach not be invidious, but rather illustrate how the UK and Ireland could be, and needed to be, partners within a peace settlement. Donlon elaborates:

> What John Hume and Michael Lillis achieved was to get the Americans to come to the table and to be part of a process. But we were very careful not to ask the Americans to take sides because we knew if we did, we would get a 'no', because the American–London relationship, the so-called Special Relationship, was so strong that we were never going to crack that nut by saying 'side with us'.

That formula worked, and with a successful formula the will to form a policy followed swiftly. To this end, the Chiefs of Staff who supervised the Irish Question for the Four Horsemen were critically important. Highly talented people, they were Carey Parker, for Senator Ted Kennedy; Kirk O'Donnell, for Speaker Tip O'Neill; Tim Russert, for Senator Daniel Patrick Moynihan; and David Burke, for Governor Hugh Carey. They met and communicated regularly with Michael Lillis and worked on engaging the interest of the Carter White House in an initiative which became known as the Carter Statement, which took six months of hard negotiation. All of the elected politicians from Georgia, Carter's home state, opposed it, as did the National Security Council and, naturally, the State Department. The relationship between the White House, National Security and the State Department was tight; the latter organ of government, being bound by hoops of steel to British policy, never supported any initiative on Ireland unless it was seconded by the British Embassy. Breaching that long-established precedent was a huge challenge.

The Chiefs of Staff also worked on what was to become a Washington institution, the St Patrick's Day statement from the Four Horsemen. Their first St Patrick's Day statement was issued in March 1977 and it read:

> The world has looked with increasing concern in the past eight years on the continuing tragedy that afflicts the people of Northern Ireland.

Each of us has tried in the past to use our good offices to help see that the underlying injustices at the heart of Northern Ireland are ended, so that a just and peaceful settlement may be secured ... It is evident to us, as it is to concerned people everywhere, that continued violence cannot assist the achievement of such a settlement, but can only exacerbate the wounds that divide the people of Northern Ireland ... We therefore join together in this appeal, which we make in a spirit of compassion and concern for the suffering people in the troubled part of Ireland. We appeal to all those organizations engaged in violence to renounce their campaigns of death and destruction and return to the path of life and peace. And we appeal as well to our fellow Americans to embrace this goal of peace, and to renounce any action that promotes the current violence or provides support or encouragement for organizations engaged in violence.[4]

Given that it was a Joint Statement from the Four Horsemen, it was persuasive. While condemning violence and urging Americans not to give money for arms (the 'negative message' in Hume's vocabulary), it also undertook that the American government would become involved politically in Ireland, 'the positive message', if peace were secured. From 1977, St Patrick's Day Joint Statements, issued in Washington and covered by the national press in the USA, became an annual feature of the Four Horsemen's involvement in Irish matters.

To build on this statement, Senator Kennedy recalls meeting John Hume at the St Patrick's Day 1977 American Ireland Fund (AIF) dinner, a philanthropic organisation part of whose mission is to help to reconcile Irish political division, during which they discussed the need to enlist the support of the President: 'Both John Hume and I were going to speak at that fund [American Ireland Fund dinner]. We talked about trying to persuade President Carter to appeal for a partnership in the North with a promise of substantial economic aid linked to accepting a political solution.'[5] On the platform at such events, Loretta Brennan Glucksman, wife of Lewis L Glucksman, philanthropist and former chief executive officer and chairman of Lehman Brothers, remembers that Hume was a novel and welcome voice:

In the early years, it was crucial for our Irish-American community to believe that there was an alternative to the Troubles, that we could find a different way than the bombs and the bullets. John Hume was the single figure who presented, especially to Irish-America, an alternative to the violence. He was so ahead of his time to understand that, sure it was tribal, sure it was the reaction to years of colonization, and it was Protestant and Catholic. But it was at the end of the day economic. And he always got that message into his talks, whatever the constituency was. Give us a chance to have jobs and we will break this cycle of violence.

Hume persuaded his audiences in the US to focus on these core issues. He sought to bring divisive elements to the table. He became *the* man for many in the US, who admired his talent to synthesise the situation in Ireland and his instincts to calm the churning waters. The AIF dinners provided Hume with an ideal platform to educate Americans and encourage investment in the North of Ireland – both central concerns for Hume.

Northern Ireland concerns took precedent in the late 1970s and into the 1980s. Hume spoke very convincingly at an early AIF fundraiser in Boston. The AIF saw itself as the antithesis of the IRA: being focused on reconciliation and working with Hume. Dealing with business people who were not steeped in the Northern Ireland Troubles, they tried to get away from the view that the evil English were persecuting the woebegone Catholics in the North, and to give perspective to the Protestant side of the story. Hume was a social democrat and thought that the government should do more to educate people. As Ambassador James Sharkey further illustrates: 'Reconciliation became a very, very fundamental drive in my personality, to try and bring the two communities to a closer view of their own identity, their own place in Northern Ireland, their own place in Ireland, and their own grievances … The great success of John Hume, I would argue, has been his persistent focus on the concept of reconciliation.'[6]

There was a vigorous social dimension to channelling US support for peace, in considerable part instigated by Michael Lillis. In what amounted to an almost unprecedented coup in Washington, Lillis persuaded Tip O'Neill, who had become Speaker of the House of Representatives in January 1977 (also in January 1977, Jimmy Carter, was inaugurated President of the United States), to attend house parties at Lillis's residence in Georgetown, where Hume stayed during his visits to Washington during this period. With the Speaker in attendance, members of the National

Security Council, the White House and US Congress followed in tow. O'Neill made the most of Lillis's diplomatic immunity by helping himself to Lillis's contraband Cuban cigars. The high jinx, Irish stories and Irish jokes and poetry recitals made the parties legendary. Yet, as Irish historian Ronan Fanning, who was a Fulbright Fellow at Georgetown University in 1976–7, recalled, the parties were also very much 'an instrument of policy'.

Back in Ireland in 1977, Hume became an occasional visitor to William Shannon, Ambassador to Ireland from 1977–81 under President Jimmy Carter. Ted Smyth, Michael Lillis's successor as Press Officer in New York, relates that:

> Michael Lillis got very close to Shannon and introduced him to Hume and to many new dimensions in Irish thinking: that it was no longer just a case of 'Brits out'; it was a case of Brits in and the Irish in and we would have an Agreed Ireland. It was immensely important to present the Irish problem as a civil rights problem where there could be equality between Protestants and Catholics in Northern Ireland. That resonated with Americans in a way that the old football game, Brits versus the Irish, did not.

It was clear to those close to President Carter that with the newly unified Irish influence in the US Congress, and with President Carter installed in the White House with a mission to protect and defend Civil Rights issues, the time was right to push for a new initiative.

It would be fallacious to portray the background to the Carter Statement exclusively as a tug-of-war between purely constitutional pro-Irish and pro-British pressure. There was a significant threat posed by proponents of Fourth Green Field nationalism, entities such as NORAID, the Irish Northern Aid Committee, which was forced in 1981 by the United States Department of Justice to name the Provisional IRA as its foreign agent under the Foreign Agents Registration Act, also had a nascent presence in Washington and a cohort within the media who championed their exertions. These activities risked distorting the work of the Four Horsemen by association, given that both constitutional politicians and those ambivalent on the use of force were conveniently lumped together in news reportage on Northern Ireland.

Hume making a documentary film in Derry in the 1960s. (Courtesy of the Hume Family Collection)

ne on his graduation from
nooth University, 1958.
urtesy of the Hume Family
ection)

As a history teacher at St. Columb's College in Derry in the 1960s, John Hume brought his students to visit the President of Ireland (above) and to visit the Prime Minister of Northern Ireland. (Courtesy of the Hume Family Collection)

John Hume addressing a crowd, 1969. (Courtesy of *The Derry Journal*)

John Hume giving a speech, 1969. (Courtesy of *The Derry Journal*)

John Hume confronts a British army soldier at Magilligan Strand on 23 January 19 during a protest against Internment Without Trial. (Courtesy of *The Derry Journal*)

The first extensive meeting between John Hume and Senator Ted Kennedy, at the residence of the Irish Ambassador to West Germany, Sean G. Ronan, in 1972. (Courtesy of the Hume Family Collection)

The Four Horsemen grouping was formed in 1977: Governor Hugh Carey, Speaker of the House of Representatives, Tip O'Neill, Senator Ted Kennedy and Senator Daniel Patrick Moynihan. (Courtesy of the Hume Family Collection)

Senator Ted Kennedy showing Speaker Tip O'Neill a photograph of the Four Horsemen, 1981. (Courtesy of the Seán Donlon Collection)

John Hume and Speaker Tip O'Neill, 1980s. (Courtesy of the Hume Family Collection)

John Hume, Irish diplomat James Sharkey and Speaker Tip O'Neill, 1980s. (Courtesy of the Hume Family Collection)

John Hume and Speaker Tip O'Neill, at O'Neill's ancestral home place in Drumfries, Co. Donegal, 1979. (Courtesy of *The Derry Journal*)

John Hume and Speaker O'Neill, 1980s. (Courtesy of the Hume Family Collection)

United States Senate

November 9, 1981

Mr. John Hume
6 West End Park
Derry, Northern Ireland

Dear John:

A great deal has happened since these Four Horsemen mounted up for their first ride together on St. Patrick's Day 1977.

You know how much we have valued your counsel in the past, and we look forward to your wisdom in the future as we work together in the cause of peace.

With our thanks and best regards,

Sincerely,

Edward M. Kennedy

Letter from Ted Kennedy to John Hume, 9 November 1981. (Courtesy of the Hume Family Collection)

Left to right: John Hume, Garret FitzGerald, Colm Ó hEocha, Charles J. Haughey and Dick Spring at the New Ireland Forum, 1983. (Courtesy of the Hume Family Collection)

Ambassador Seán Donlon and President Ronald Reagan, 1978. (Courtesy of the Seán Donlon Collection)

John Hume and President Reagan, 1980s. (Courtesy of the Hume Family Collection)

Left to right: Tip O'Neill, Ronald Reagan, John Hume, Ted Kennedy and Peter Barry, St Patrick's Day, 1983. (Courtesy of the Seán Donlon Collection)

December 13, 1984

The President
The White House
Washington, D.C.   20500

Dear Mr. President:

I understand that you will be meeting with Prime Minister Thatcher next week. I am certain that there will be a number of important issues that will be addressed in your discussions with her.

I have signed a letter with several of my colleagues requesting that you address the issue of Northern Ireland and the future of the New Ireland Forum in your meeting with her.

Nevertheless, I want to personally share with you my deep concern that the Forum, which is the best hope for a peaceful, lawful and constitutional resolution to the tragedy of Northern Ireland may be in serious jeopardy as a result of Mrs. Thatcher's public statements about the Forum's Report.

You have been outspoken in your condemnation of the forces of violence in Northern Ireland and in your statements to Americans imploring them not to support the men of violence in Ireland. Your statements have been very helpful in educating Americans to the real threat posed by Irish terrorists.

The way forward in Northern Ireland must be peaceful and political. It clearly must involve the reconciliation of the two identities in Northern Ireland and the active participation of the governments of Ireland and the United Kingdom in bringing about such a resolution.

The Forum Report represents a sincere, comprehensive and realistic assessment of future alternatives for Northern Ireland. It represents the best efforts of moderate elements in Northern Ireland and in Ireland to fashion a political and constitutional framework for achieving a political solution to the tragedy of Northern Ireland.

If the Forum Report is not acknowledged by Prime Minister Thatcher as a basis for discussion and dialogue between the United Kingdom and Ireland, then I fear that the forces for moderation in Ireland and here in the United States as well will suffer significantly.
Consequently, I ask that you encourage Mrs. Thatcher to renew the Anglo-Irish dialogue over the Forum Report and that the Prime Minister recognize that the Forum has significant support in Congress and among Irish-Americans interested in bringing peace to the beautiful land of their forebears.

Sincerely,

Thomas P. O'Neill, Jr.
The Speaker

The founder of the Irish National Caucus (INC) lobby group in Washington, Fr Seán McManus, whose clerical collar and Northern Irish background some on the Hill found hard to disregard, was also intent on exerting influence on the White House administration. The National Security Council Director of West European Affairs Robert Hunter explains:

> What really helped to jump-start this [White House cooperation with the advocacy of John Hume's principles] was an individual called Father McManus, who was involved with NORAID, and some of the other people who were trying to be helpful to the Provisional IRA. I knew none of this but I had come off Senator's Kennedy's office in Capitol Hill where we saw everybody; we were an open shop. And I had received a message that this individual, Father McManus, would like to come and meet with me. I said, 'well, why not'. A few minutes before he was going to come into the White House, the phone rings, I pick up the phone and there's a voice at the other end. He says: 'My name is Michael Lillis. You've never heard of me, we've never met. Listen to me carefully. I am the number two, the Deputy-Chief of Mission, at the Irish Embassy. You're about to meet somebody called Father McManus'. I said, 'yeah, that's correct'. 'Listen to me,' he said, 'You don't know me, but that would be a big political mistake'. I said, 'OK, I don't know you but I'm going to take you at your word'. So I put down the phone, I called my secretary and I said: 'Cancel the permission of this man to come in the White House,' which was then done. He didn't get in the White House. I then called Lillis back. That began a relationship which we then built upon, with his lead, which led in August of 1977 to the President himself deciding the time had come for the United States to take a stand.

Lillis was equally interventionist on Capitol Hill. He was solicitous to ensure that the good-will of O'Neill be channelled to the maximum effect for the new agenda on Ireland led by John Hume. Christine Sullivan Daly, Tip O'Neill's scheduler, relates:

> Michael Lillis would never let you up for a minute. If Michael had somebody in town from Ireland or Northern Ireland, and if he thought

it was really important that they come in and brief the Speaker, even to come in and meet him and shake hands, there was no way Michael was going to go back to the Embassy without you agreeing to that meeting. If you were not coming along quickly enough, all of a sudden there would be stories about blood in the streets and this was going to be the end of things as we know them in Western civilisation. He was a very dramatic guy. The Speaker would always say yes because he was interested and he always wanted to be helpful.

The Speaker's help extended to his influence on President Carter. As well as dovetailing with Carter's vision of the United States' role in the world, it was also in President Carter's best interests to concede to O'Neill's strong preferences, since he needed O'Neill's facilitation to govern. Lillis elaborates:

> The president of the United States, in order to pass his legislative programme on anything from social security to very controversial issues in Central America such as the *Sandinistas* in Nicaragua, needed the support of Tip O'Neill. And Tip O'Neill had a very different view on these issues from Carter. But they negotiated and Tip O'Neill put at the very centre of his negotiation the programme of John Hume. Hume had an extraordinary effect on O'Neill (as he did on the other Horsemen), but on O'Neill in particular and O'Neill was the most powerful of the four of them. He was the second most powerful politician in the United States. And he took the Irish issue on as passionately as any basic American priority for the American people.

The Carter Statement

What, from President Carter's own point of view, led up to what became the famous Carter Statement on peace in Northern Ireland? President Carter relates:

> When I was elected President and gave my inaugural address, I called for the United States to be a champion of human rights and to promote peace everywhere we could in the world. Obviously, I learned very

quickly that one of the main challenges for peace and human rights was in Northern Ireland, in its relationship with the rest of Ireland and also with Great Britain. Soon, Governor Hugh Carey from New York, Pat Moynihan and Ted Kennedy in the Senate, and Tip O'Neill started giving me information about it quite often. Pat Moynihan and the others, Tip O'Neill, would quote John Hume and his efforts for a peaceful resolution of the Irish problem. I became convinced that the United States should speak out for change on this issue and call for honouring the desire for the Northern Ireland people for peace – with Great Britain and the rest of Ireland – and also for recognition by the international community. So I drafted a statement that was issued the first year I was in office, not only calling for the United States to be directly involved but also to promise that if peace was achieved, the United States would join with others in giving financial assistance to job creation.

It was a very supportive and very benign one-page statement. Yet what was striking about the 1977 Carter Statement was quite how much it seemed to antagonise the State Department and the British Embassy, whose resistance was vehement. President Carter provides the political context:

> Well, the State Department was not in favour of what I did, as you may know. But I didn't really consult with them too thoroughly. I had a lot of confidence in Pat Moynihan, and Tip O'Neill was visiting me every day. Hugh Carey was very important to me as a politician, so was Ted Kennedy. So those four people, who had connections directly with Ireland, were good.

The Four Horsemen were in a position to convey the intricacies of the problem to Carter – the provocations and injustices felt by the Nationalist community in the North, and not simply the IRA response to them. Yet, while some commentators, both in the United States and Ireland, equivocated on the use of violence to settle the Northern Irish issue, Carter's statement was clear that if the White House was to play a role, absolutely no tolerance of violent methods was acceptable. It is a statement of non-violence and that was in absolute accord with John Hume's view of things, and President Carter was adamant that violence from either side had no place in resolution of the Irish Question:

Well, there was violence on both sides. I think the British exhibited unnecessary violence in trying to control the Northern Irish citizens, and the IRA obviously committed acts of violence against Great Britain, including some of the top people who lived in Great Britain. Lord Mountbatten, I remember, was killed. So the violence on both sides caused me to be very careful, to make sure that my statement back in 1977 did not encourage either side to continue with their violent acts. Peace was very important to me as well as human rights, those were the two things that were important to my whole administration.

In addition to conveying the urgency and necessity of action to President Carter, Hume and the Horsemen were at pains to find a way through the State Department bureaucracy, as Senator Ted Kennedy recalls:

My conversations, and I believe John [Hume]'s, were with Cy Vance [Secretary of State Cyrus Vance] and a number of the people who were advising and guiding him [Jimmy Carter] at that time ... In early June, Tip and I and Pat Moynihan went to the State Department to present a proposal to Cy Vance. This was the proposal – if there was going to be progress made in terms of the two different traditions in the conflict, the United States was prepared to offer economic aid and assistance in order to try to move the conflict into the political sphere and political resolution. We had a proposal and we pointed out that it fit perfectly into President Carter's commitment to a moral foreign policy and his strong commitment on human rights.[7]

Despite all the ways in which an intervention from Carter chimed with the mission of his presidency, the Four Horsemen received the following letter from Hodding Carter of the State Department in late June 1977:

To the friends of Ireland ...

If all the parties were to conclude the U.S. could play a useful role, we would naturally consider what we might do. However, none of the parties concerned has requested U.S. to take an active part. In the absence of such a request, the U.S. Government is convinced that U.S. intervention could be both inappropriate and counter-productive.[8]

The tone of this letter was designed to appear as the picture of reasonableness. Yet 'all the parties' would necessarily include Britain and, as the State Department well knew, the British were using their every weapon to frustrate the US from playing an 'active part' in Northern Ireland. In short, the State Department was patiently waiting for a request which they knew would come in only after hell had thoroughly frozen over. (Similarly, after the Bloody Sunday massacre, the President Nixon White House had issued a statement, 'The United States government would play a role only at the request of both British and Irish governments.')[9]

Robert Hunter heard first-hand from the State Department about their misgivings:

> There was no doubt the State Department did not like the idea of the President getting involved, and if I may say so, to heck with the State Department, because this was about bigger issues. This was not about day-to-day matters and how do you keep people happy. This was about change. One thing I believed in, always have believed in and certainly did in regard to everything I did in the White House, [is] how do you make things happen? How do you make things change? Dr Zbigniew Brzezinski [President Carter's National Security Advisor] was probably going to take my word for what happened and the President would take Brzezinski's word.

Yet Kennedy had great faith in Cy Vance's skill as a diplomat and he continued to work with him in tandem with O'Neill's quid pro quo propositions to President Carter. By August they had their statement, which in Robert Hunter's words 'was the breakpoint, suddenly the United States was on the opposite side of the issue'.

On 30 August 1977, President Carter issued his statement through a spokesperson, who read it on the White House Lawn:

> Throughout our history, Americans have rightly recalled the contributions men and women from many countries have made to the development of the United States. Among the greatest contributions have been those of the British and Irish people, Protestant and Catholic alike. We have close ties of friendship with both parts of Ireland and with Great Britain.

It is natural that Americans are deeply concerned about the continuing conflict and violence in Northern Ireland. We know the overwhelming majority of the people there reject the bomb and the bullet. The United States wholeheartedly supports peaceful means for finding a just solution that involves both parts of the community of Northern Ireland and protects human rights and guarantees freedom from discrimination – a solution that the people in Northern Ireland, as well as the Governments of Great Britain and Ireland can support. Violence cannot resolve Northern Ireland's problems; it only increases them and solves nothing.

We hope that all those engaged in violence will renounce this course and commit themselves to [the] peaceful pursuit of legitimate goals. The path of reconciliation, cooperation, and peace is the only course that can end the human suffering and lead to a better future for all the people of Northern Ireland. I ask all Americans to refrain from supporting with financial or other aid organizations whose involvement, direct or indirect, in this violence delays the day when the people of Northern Ireland can live and work together in harmony, free from fear. Federal law enforcement agencies will continue to apprehend and prosecute any who violate U.S. laws in this regard.

U.S. Government policy on the Northern Ireland issue has long been one of impartiality, and that is how it will remain. We support the establishment of a form of government in Northern Ireland which will command widespread acceptance throughout both parts of the community. However, we have no intention of telling the parties how this might be achieved. The only permanent solution will come from the people who live there. There are no solutions that outsiders can impose.

At the same time, the people of Northern Ireland should know that they have our complete support in their quest for a peaceful and just society. It is a tribute to Northern Ireland's hard-working people that the area has continued to attract investment, despite the violence committed by a small minority. This is to be welcomed, since investment and other programs to create jobs will assist in ensuring a healthy economy and combating unemployment.

It is still true that a peaceful settlement would contribute immeasurably to stability in Northern Ireland and so enhance the prospects for increased investment. In the event of such a settlement, the U.S. Government would be prepared to join with others to see how additional job-creating investment could be encouraged, to the benefit of all the people of Northern Ireland.

I admire the many true friends of Northern Ireland in this country who speak out for peace. Emotions run high on this subject, and the easiest course is not to stand up for conciliation. I place myself firmly on the side of those who seek peace and reject violence in Northern Ireland.[10]

The Statement *looked* neutral, but given the foregoing account of the negotiations leading up to it, it was anything but. The ingredients of the peace process were present in the Carter statement: bringing jobs and investment to Northern Ireland, enabling people to transcend their division through working together, 'spilling their sweat not their blood' – as Hume repeatedly urged – and the need for more equitable and accountable institutions in Northern Ireland. How did the President view that? 'It was a rare thing for the United States to take a position against the policies of the Great Britain government,' recalls President Carter, 'because some people, most people, considered that to be an internal affair just for the people in London to decide ultimately. I did not really feel that way. I thought it was a challenge to human rights.'

This statement from the White House, against the wishes of the British, was without precedent in history. As Lillis put it:

This was one of the things that changed our history in the last fifty or sixty years. I think the phrase 'tectonic plates' is appropriate here. Hume succeeded in removing the influence of Britain and the State Department on the Northern Ireland Question, with the White House preventing them from completely controlling the situation. It balanced the situation out. We did not get from our side everything that we wanted, that is never possible in diplomacy, but we actually got a voice and considerable influence. This was resisted in the most bruising possible way by the British. The key thing here was that the President of the United States, for the very first time, had said something more than 'we will not get involved'.

When the Carter Statement was issued, the British ambassador to the US was Peter Jay. That President Jimmy Carter was taking a step by making a statement about what was part of Britain's jurisdiction, Northern Ireland, was for some people a terrible arrogance and none of the US president's business. Yet Peter Jay recalls that the British were prepared to make an accommodation if the benefit was less weapons and money getting into the hands of the paramilitaries:

> I think the government in London had needed to resolve in its own mind a dilemma. If, on the one hand, you stand pat on the doctrine this is none of anybody's business except ours: Americans keep out, Dublin keep out, you are not going to get any helpful results in relation to the problem you have – which is that significant amounts of money [were] reaching paramilitary organisations. The British Government had reached the conclusion that the help and support of those four very heavy-hitting Irish-American politicians in discouraging misguided people, or people anyway, from sending arms and money to support terrorism on the island of Ireland was a very important objective, an objective shared by the government in London and the government in Dublin. If it meant swallowing a bit of antique pride about having comments on the domestic affairs of the so-called UK, well that was a very modest price to pay for a very important objective.

Some deconstruction: First, it is moot that the root of the problem was 'significant amounts of money reaching paramilitary organisations', as the British frequently claimed. Even restricting that analysis to America, it is questionable that the kernel of the problem was 'jars on the bars' funding 'widows and orphans' in the Six Counties. While NORAID funds were a big part of the problem, the failure of policy in Britain and in Northern Ireland to enable the Nationalist minority to identify with, and participate in, their state certainly lent a perceived legitimacy to the Republican dimension of the armed struggle. This in turn gave strength to the propaganda activities of NORAID supporters in the US. Secondly, while the Four Horsemen stood for resolutely constitutional means to address the Northern Irish crisis, they stood for a lot more besides. They were convinced that they could – and should – use their political clout to take active measures to bolster Hume's approach; these measures included passing resolutions in Congress, prioritising the Irish Question in their negotiations with the White House, and using their status with the American media to communicate that the Northern Ireland crisis was not nearly as monochrome as news reports from London tended to paint it. Thirdly, the ex post facto rationalisation that London and Dublin shared the objective of ending terrorism in Northern Ireland disguises the fact that the British were forced to concede the involvement of Ireland and the US in Northern Ireland.

The breakthrough that the Carter Statement constituted was irreversible. Carter himself is quite clear on the point:

> It was very important for me to express myself personally to the prime ministers of Great Britain, to let them know that this was not just a superficial statement on my part but I really meant it and it was an important part of American policy. That is why I talked mostly to Jim Callaghan, and then after a couple of years he was replaced as prime minister by Margaret Thatcher and I also discussed it with her. So I let it be known, both to the British leaders and also to the general public and to my Irish supporters in the United States, that I had one policy toward Ireland. That was peace, human rights and an absence of violence.

The Statement had a lasting effect on America's relationship with Britain, and it formed the framework for future discussions. A handwritten letter on White House-headed paper, dated 25 July 1979, from President Carter to Senator Kennedy read: 'To Ted Kennedy, I discussed Northern Ireland with PM Thatcher and will report results of our conversation next time I see you, Jimmy.'

When Prime Minister Callaghan visited Washington, he stood alongside Jimmy Carter on the South Lawn of the White House and stated the mantra of the special relationship between the United Kingdom of Great Britain and Northern Ireland and the United States. But the mould had been broken and the Carter initiative mapped out what could happen in the North of Ireland if peace were secured; in the words of Seán Donlon, 'every subsequent US president derives his interest in Ireland through the Carter Statement'.

Consequences of the Carter Statement

While the British Embassy reports to headquarters in London on the defeat in the US Congress of the Fogarty Resolution on Irish reunification a generation earlier were jubilant, representing it as a defeat not only of the Irish on the Hill but as put-down to any upstart ethnic group, with the Carter Statement things had come full circle. Robert Hunter argues: 'It was one of *the* important moments in which the United States took an issue of importance to an ethnic community and turned it on its head and helped with the education of people.'

Although the formation of the Four Horsemen and the Carter Statement represented a milestone for Hume's political agenda, it came at a cost. Unsurprisingly, during the SDLP annual party meeting in December 1976 Hume was sternly criticised for his absence in the United States. He did not defend himself on the grounds that in his absence he had been relentlessly active for peace and for the principles of the party, and that facet of Hume's personality, his discretion, was distinctly upsetting to some of his colleagues. Yet it shows that Hume managed to leverage the power of the US and not be bewitched and consumed by the popularity that association with it could afford; he kept his objective of peaceful reconstruction absolutely clear.

4

Washington: Shifting Policy in London on Ireland, 1977–81

The formation of the Irish National Caucus to influence US Congressmen made it clear that two opposing blocs, differing principally on what constituted an acceptable mode of response to the Northern Irish crisis, would form in Congress. The Ad Hoc Committee on Irish Affairs, created in 1977 in large part by the Ancient Order of Hibernians (AOH) and led by Congressman Mario Biaggi, was to a considerable degree the congressional arm of the INC. The alternative bloc – formed in 1981 with the support of the Four Horsemen – ultimately became known as the Friends of Ireland. Congressmen and Senators from both the Republican and Democratic parties were invited to join the Friends of Ireland and respect its founding charter, which strongly affirmed the ideals of peaceful settlement and reconciliation in Ireland. The Friends of Ireland replaced the Four Horsemen, who ceased to operate during the Reagan's Republican presidency; and the emphasis henceforth was on bipartisan engagement. Seán Donlon gives the background to the formation of the organisations:

> Biaggi was available to lobby groups. He was a 'bought' congressman. Now I am not suggesting that the Irish National Caucus or NORAID bribed him or bought him. But it suited him, given the Irish-Americans in his constituency back in New York, to take the Provo/IRA line, basically 'Brits Out'. He formed an Ad Hoc group of Congressmen who basically signed a piece of paper and rarely did anything. But it looked good on paper; he had a hundred members of Congress signed up to this group. Tip O'Neill felt that he better build up a corresponding

group. So he contacted a fellow congressman, a friend of his, Tom Foley, to head up the group and it became the Friends of Ireland.

Nancy Soderberg remembers: 'What Ted Kennedy did in the early stages, in the 1970s and 1980s, was to try and build up a political base for John Hume here in the United States that opposed the IRA method. The IRA had great support here in the United States.'

But where exactly did the fault lines lie? Who created momentum within Congress for the Sinn Féin–IRA point of view, and who led the John Hume approach? Nancy Soderberg again:

The House of Representatives is designed by our Constitution to be closer to the grassroots. So that's exactly what you saw, it was very much a grassroots movement which filtered out through the members of Congress. The Senate was more attracted to the John Hume, more thoughtful approach. The grassroots filtered out through the IRA wing but then you had the more senior statesmen creating a counterweight, really led by John Hume behind the scenes. So it was Ted Kennedy, Tip O'Neill, Hugh Carey of New York and Senator Pat Moynihan also of New York.

Chris Dodd, a Democrat from Connecticut first elected to the US House of Representatives in 1975 and to the US Senate in 1981, recalls that he, 'gravitated to John's approach. I understood the passion of the Caucus's view. But it appeared to me that John had a longer view'. It was Tip O'Neill who facilitated an introduction between to Hume and Dodd. As Dodd recalls:

I met Hume through Tip in the late 1970s during a very difficult period. Northern Ireland was not a compelling issue on Capitol Hill at the time. There was not a burning need to immerse oneself in its politics. The activist element, Fr Seán McManus, periodically came to Congress to coax a group of us into taking a stance on Northern Ireland. Hume provided an alternative space where people could go, and not be stigmatised for being against NORAID. Hume was critical in providing this alternative, which would not have worked without him. He was clearly gifted intellectually and politically, and he was consistent. He knew that this would not happen without outside assistance, probably Irish-American and Catholic. He never sought notoriety, he just persisted. He understood that history does not move forward without taking risks. So he did what someone needed to do. He insisted on accommodations.

Hume's frequent trips to the US focused on the potentiality of Congress to repulse the facile solutions offered throughout Irish-America. Hume had resolved early in his campaign that his efforts were best channelled at the level of federal power. Yet Congressmen encountered animosity to the perceived cowardice of the constitutional approach when they returned their constituencies. A taste of that animosity is captured in the following encounter experienced by Seamus Mallon (Hume's SDLP colleague who occasionally travelled to the US to speak to grassroots organisations in Philadelphia, Pittsburgh and Detroit):

I had to speak at a meeting in the Emerald Club in Detroit on a Friday evening, about two hours after work ended. Anybody who knows that score knows that's not a good time – those two hours made people more vocal. Anyhow, the Irish Consul-General, Liam Cuniffe, spoke before me. He was treated very badly. There was a guy at the back of the room and I knew when I'd walked in that he was the Provo IRA plant. He gave Liam such abuse. I'm sitting up there and this voice is away at the back of the hall. So I said to him, 'would you like to come up here and say that?' He stood up. He was about six feet five tall, broad as a ditch. Here was I, shaking in my shoes, not showing it and had to stand. I could not back off. He got up to me and he told me what he would do if he had his gun (not *a* gun) with him: 'If I had my gun, I would shoot the head off you'. And then he left. That only increased my recognition of what had to be done. I threw down a challenge that night. I said, 'many of you are in favour of violence, killing people, trying to solve political problems with the wrong means. I'll tell you what I'll do. I'll get somebody with money to hire a plane to leave Detroit, taking all your young sons and daughters over the age of fifteen to Northern Ireland to do the fighting. That is the test I'll put to you'. The result was obvious from the word go.

For congressmen representing such constituencies, the equation could be as stark as political survival, particularly for those who fought for marginal seats and who needed the support of hardliners. For some congressmen such recrimination led to being punished during re-election bids; they were scapegoated by a frustrated and often ill-informed electorate.

If the fight for the conscience of Irish-America needed one symbolic embodiment, there is scarcely one better than Congressman Charlie Dougherty. As Republican State Senator running for the US Congress in 1978 in a resolutely Democrat area, North East Philadelphia, Dougherty needed Democrat votes. A trade union leader, Johnny Morris, approached Dougherty to make a pact: that he publicly support the IRA and NORAID, and publicly state that he would join the Ad Hoc Committee under Congressman Mario Biaggi on entry into the US Congress, and in return Morris would deliver the Teamsters Union support. Dougherty had happened to hear Taoiseach Jack Lynch make a remarkable statement (unique in the history of Irish Taoisigh) denouncing Congressman Biaggi, and he was firm that he would not back Biaggi: 'When I wouldn't support the IRA and join the Biaggi committee, let's say I was greeted by him on a number of occasions less than friendly.'

Even without Morris's support, Dougherty was elected to Congress in November 1978, and took office in January 1979. Within days of being sworn in, he received a telephone call from Irish Ambassador to the US, Seán Donlon, inviting him to the Irish Embassy to meet John Hume. Dougherty readily accepted:

John and I really hit it off. John was real. He was an average working-class guy. He didn't have an agenda that was hidden. I had a very long conversation that day with John and Seán Donlon, but John did a lot of the talking about the reality of Northern Ireland. From that day on we were locked in. Seán Donlon said to me: 'We have a consulate in Boston, we have a consulate in New York, we have the embassy in Washington. But we have nothing in Philadelphia, and it is a hotbed for the IRA. Will you stand up and defend the Irish Government, will you support John and the SDLP?' I said 'yes, I will do that'. I agreed to be the spokesperson in Philly for the position of the Irish Government and John Hume.

Commenting on the two competing narratives on the Ireland Question in Congress at the time, Dougherty noted:

> Tip O'Neill created what was called the Friends of Ireland and it was a membership made up of Congressmen who would support the Irish government and support John Hume. I joined it as soon as it was formed. I eventually got to be the ranking Republican on the committee. So from that point on, nothing happened on the floor on Ireland of any significance without the Friends of Ireland because a majority of people in Congress identified with Tip O'Neill. The best Biaggi could do was make speeches.

Wielding the gavel as Speaker of the House, O'Neill had an enormous role in steering Congress. While Tip was from the Democratic side of the House, he trusted Dougherty profoundly and collaborated with him extensively. This was a time of significant bipartisanship in the US Congress on Ireland, which has endured in the Irish context despite the progressive collapse of bipartisanship between Democrats and Republicans in recent years. At the Congressional lunch on St Patrick's Day in 2016, President Obama praised the bipartisan nature of the annual gathering, saying: 'It's a welcome break from politics as usual, a moment when we all trade in our red and power blue ties for our green ones.'[1] Dougherty recollects that the Irish issue was an issue which both Republicans and Democrats could rally around and transcend party affiliation:

> Yes, it was an interesting time. Tip didn't preside all the time. The Speaker presides when there's something significant, but other people preside and I would walk on the floor and occasionally Tip would say: 'Brother Dougherty, come over here'. He'd be sitting in the front row, I would sit down next to him and he's said to me: 'Now, what are you doing over there with those [Republican] guys? You belong over here with us'. I would say, 'ah, Mr Speaker, I appreciate that'. Tip O'Neill was a guy that you had to like. He did not have any vindictiveness like you may have today in Congress.

Moreover, O'Neill ensured that delegations to Ireland reflected both the Republican and Democrat make-up of the House. Dougherty was the sole Republican nominated by Tip to send on official delegations to Ireland:

When the decision was made to have the exchange group between the Irish Parliament, the Dáil, and the US Congress, Tip put together a five-member team. Tom Foley was Majority Leader, who was a Democrat from Washington. He would eventually become Speaker. Jim Shannon was a Congressman for Massachusetts, he went on to become the Attorney General of Massachusetts. Chris Dodd went on to become a United States Senator. I was the Republican and then there was Kirk O'Donnell, who was Tip's counsel. So that was the five of us. We had a great time visiting Ireland. I went to Ireland in '79, '81 and '82 for the exchange between the Irish Parliament and the United States Congress.

Being an astute politician, O'Neill understood how hard it was for Dougherty, coming from North East Philadelphia, to adopt the Hume line on the North. Despite being a partisan Democrat, he always managed to be supportive of Republican Dougherty in covert ways. For example, Dougherty recalls:

There was never a presence of anything from Tip O'Neill in my district in the re-election campaign. When I ran for re-election I was endorsed by the state CIO and by the US Chamber of Commerce. So I had labour and business both supporting me. But there was a movement by some of my labour guys to get Tip to call me and ask me to switch parties. And he didn't call because the message back was I pretty much wasn't ready to become a Democrat. But I know for a fact that if I had said, 'yes, I'll take a call from the Speaker', I would have heard from Tip.

A central instrument to propound the Hume line was the St Patrick's Day Statements. The first St Patrick's Day Statement emanated from the Four Horsemen, but by 1981 it has become a statement from the Friends of Ireland, which involved robust criticism of IRA violence as well as British excesses and pressure toward a new agreement. Equally, British policymakers, in coordination with the British Embassy in Washington, attempted to frustrate the Friends of Ireland's efforts to reconfigure Anglo-Irish relations. For the most part Britain was powerless to stymie the work of the caucus. The best resistance it could muster was an annual smear campaign, timed to coincide with the St Patrick's Day statements, in which Ted Kennedy was singled out for characterisation as an IRA fellow traveller in the British press.

In *The Irish Times*, the British Secretary of State for Northern Ireland, Humphrey Atkins, called on the SDLP to stop 'using Dublin and Washington to influence British policy in Northern Ireland'.[2] Similarly, in Dublin, Conor Cruise O'Brien, in a head-to-head television debate with Hume on RTÉ after the Carter Statement in 1977, argued that it was undesirable for Washington to play a role in Northern Ireland and persistently attempted to draw Hume out on the Washington dimension of Hume's programme. Hume ignored him. The predictable sources of attrition notwithstanding, a fatal threat to the Hume line in Washington was to emerge from an unexpected quarter. In 1970, an Irish government minister had been brought to trial on charges of conspiracy to smuggle arms from the South of Ireland to the IRA in the North. Although the charges were dropped, he was fired from government. In December 1979, in a dramatic comeback, Charles J. Haughey became Taoiseach of Ireland.

The Donlon Incident

Seán Donlon was appointed Irish ambassador to the USA in July 1978 by Irish Taoiseach Jack Lynch. Donlon found a significant 'overlap of leadership' between NORAID and the Irish National Caucus, including eight INC board members who readily identified with NORAID; the former was a fundraising organisation for the IRA and the latter 'did not find it possible to condemn the violence of the Provisional IRA'. Additionally, Congressman Mario Biaggi's Ad Hoc Committee on Irish Affairs often covertly took the Provisional IRA line on Northern Ireland.

From the time Charles J. Haughey was elected Taoiseach, on 11 December 1979, he repeatedly stated that 'the first political priority' of his administration was the unification of Ireland. At the very same time, Neil Blaney, a maverick TD from Haughey's political party, who sought to outflank him in nationalism, was visiting Washington. Blaney had been invited by the INC, and he issued a statement stating: 'it is the wish of all the friends of Ireland that the government will work with the INC in the important task it has undertaken ... it is doing the job that our embassy in Washington should be doing but is not doing'.[3] In a memoir of his time as

Irish ambassador in the US, Seán Donlon registered quite how badly that stance was viewed by Tip O'Neill:

> O'Neill had sought me out – at his birthday party – as early as December 11th. There were, he said, two Irish positions in the US, that of the Four Horsemen and that of Biaggi and the INC. The positions were in conflict. The basis for the Horsemen's position was the Irish government and John Hume. If that basis was removed, they were no longer interested in being involved … Then British Prime Minister Margaret Thatcher was due to visit Washington on December 17th and O'Neill wanted to know what he and Carter should say to her about Northern Ireland.

Among the messages conveyed to Donlon by Haughey by phone on 14 December was: 'As far as the Carter statement of 1977 was concerned, we should not press for any official US commitment to invest in Northern Ireland in advance of the creation there of acceptable political institutions.'[4] Haughey's stated agenda – to unify Ireland – was hardly a political agenda with which Unionists would make common cause.

In Washington, Donlon relates, 'because of his [Haughey's] background, particularly the attempt in 1969–70 to import arms, and the reputation he had in the United States as somebody who had been very close to the Provisional IRA, there was a concern particularly on the part of the Four Horsemen, that Irish government policy would now change'. Donlon had to adopt the classic diplomat's role of reassuring the Americans and gently steering his government's position. But Haughey was not inclined to take directions from his representative. His thinking on the North of Ireland was definite, as Donlon relates:

> I knew his mind on Northern Ireland and the American role: the Brits created the problem, the Brits have to solve the problem. It is not for Ireland to get involved. His view was that whatever problems there might be in the US with the IRA getting money and guns, let the Brits deal with it. They created partition. Let them deal with it.

Haughey's dogmatism blurred distinctions, which for the Four Horsemen were clear and non-negotiable boundaries. On 22–3 January 1980, during extensive meetings with Haughey in the presence of other diplomats in Dublin, Donlon heard from Haughey that 'he wanted to end the divisiveness of the Irish effort in the US. He wished to see a unity of effort involving the Four Horsemen, Biaggi's Ad Hoc Committee, the INC, and NORAID'. Donlon took pains to convey quite how impossible that ambition was. However, it was clear that the Taoiseach was not amenable to such perspectives because Donlon was called to Dublin to meet Haughey and he was instructed to leave Washington:

> In July of 1980, Haughey sent for me yet again and this time I knew that I was being fired because when I arrived all the other chairs had been removed. There was only his chair behind his desk and I had to stand. Someone had tipped me off that if you walked into Haughey's room and there were no chairs it was going to be a short meeting, he was going to tell you something. That is exactly what happened. He said, 'I'm asking you to leave Washington with immediate effect'. There was no discussion at that point.

Speaking in Strasbourg, Neil Blaney could not contain his pleasure at Donlon's removal: 'I'm delighted if he's going to be moved.' Blaney alleged that Ambassador Donlon 'went out of his way to make clear to Irish-Americans that they shouldn't have anything to do with the Irish National Caucus. He also discouraged members of Congress from joining Biaggi's committee, which is the brainchild of the caucus'.[5] In contrast, Seán Donlon recalls that Hume's response to his removal by Haughey was swift and immediate:

> Haughey's priority was to gain more political support in Ireland. If in the process he had to dump Washington, he would dump Washington. It did not come to that mainly because of the Horsemen and because the only time that John Hume intervened in a domestic political situation in Dublin was in relation to my removal from Washington. Hume told Haughey that this would be unacceptable.

It was an example of John Hume effectively instructing the Taoiseach, which was something he was very loath ever to do, and only did *in extremis*. It is nevertheless illustrative of Hume's power in Dublin when he decided to exercise it. When the news reached Washington, the Four Horsemen were also very quick to react. Donlon relates that: 'They made their views known both publicly and privately. Both Tip O'Neill and Ted Kennedy phoned Haughey and said "if you're changing your policy you are losing us, and if you lose us you will lose the White House". It was as blunt as that.'

A Taoiseach recalling an ambassador is seldom in itself enough to be the cynosure of international news. Still, the 'Donlon Incident', as it became known, was a serious crisis inasmuch as it jeopardised the continued involvement of the Four Horsemen. Donlon, in the eyes of the Horsemen, was the embodiment of Hume's agenda through the Irish government's representative. If he seemed to be removed on policy grounds, it suggested to the Horsemen that policy had changed, and from the Horsemen's point of view, no change of policy was possible: any ambiguity whatever on the use of violence to achieve political objectives and they were out. Haughey's commitment to Donlon therefore became a barometer for the Irish government's continued commitment to constitutional methods (and condemnation of violent fundraising groups).

The threat of losing the Horsemen, combined with losing Hume's support, caused Haughey to climb down. He publicly stated that there was no truth in the rumour that Ambassador Donlon was to be removed. At this point, Hume made an intervention that forced Haughey's hand: 'In order that all shades of suspicion be removed and this unfortunate affair closed, it is necessary that it be made absolutely clear that the activities of Congressman Biaggi and the organisations with which he is associated enjoy no support whatsoever among any substantial section of Irish opinion.'[6] Haughey made the requisite statement in Cork on 27 July, asking:

> [A]ll in America who have the interests of Ireland at heart not to give this body any support … associations that exist between NORAID and the INC casts grave suspicions on the latter organisation … I say now to all supporters of the bodies I have mentioned [NORAID and the INC] that they should carefully consider whether the cause they profess to serve would not now be best served by uniting in firm support of the policy of the Irish Government.[7]

Seán Donlon elaborates:

As far as I know, that was the only speech that Haughey made in order to get Hume's continued political support, because if Hume had broken off relations with any Irish government, particularly with Haughey, there would have been no basis for an Irish government policy. When it came to Irish government policy at any stage since the foundation of the State, formulating a policy in relation to Northern Ireland required some basis for that policy. At that time, the obvious basis was the SDLP, because they were the elected representatives of the Nationalist community in Northern Ireland and in the front line.

As stated earlier, the Four Horsemen was a system of power politics, and the 'Donlon Incident' served to reinforce the roles particular actors could play and had to play. In Washington, there was an apparent contradiction on the Ireland Question in that Hume, the central authority on Ireland in the eyes of the Horsemen, was not the head of the Irish government. Rarely did the two come into contest, but the conclusion was foregone when they did. Subsequently, Fianna Fáil party leader, Charles Haughey, asked Bertie Ahern to be part of a delegation to Washington. Ahern relates what he encountered in terms of Hume's influence on Washington:

The Irish living in America were putting their hands in their pockets every week and giving dollars to fund the cause [the armed struggle to unite Ireland]. As I got older in politics, I realised that this was not the right message. John Hume had realised that a long, long time earlier and he had explained that to Tip O'Neill. So when you were talking to Tip he very much said what the underlying causes were, why people were doing this, why people were being killed, why people were joining the IRA, why they were being supported and why communities were not given any information. Tip O'Neill had an amazing insight into all that, which he got from his relationship with John Hume.

For Tip O'Neill, and for senior politicians in America, it was on their desk every day because they got reports from the State Department on Northern Ireland. And Tip took his lead, and Tip took his politics, and Tip took the view of what John was saying. I would say in those days he was taking it far more from John than he was from the Irish government.

Tip O'Neill's Visit to Ireland, 1979

Speaker Tip O'Neill's celebrated visit to Ireland in April 1979 was memorable above all for his comments in relation to British policy in Ireland. Speaking in Dublin Castle in April 1979, Tip O'Neill said, 'we do insist on an early, realistic and major initiative on the part of the incoming British Government so as to get serious negotiations moving quickly towards a just, realistic and workable solution'.[8] It transpired that O'Neill's comment was aimed at Margaret Thatcher, who was to win a landslide victory and become Prime Minister of Britain the following month. The comment caused furore, even in the leftist British press. As James Cooper observed, 'the *Guardian* was rejecting O'Neill's intervention as neo-colonialist language that the UK had moved on from'. Further criticising O'Neill, the editorial noted how he had 'a privileged status in these matters', given his position as 'a man of influence in the White House' who could 'gain attention denied to others struggling behind him on that same path to righteousness'.[9]

True, O'Neill's use of 'we do insist' exceeded reasonable restraint for a foreign politician commenting on another country. However, viewed from another perspective, what is more compelling is that even before proroguing the Northern Irish Parliament, the British government had deployed troops in Northern Ireland, which had routinely abandoned professional standards and partaken of 'high-speed driving of armoured cars through heavily populated areas, day and night, but often without lights and often with two wheels on the footpath',[10] culminating in the massacre of Bloody Sunday. Consternation about Speaker O'Neill's use of the word 'insist' happened against that backdrop.

Speaker O'Neill's insistence extended to pushing small but symbolic acts of legislation through Congress, which ensured that American pressure continued to be felt. As Cooper further notes: 'Much to the displeasure of the UK government and U.S. State Department, in August 1979 O'Neill allowed the amendment banning the sales [of weapons to the Royal Ulster Constabulary] attached to the State Department annual appropriations Bill to pass through Congress. The Carter administration accepted the ban.'[11] Implicit in O'Neill's move to ban the sale of weapons to the RUC was a critique of policing in Northern Ireland. Hume had, from the early 1970s, been outspoken about the bias in the police force, which was abetted by a paramilitary wing, the B-Specials. The unrepresentative character of the police force augmented in proportion to the Nationalist minority's flight from its ranks after Brian Faulkner's 'internment without trial' policy was introduced in 1971. The non-identification with the police on the part of the Nationalist community destabilised Northern Irish security a great deal, and O'Neill's protest ban on weapon sales highlighted the matter. What was also implicit in his stance was that this was a counterpart measure to the Friends of Ireland members' bid to thin the flow of weapons from the US to the IRA. That vague association rankled London.

Yet, in the form of Margaret Thatcher, the UK had just elected a thoroughgoing Unionist, whose imperious manner was deeply unsettling. Hume was always anxious to convey to Thatcher the complexities of the Northern Irish situation, given her famous touchstone, that 'Ulster is as British as Finchley.' On 13 May 1980, a meeting between Hume and Thatcher in 10 Downing Street lasted from 11.35 to 12.15, and revolved around Thatcher's insistence on protecting the Unionist minority and Hume's insistence that the absence of agreement fed the terrorist campaign, which was a menace to both the minority and the majority. He stated that he was leaving the meeting in a worried state of mind, and that Northern Ireland was unlike an English constituency, which needed to be understood since in England, even if one party dominates at a local level, at the national level there are frequent changes in government. As relations soured between Dublin and London during the early 1980s, Hume would try to meet Thatcher ahead of the Taoiseach's scheduled appointment to put his point across.

The Reagan Landslide

When James Sharkey, Michael Lillis's successor, arrived in Washington as Irish Political Officer on 12 July 1980, Seán Donlon was the Irish Ambassador and still energetically collaborating with John Hume on the Irish Question on the Hill and in the White House. Sharkey witnessed Ted Kennedy's Concession Address at the Democratic National Conference in New York on 12 August 1980, following his defeat to Jimmy Carter for the Democratic nomination as President. Tip O'Neill, Senator Moynihan, Governor Carey and others all made clear that they identified with John Hume and would continue to work with the Irish government on the basis of Hume's principles. In Washington, a legislative assistant to Ted Kennedy, Matthew Murray, remembers:

> I was invited ... to The Dubliner, which is a bar on the Hill, by Ambassador Donlon and James Sharkey, and John Hume was there. It was the four of us to discuss what we were about to do and John Hume turned to me and he said 'do you know what the most amazing thing is about the United States?' I said I'd like to know. He said, 'that it's one country'.

James Sharkey remembers:

> One of the most important meetings that I attended was on January 20th 1981, the day of the Inauguration of Ronald Reagan. It was in the Ante-room of the offices of Tom Foley, Senior congressman in the Capitol Hill. Tom Foley had just been appointed Majority Whip. Present on that occasion was John Hume; also present was Kirk O'Donnell, who was a Senior Advisor to the Speaker; there was a young congressman from Massachusetts, called Jim Shannon; there was a newly elected congressman from Pittsburgh, called Bill Coyne; Joe Moakley, from Massachusetts, was there. Naturally, in the presence of John Hume they were discussing what should be done on Ireland in the context of the Reagan election and that the Democrats for a long time had lost control of the Senate. Naturally, the talk came out about the Big Four, the Four Horsemen, and also about the fact that Hugh Carey would be retiring soon. So the Big Four would become the Big Three. We also discussed the fact that bipartisanship would have to be the order of the day henceforth, and that absolutely the Irish lobby in Congress should be free from any taint or association with violence if it was to have any impact on the White House and on the Reagan Administration.
>
> They were uncomfortable with the Ad Hoc Committee for Congressional affairs, which had been founded by Mario Biaggi, and they wanted their own grouping, their own base to include Republicans and Democrats which would establish close connections with the Irish government and with Irish elected representatives, which would also be close and sensitive to the SDLP's position in the North and the

position of Unionists. This was ultimately what they set in motion. Their name, which they were given by John Hume, was the Friends of Ireland, and it became the dominant force in Congress on the Irish issue during the 1980s, and indeed the dominant point of reference for the White House on Irish affairs.

At another crucial meeting with James Sharkey, Werner Brandt (from Tom Foley's office), and Kirk O'Donnell it was agreed to outline five recommendations for policy for the Friends of Ireland. Those recommendations became the founding principles of the organisation. Carey Parker gave additional help with drafting the principles and they made clear support for non-violence, reconciliation, persuasion and radical reform. The Friends of Ireland was ultimately launched on St Patrick's Day in 1981, the same day a major lunch was hosted by Ambassador Donlon at his residence at which President Ronald Reagan was Guest of Honour.

The Four Horsemen, four senior Democrats, was an unproblematic grouping during the Presidency of Jimmy Carter. However, after the Reagan Landslide and the loss of the Senate to the Republicans, a new broad-based formation was necessary. As Sharkey recalled, 'given the huge shift in American politics which the Reagan victory represented, it was vitally important that the Irish Question in America should no longer be seen as the exclusive preserve of urban Democrats'. Therefore it was very welcome that senior Republicans, such as Senator Paul Laxalt of Nevada, Senator Orrin Hatch of Utah, Senator John Heinz of Pennsylvania and Senator John Danforth of Missouri, were founding members of the Friends of Ireland.

By June 1981, Garret FitzGerald had become Taoiseach. FitzGerald overcame some initial hesitation over the Friends of Ireland – perhaps attributable to the confusion and scandal over the 'Donlon Incident' the previous summer – during a visit to Washington, when he embraced the Friends as the de facto supporter of constitutionalism and the Irish government. Hume, for his part, worked to support the Friends of Ireland. James Sharkey remembers that:

[Hume] lobbied on behalf of the Friends of Ireland, at least in commending some people to join. I remember a meeting with Chris Dodd, who had been just elected a Senator for Connecticut, and John made the case – because Connecticut was of course an extension of

New York, especially in a political sense – that Senator Dodd should join the Friends of Ireland, and Senator Dodd became one of the leaders of that organisation. John also, I remember very well, went out to National Airport in Washington, and I went with him, to meet Al D'Amato. Al D'Amato was the new Republican Senator for New York. John made the case again and briefed him on the pragmatic approach to Northern Ireland. Certainly Al D'Amato was impressed with John's sincerity, his commitment and perspective. But Al D'Amato was an Italian-American, and a close friend of Mario Biaggi. So, in the end, he never associated, at least not openly, with the Friends of Ireland, although he did support at least some of their initiatives.

I remember very well a meeting with Paul Laxalt, a senior Nevadan senator, who was very close, even a friend, of Ronald Reagan's. John had just been elected to the European Parliament when he met him. Laxalt was extremely impressed both by John's knowledge of the European Parliament and by his awareness of the Basque problem, because the Nevadan Basques and the New Mexico Basques were a significant minority group since they emigrated to those two states at the end of the nineteenth century. Paul Laxalt became a member of the Friends of Ireland and became a very senior figure in that movement.

One Congressman from Connecticut, Bruce Morrison, who was not at all inclined to support the IRA, joined the Friends of Ireland but later left for the Ad Hoc Committee because he did not consider the Friends of Ireland as a worthwhile or effective caucus. Partly what motivated his change was the focus of the Ad Hoc Committee on human rights abuses:

As time went on, I learned that the other group, the Ad Hoc Committee, had a reputation of being too radical or too aggressive in its positions. But I also found that it really was focused on the human rights issues that were foremost in my mind and over time I switched. I felt that, whatever the reputation issue, I was more concerned about sending messages about human rights than the other things that I saw being done which were more of a celebratory or a congratulatory nature.

Yet Tip O'Neill, Ted Kennedy and others did – through legislation, through supporting initiatives in Ireland and particularly through the Dublin government – support the achievement of peace through legislative and constitutional means. However, Morrison was adamant that 'the problem that had to be solved was to bring the [Irish] Republicans out of their armed struggle, as they would call it, and into the democratic process. They were not a splinter group; they were a group that was supported by a significant number of people in Northern Ireland'.

The Media and the Message

In the United States, the campaign to communicate a new approach to Ireland in the media was the inevitable corollary of the campaign within the US Congress. There were myriad challenges to this undertaking. For one thing, this was a period in which foreign news in the US was overwhelmingly focused on the US–Russia superpowers and on the Middle East. What reportage there was on Ireland was riven between a knee-jerk sympathy for the beleaguered Nationalists in the North, on the one hand, and on the other, a tendency in less Irish-leaning media publications to adopt the British view on matters based both on proclivity and force of habit. Neither of these narratives were adequate to address the Northern Irish Troubles. Consequently, the need to communicate a 'third way' was overwhelming.

When he was then posted to the US in the mid-1970s, first to New York, Michael Lillis found that:

> *The New York Times* and the television networks were very influenced by US State Department Policy, and by the British. But their position evolved, as did that of the position of the Four Horsemen under the leadership of John Hume. The Four Horsemen's Statement led front page news and led the evening news on CBS television, and also featured on NBC and on PBS.

That was the scope of the change which occurred in just a few years. As John A. Farrell, Tip O'Neill's biographer and respected journalist, puts it:

> Irish-American journalists were, like Irish-Americans, great romanticists, maybe even greater romanticists than the average Irish-American fellow on the street. You had columnists like Jimmy Breslin

and Pete Hamill up in New York. You had columnists like Kevin Cullen at the *Boston Globe* and his predecessors, Marty Nolan and David Nyhan; Mary McGrory in the *Washington Post* – a bunch of Irish names sprinkled throughout journalism in the United States – and our first reaction was to be sympathetic; anti-British, 'Brits Out', and even sympathetic to the IRA – despite the horrendous terror campaigns and bombings in Northern Ireland. So there was a process of education that had to be undergone, not just for American political leaders but also for the American press, and John Hume certainly played a role in that.

Overcoming the near monopoly that the British had on news and communication lines was the first step, Seán Donlon relates:

One of the difficulties for anyone in those days dealing with the media in the US was that all the foreign news was generated outside the United States. Northern Ireland news coverage came through London. So the news coverage of what was happening in Northern Ireland was very heavily influenced by the British view. That was particularly evident after Bloody Sunday, when the British had essentially fed to the British journalists in London a particular line about what happened in Derry that Sunday, and that turned up in the US media.

Some serious newspapers, *The Los Angeles Times* for instance, could not cover the Ireland Question other than through its London sources. Its London-based correspondents, Marjorie Miller and Tyler Marshall, covered Northern Ireland when a story emerged, but the Ireland Question was always considerably subordinate to the bigger foreign policy questions of the day. However, it was possible to put Ireland more centrally on their agenda, in East Coast publications in particular, and to create an awareness of the Irish Question as having been distorted by the consensus view among journalists in London. In the case of those newspapers and serious political magazines, Hume was able to meet senior writers and editors, and to impart not only his perspectives about British misrule in the North of Ireland and about the IRA, but the solutions required to address the crisis. Largely due to Hume's influence, a modification in the way Ireland was portrayed in the American media began.

With the status of Ambassador to the USA, Seán Donlon was in a position to cultivate these senior journalists and to introduce them to Hume. It was, as Donlon relates, important to have picked targets:

> What was possible was to get in touch with the editorial types, the people who wrote the editorials and in particular who wrote opinion columns. You would go and meet the editorial board, have lunch with them [and] talk about Ireland, and it was particularly helpful if John Hume was visiting to bring him along because that gave legitimacy, a first-hand account from a man who was a leader at the coal face in Northern Ireland. So, from the mid-1970s on, that became a regular feature of John's visits to the US. Over the years, a small but very influential group of journalists emerged who became specialists on Ireland; people like Michael Kilian in *The Chicago Tribune*, Mary McGrory in *The Washington Post*, Ron Apple in *The New York Times*, Nolan in the *Boston Globe*.

Other prominent journalists who reported on the Irish Questions included Ben Bradlee and Lou Cannon of *The Washington Post*, Roger Mudd of NBC, Michael Pakenham of *The Philadelphia Inquirer* and Sam Donaldson of ABC. Hume's message was very clear, as Ted Smyth, Irish Press Officer in New York in the 1970s, relates:

> Most of his value was in off-the-record briefings. You would take him to *The New York Times* editorial board, the *Daily News*, *The Washington Post*, *Time Magazine*, *Newsweek*. We focused on the editors and journalists there and John really knew how to speak to them and influence them in a way towards an Agreed Ireland. It was a novel story in a way because it was easier to write about the bombs and the bullets and the conflict and why are Catholics killing Protestants and Protestants killing Catholics, as if it was some sort of medieval story. So to turn that around and make it into a failure of policy, which it was. And John pointed that out, that there actually was a better way forward and here it is. He just kept on telling that story until enough people believed him and began to write it in editorials.

Hume's approach was to identify the education level (on Ireland) of the editorial team. If he judged that he was speaking to people who did not know the background or the causes of the Conflict, he would open them up by telling them stories before he got to policy matters.

Aside from the elite media, many of the American Irish and expatriate Irish newspapers traditionally were promulgators of a diehard approach and wholly focused on the question of partition; most, but not all. One which was more nuanced was *The Boston Irish News*, which consciously sought to become part of that education process by recruiting in a very able senior staffer from Daniel Patrick Moynihan's office, Tom Melia, who wrote a monthly column from 1985–8 providing an alternative view to the pro-NORAID publications. He relates:

> The editors of *The Boston Irish News* sought me out and asked me if I would do a report from Washington from time to time about Capitol Hill politics on Irish questions. So I did. It was a monthly publication and it was distributed around the wider Boston area, so I had a pretty regular opportunity to do a presentation of what was going on in Irish-American politics – visitors from Ireland, cabinet members from Ireland visiting or about some of the politics on Capitol Hill. I remember doing a profile of Ambassador Heckler when she was appointed and went to Ireland and did an interview with her. It was just really an occasion to do less controversial, less provocative writing and to normalise the question of Irish-America, make it more the diplomatic back and forth.

Tom Melia and James Sharkey shared perspectives on Northern Irish realities and knowledge dissemination. During one such interaction, Melia gave Sharkey a valuable idea about how best to communicate on the Hill:

> Given the difficulty of educating more people in Capitol Hill about what was going on in modern day Ireland, I said to Jim Sharkey, maybe you guys should do what the Pentagon does: they have a news clippings service that they provide on Capitol Hill. The Pentagon would, with scissors, cut and paste out articles from newspapers that related to their issues and agenda, put them in a packet and photocopy them in their hundreds and distribute them all over Capitol Hill. That is what Sharkey did.

Sharkey worked with the Four Horsemen, but also met with their staffers and with journalists, forming a second circle around the big lions. Arguably the greatest coup, though, was in accessing editorial boards, since their editorials reflected a newspaper's stance and, in the case of *The New York Times*, that held huge sway in American opinion. Once the momentum had begun, Sharkey encouraged Irish-American politicians to articulate the constitutional alternative in the US Congress and in turn endeavoured to bring those speeches to the attention of the press both in the US and in Ireland.

The New York Times editorialist on Ireland (1979–99) was Karl E. Meyer. Meyer had reported on the Troubles in Belfast from 1965–70, while a London bureau chief of *The Washington Post*, and he had immersed himself in Irish history. In many of his editorials, the titles alone spoke of a determined and non-partisan probing of the root causes of the violent conflict in the North of Ireland: 'The Right Response to Irish Terror'; 'In Europe, Hope for the Irish'; 'A Creative Bid for Ulster Peace'; 'Where Mrs. Thatcher Faltered'; 'Papering Over Ulster's Strife'; 'To Live for Ireland'; 'The Sharing of the Green'; 'Don't Let Clothes Make the Martyr'; 'Ireland's Friends'. Meyer recalls the effect that Hume had on *The New York Times* editorial board:

> What John Hume was trying to say – what he did say as a matter of fact, and he persuaded a lot of us to agree with – was that despite the war of words and despite even the war of deeds on either side, there were factions that were looking to a future for their children, their grandchildren, in which the war of words would give way to some kind of reconciliation process. But that reconciliation depended on the granting of political rights, religious rights and other rights; and to some kind of promise that all of the communities would have a voice in the future.

The jolt that a well-informed Fourth Estate in the United States gave to coverage of Ireland was striking. For a long time, 'Green Army' rhetoric had been dismissed because its goals seemed completely unrealisable. As Ted Smyth, former advisor to Garret FitzGerald on Northern Ireland, recalls:

NORAID played into British hands in New York. They put forward a solution based on 'Brits Out', ignoring the rights of one million Protestants in Northern Ireland. Many Americans saw the flaw in that, and so it was easy for them to ignore the NORAID position and the IRA position. When Hume said actually the British should be promoting a solution recognising both Protestant and Catholic rights, then it became more complex for the British. Many of the British did not know how to respond to that.

The silent influence Hume managed to exercise through his work with editorialists and journalists cannot be overstated. It was absolutely fundamental to realising his objectives. Hume's strategy was to win the media, which would in turn ease the way for political change, because the newly educated editorialists, as Ted Smyth put it, 'became immensely influential in policy in Washington and most of that was guided by what they learned from Hume'. In effect, by putting an educated media out in front, Hume pressured politicians to keep well briefed and prepared to debate. Those who were not initially amenable to Hume's view would have to provide a plausible alternative, not so much to him but to reporters in the most important publications in the country; those who could not do that found themselves aligning with Hume by default. Therein lay the subtlest aspect of his programme with the United States media, and it was a manoeuvre that had the true stamp of Hume's political personality: it was an outstanding example of his ability to vicariously create a channel of influence through people whose words and deeds had considerable impact. His work with those media professionals was almost as strategically important as his work with Congress; they formed the twin tracks of his strategic vision of how to bring American power to bear on the process for peace and reconciliation in Ireland.

But all this work of the cultivation of the US media, as well as Hume's access in Congress, was about to be severely tested when Northern Ireland reached the nadir of its civic, political and judicial history.

A Politics of Conscience:
Human Rights and Democracy

The Hunger Strikes

On 1 March 1981, IRA prisoners in Long Kesh Prison began a hunger strike unto death lest they were granted 'political status' within the prison. The prisoners staged their strikes in a staggered manner, with each striker starting two weeks after the previous striker. They were led by Bobby Sands, and their action captured the attention of the world, from Teheran to San Francisco. In the US, the Ad Hoc Committee was critical of the Friends of Ireland for failing to move Prime Minister Thatcher to make the requisite concessions to stop the hunger strikes. Specifically, they challenged Speaker O'Neill and the Friends of Ireland for not convincing President Reagan to intervene with Thatcher. Reagan was instinctively reluctant to intervene, his own experience of jail unrest during his tenure as Governor of California being the chief source of his unwillingness to become involved. President Reagan informed Ambassador Seán Donlon, through his staffer, Mike Denver, that prisoners who cease to heed prison rules understand only one thing. Reagan would never be persuaded to express sympathy with the strikers. Besides, to do so would have been to defy his State Department within months of taking office: the State Department wished that the President remain neutral and non-interventionist with regard to the hunger strikes.

To make any gains in influencing US foreign policy, the Irish had to maintain an impeccably constitutional approach, and their response to an IRA prisoner strike required a policy for handling Reagan's commitment to combat 'the international terrorist network'. The policy of uniting Ireland remained foremost on Haughey's agenda. Replying to journalist Tim Pat Coogan on a BBC Northern Ireland radio programme on 21 March 1981, shortly after the strike began, Haughey's Minister for Foreign Affairs, Brian Lenihan, stated that he understood the 'totality of relationships within these islands' to mean that there would be a United Ireland within ten years.[1] The next time Haughey met his British counterpart, he was carpeted by Thatcher for implying that the wishes of the majority in Northern Ireland would be ignored and for Lenihan's statement that a United Ireland was imminent. Haughey in turn carpeted Lenihan, and chose to do it in front of the Fianna Fáil cabinet. It was to be a costly diplomatic error at a time when Anglo-Irish relations badly needed a better framework for cooperation.

Haughey and Thatcher

The new leaders of Ireland and Britain, Charles Haughey and Margaret Thatcher, met twice in 1980. From the first their relationship was tense. They both came to the issue of the North of Ireland from staunch and opposed positions, nevertheless they attempted to sustain an ongoing dialogue. In May 1980, at their first summit in London, Haughey presented Thatcher with a silver teapot and they seemed to foster an entente. However, Thatcher noted privately that she felt Haughey expected much more than she was willing to concede in his concept of the 'totality of relationships'. The British side endorsed the idea of a unique relationship between Ireland and Britain and agreed to undertake a study of the 'totality of relationships' between the two countries, promising a commitment on both sides to a new phase of cooperation. The Unionists were upset both by the opacity and potential open-endedness of the term; and alarmed that the possibility of the study of the totality of relationships might have also implied re-examination of the constitutional status, North and South. There was considerable mystery as to everything that the term 'totality of relationships' implied. There was speculation that it might have involved a military security dimension, with Haughey perhaps hinting at some form of closer military cooperation.

After December 1980, relations deteriorated between Haughey and Thatcher for three reasons: the hunger strikes, which Haughey reacted to in a somewhat sympathetic vein (in contrast to Thatcher's insensitivity), partly because his party had to contest TD seats on the Irish border it ultimately lost; secondly, Brian Lenihan, Haughey's Minister for Foreign Affairs, whether through his own over-enthusiasm or at Haughey's prompting, oversold the notion of the 'totality of relationships' as relating to constitutional rather than institutional change and linked it directly to a United Ireland, which outraged Unionists and consequently Thatcher gave Haughey a withering reception; and lastly Haughey's opposition to the British resolution to fight the Falklands war (April–June 1982).

The third issue was by far the most devastating. With Thatcher, the irritation factor was always high and when Haughey opposed her policy on the Falklands he comprehensively poisoned her against a renegotiation of Anglo-Irish modalities. It was a very dilettantish move, going in feet first and causing problems for the Irish in the United Nations (UN) that rippled to domestic issues. A little like a general who does not reconnoitre the battlefield, Haughey did not fully consult Noel Dorr, Ireland's Ambassador at the UN, about the matter (Ireland at that moment was a member of the Security Council of the United Nations). The hunger strikes were next in significance to the Falklands war in determining Anglo-Irish relations in the early and mid-1980s. These setbacks froze Anglo-Irish relations for a period. Where subtle diplomacy was required Thatcher and Haughey inexorably brought out of each other an animal aggression and inflexibility. The souring of relationships between Thatcher and Haughey caused anxiety to the protectors of Irish interests in Washington, where Anglo-Irish developments were, by now, being keenly monitored. On top of all this, Haughey's perceived reluctance to specifically condemn Republican violence in the North posed further difficulties to the Congressional Friends of Ireland.

Hume tried many times to persuade Haughey against that position. Peter Gallagher, a Derry school teacher, remembers meeting Hume at a function in Dublin. Hume asked Gallagher for a lift back to Derry. On their way, just into North Dublin, Hume informed Gallagher that they would be stopping to speak to Haughey at his estate at Abbeville. When they arrived at Haughey's estate, Gallagher was sent into a library and remembers Hume being very straight with Haughey and very determined to express his views on the North. When Haughey came to Derry, Hume would drive Haughey around the city to survey the worthless wreckage that the IRA had caused the city: their 'economic targets'. Hume made a habit of stepping in decisively with Haughey: he would arrive unannounced to Haughey's office and he could be gruff and relentless. He retained a schoolmasterly severity which was necessary with Haughey.

As the hunger strikers began to die of starvation in Long Kesh prison, extraordinary levels of morbidity and tension prevailed not only in the North of Ireland but throughout the island of Ireland. The anti-British sentiment spilled into riot fervour, not only in the North, which was routinely the case, but also in Dublin. On 18 July 1981, 1,000 members of the Garda Síochána (the Irish police force) repelled protesters who attempted to assail the British Embassy in Dublin, chanting 'burn the embassy!' It was a moment redolent of the crowd that had assembled in Dublin on 2 February 1972, days after Bloody Sunday in Derry, who that time succeeded in burning the embassy.

John Hume's statement on the death of Bobby Sands was sombre and reflective, but clearly unsympathetic to the continuing hunger strike: 'SDLP leader, John Hume, said that Sands' death was so unnecessary and could have been avoided … "The British government wanted Bobby Sands to die or to surrender … The Provisional IRA had to have victory or Sands had to die … The only people who wanted Bobby Sands to live were the ordinary people [of Northern Ireland]'.[2] Such was the message Hume attempted to convey to the British prime minister a few days later. Hume met Thatcher at 10 Downing Street on 13 May 1981 and failed to convince her to intervene and play a constructive role in the situation in the Maze Prison. Sean O'hUiginn, who was Irish Consul-General in New York 1979–83, remembers that his posting was evenly divided into two phases; before the hunger strikes and after the hunger strikes:

> Starting in the early 1970s, successive Irish governments had realised the importance of Irish-America. Either for good, if that influence was harvested in the search for political progress, or indeed for damage if that influence was used to foster an armed campaign in Ireland. Suddenly, with the hunger strikes, the mythology of total victim and total tyrant oppressor was resurrected with a vengeance. You had hunger strikers on one hand, the morbid death-watch of a young person going for sixty, seventy days would engage anyone, on humane grounds. It had echoes of Christ's Passion, echoes of ancient Celtic systems where the hunger strike was the ultimate weapon of protest.

In the United States, there were huge demonstrations in which the British did not dare fly their flag. Massachusetts asked the State Department to remove the British Consulate. Subscriptions from NORAID went up. In the Irish Consulate in New York we got to death threats, some of which were taken seriously by the police. One I remember, though that did not come to fruition because we had a redoubtable Leitrim woman working for us. When she got the threat she snapped at the caller and said 'are you ringing from a pub?' Then she proceeded to give him a tongue lashing in the best Irish Mammy fashion. So at least one putative assassin was disempowered for the day.

Congressmen who had aligned with Tip O'Neill's Friends of Ireland faced similar pressure and even intimidation. Those who were elected from heavily Irish constituencies faced particularly astringent challenges when NORAID was at its peak. Congressman Brian Donnelly from Dorchester, representing South Boston in Congress, remembers even mild-mannered constituents and neighbours haranguing him in the early 1980s for the perceived inaction of the Friends of Ireland, as young prisoners grew emaciated within the excrement-strewn walls of Long Kesh: 'what are we sending you to Washington for?' Congressman Charlie Dougherty's family and his home were prey to intimidatory tactics, peaking during the hunger strikes of 1981. He remembers:

I would not support a hunger strike. So there was a big rally in my district – I'm told 5,000 people – at a major crossroads, which was the heart of the district. Then they marched down to where I lived. We were not at home. The police had said, 'just don't be home, just take your family and go away'. We were told 5,000 people marched by carrying coffins saying I was supporting the British in killing Irish Patriots.

Threats to his life almost inevitably accompanied such protests:

They couldn't get me as a sitting Congressman because it would be politically stupid, so they put pressure on my family. One of my daughters worked at a local bank as a teller. One day she was working at the bank and a guy came in and said: 'Did you say goodbye to your father this morning, before he left for work?' and she said, 'yes, why do you ask?' 'Well, he won't be coming home tonight'.

I also had some staffers who were Irish Catholics and who went to the local bars at the weekends, and they were subjected to harassment. My parents were elderly … and at three o'clock in the morning the phone would ring and there was silence on the line. I got concerned because my mother had a heart problem. I was dealing with an Irish Catholic constituency that had not heard any point of view other than the IRA. My job was to advance the flag for the peace and reconciliation in Northern Ireland.

During one of the delegation trips to Northern Ireland, Congressman Dougherty saw at first hand the threats that Hume and his family faced:

John Hume was dealing with much more dangerous, high-level, multiple kinds of risks. I remember being in his house in Derry and he was saying to me, pointing at the windows, 'they are bullet-proof windows'. I remember standing outside John's home in Derry. He was about to leave, but they stuck a pole with a mirror under his car. Pat said, 'this goes on every morning'. They were very concerned somebody would have planted a bomb. So I had a great deal of affection and respect for Pat Hume, in addition to John.

Notably, the slurs to his reputation Dougherty encountered in his constituency – 'Charlie Dougherty is a Traitor', 'Charlie Dougherty is pro-British' – were identical to the slurs Hume encountered on his front door. For a time 'Hume Traitor', as well as featuring prominently in electioneering propaganda, was graffitied across Hume's house every day. Hume's response was the same as Dougherty: it is deeply unfair and it is an irritation, but it will not prompt a change of policy.

Two years later, in 1983, the bitterness which arose from the hunger strikes in the US endured and surfaced in New York during the build up to St Patrick's Day.

The New York St Patrick's Day Parade, 1983

Tom Melia provides some background to an incident that brought to a head many of the underlying issues which lingered from the time of the hunger strikes:

In 1983, the St Patrick's Day Parade Committee, which is a private organisation in New York City, elected as the Grand Marshal of the St Patrick's Day parade a man named Michael Flannery, who was well known in New York City as an officer of NORAID. Senator Moynihan was firmly opposed to terrorism and he said that he would not march in the St Patrick's Day parade in New York that year. That created a firestorm in New York City politics and media. He was very resolute and said, 'I'm not going to be associated with an advocate for the Provisional IRA'. That New York City's most prominent Irish-American politician would not march in the St Patrick's Day parade was headline news in all the major dailies. His colleagues, Ted Kennedy and Tip O'Neill, and New York Governor Hugh Carey joined him in that boycott and the editorial board of *The New York Times* backed him very strongly. It captured a lot of popular attention that such a prominent Irish-American would not march in the St Patrick's Day parade. It was an important learning moment for a lot of New Yorkers and we were helped in that by *The New York Times* and other sober commentators, who understood what was at stake and why it was important for Americans to shun those who would tolerate or endorse the use of violence to pursue political objectives.

The naming of Flannery as Grand Marshall also presented a problem for the Irish government, which considered that it had to act in step with the boycott of the parade by Hugh Carey, Daniel Pat Moynihan and by Cardinal Terence Cook of New York. As Sean O'hUiginn recalls:

> The selection of Michael Flannery, who was diehard among diehards in terms of the old Republican IRA campaign, was a foursquare challenge which we had to face up to and say that gunrunning was beyond the pale of what the Irish government would cooperate with, or to say that gunrunning did not matter on some level. It was the first time that an Irish government had boycotted the New York parade.

As the political temperature peaked in the aftermath of the deaths of the IRA hunger strikers, Congressmen who had not supported the hunger strikes and who sought re-election in heavily Irish districts faced palpable hostility. Congressman Charlie Dougherty was to pay a price electorally for his support of Tip O'Neill's Friends of Ireland in Congress. For his stance against violence and in favour of constitutional methods, Dougherty lost his Congressional seat in 1982:

> John had an idea that they needed somebody who would take the flag and advocate the issues that the government supported, and that the SDLP supported, to offset what had been years of this folklore about the glory of the IRA. I was trying to make Irish Catholics understand that the violence of the IRA was not the way to go. I lost the seat in 1982 by 1,800 votes. If I had supported NORAID and the Irish National Caucus, joined the Biaggi committee in Congress and done nothing, I probably would have been re-elected.

Dougherty had been elected in 1978 despite the opposition of the Teamster Union boss, Johnny Morris, and a few years later, Morris again chose to play the spoiler. He could have delivered the Teamster Union vote to his fellow Republican running against a Democrat, but Morris would sooner have supported a Barabbas figure than Dougherty:

> Some years later, I made an attempt to recover the seat. The Republican leader said, 'meet with Johnny Morris'. So I met with Morris. Morris could have been helpful. The decision was whether he would support me against the incumbent Democrat who succeeded me and whom Morris opposed and who did not like Morris. Morris's requirement was that I would publicly support NORAID. I said 'no'. That was the end of the conversation.
>
> A lot of my friends who are Irish Catholics said 'listen, just tell a certain number of people that you will be willing to support NORAID, that you will go to NORAID events, that you will show up at the NORAID dinner. You do not have to be the activist for NORAID that you were for the Irish Government. Pass the word on the street that you are no longer going to be the leader of support for John Hume and the Irish Government'. I didn't do that. No regrets.

If Dougherty were to have been re-elected, he had ideas of the tactics he would use to force the hand of the British into negotiating fairly, but he could not achieve that by being seen to support NORAID:

I had always told people that you are not going to defeat the British militarily; throwing bombs is not the way to go. You need to outthink them and outsmart them. I said to some people that if I go back for the third term, I would propose legislation which in effect would say the US Belfast Consulate is closed. All visas for the United States from anybody on the island of Ireland would have to go through the Embassy in Dublin. If that did not work, the next step would be that the US Consulate in Belfast would answer directly to the US Embassy in Dublin and not to London. The whole point here was to start using the political process to put pressure on the Brits to negotiate in good faith. It would have moved some of the discussion into the political arena of public policy as opposed to the bomb throwing.

Through its activities, NORAID–IRA played into the hands of the British and the Unionists because it allowed them to paint proponents of Irish nationalism as a radical fringe, an outrageous terrorist organisation. As long as the IRA sustained an armed struggle and left civilians dead in their wake, the British could point to the immorality and irrationality of their approach. From the moment the IRA developed an educated political approach, such dismissals became much less credible. Hume said the same thing to the IRA: 'I have repeatedly made it clear that there must be a total cessation of violence, not just a cease-fire ... I tell the IRA that their terror is counterproductive, that as long as they keep up the killing, the Unionists don't have to come up with a single proposal of their own.'[3] However, such a message was deeply antithetical to the position of many Americans. Even the American campus in the early 1980s was not easily amenable to a view that the IRA campaign of terror needed to stop forthwith. At an event held at the University of Massachusetts in Boston on 15 March 1983, hosted by Professor Padraig O'Malley, Hume faced a great deal of criticism from the audience for his portrayal of the IRA campaign as futile.

The hunger strikes had the central consequence of politicising the IRA – several hunger strikers were elected to both the British (Bobby Sands) and Irish (Kieran Doherty) parliaments, even as they were on hunger strike, and the Irish government felt pressured to respond to the political manifestation of the IRA. During the hunger strikes there was also a change of Taoiseach, part of a rotation between Haughey and FitzGerald as Taoiseach. FitzGerald had tried without success in July 1981, in a letter to President Reagan, to persuade the US Executive to move the British to a more tolerant position on the hunger strikers' requests:

> I would ask you to use your enormous influence with the British Prime Minister within the next 24 hours in the interest of averting a death which would inevitably increase support for the terrorists and further undermine the stability of our democracy in a dangerous way … I believe that an expression of your concern to Mrs Thatcher of the deterioration in the state of opinion among Americans of Irish extraction and among many other Americans and of the urgent necessity to avert the consequences which would result from Mr Doherty's death could be of decisive importance.[4]

While FitzGerald's representations were to no avail, by the mid-1980s, FitzGerald was to reach a basis for co-operation with President Reagan.

Haughey had severely blotted his copybook with O'Neill and Kennedy by attempting to oust Donlon in the summer of 1980, and they became supporters of FitzGerald. (As late as 1987, during the count for an Irish General Election, Ted Kennedy's office persistently phoned the SDLP to seek the results. It was clear that Kennedy wanted Garret FitzGerald to win the election and Kennedy berated the pace with which the Irish election results became clear.) They supported FitzGerald's visit to the US and the speech he delivered in Pittsburgh, aimed at shoring up political support for the Irish government in the wake of hunger strikes.

While Kennedy's loyalty to FitzGerald was a reflex of his distrust of Haughey dating back to the 'Donlon incident', he had other misgivings about Haughey. He remembered a conversation with Haughey in Dublin in which Haughey suggested that he had friends in Libya – something that took on a resonance in Kennedy's mind since Haughey had been brought to trial in 1970 on charges of smuggling arms:

> I had seen Charlie Haughey on one of my trips when he was Attorney General … My nephew Joe [Joseph Kennedy II] had been on a plane that was hijacked in the Middle East. They had just released him. He was on a plane in Saudi Arabia for about three days. I was in

Ireland, and ... I went by to see Charlie Haughey, and I mentioned that we had been in touch with the Algerians ... Charlie Haughey, who had just been acquitted of involvement with Libya and running guns, said, 'Well, if you run into this situation again, get hold of me. I have some friends in Libya who can help,' which was a cute little comment.[5]

His doubts in Haughey were to be confirmed when Haughey opposed the Anglo-Irish Agreement.

The Death Penalty and Human Rights

After the hunger strikes, Margaret Thatcher sustained her purblind dogmatism regarding the correct response to Northern Ireland. Her unabashedly hardline Unionist agenda stoked the ire of even moderate Nationalists, including Hume. The tendency had come to a distressing head during the hunger strikes period, but did not end there. Subsequent to the hunger strikes, her party's proposal to introduce the death penalty in the North of Ireland was yet another in a long series of ill-advised moves on the part of the Conservatives to establish law and order in the North. This motion was endorsed by Ian Paisley, but attacked by Hume. Debating the matter on the floor of the House of Commons in 1983, Hume successfully shifted British policy and persuaded Thatcher's cabinet against introducing the death penalty in Northern Ireland. Hume stated that during the hunger strike period in 1981, when Thatcher refused to concede to the demands of prisoners in Long Kesh prison, British policy inadvertently became the finest recruiting tool the IRA had ever had.

After a long *reductio ad absurdum* of the arguments in favour of the death penalty, Hume's talent for illuminating the consequences of a political policy and demanding that its proponents face up to those consequences in advance of passing legislation was devastating:

Terrorists are moving in a society that is deeply distrustful of Government and which, in consequence, is deprived of any real sense of security, the effect of the introduction of the death penalty is certain – it would destroy any hope of democracy in Northern Ireland and, in addition, would undermine the reality of democracy in the Republic of Ireland. What is now a disaster in Northern Ireland would, if the death penalty were introduced, become an unmanageable calamity throughout Ireland. There would be many more deaths, both in Britain and in Ireland. If we try to solve a problem by methods that will create even greater problems, is it sensible even to discuss the issue?

When reassessing the British decision to execute the leaders of the 1916 uprising in Dublin, Winston Churchill said that, as a consequence of that action, 'the keys of Ireland passed into the hands of those to whom hatred of England was the dominant and almost the only interest'. Hatred of Britain, the result of grisly experience of generations of Irish life, has, alas, strong roots in Northern Ireland, particularly among young people. It was magnified two years ago by the Government's handling of the hunger strike. Never in its wildest dreams could the IRA have expected to recruit the support that was won for it by the British Government's tragic mishandling of the hunger strike ... That hatred, the instability and the macabre display of that time, are as nothing compared with the reaction that would take place in Ireland if Irish men or women were hanged under British law. If the House wants the IRA to win, then hang them.[6]

Ever the IRA's 'objective ally', Ian Paisley counterargued that the death penalty was wholly necessary. Sinn Féin had even admitted that it depended on such people as Paisley and Thatcher for their power: 'Our cause has two important allies, Mrs. Thatcher and Ian Paisley. They will make a present of power to us in Ireland, in the whole of Ireland.'[7] But it was small wonder, after the force of Hume's philippic, that the House of Commons did not carry the motion. Hume added: 'Let not the House think that the leaders will be hanged. The leaders are not in gaol. It will be the young followers who are sucked into the organisations because of the desperate position in Northern Ireland' who would be sentenced to death. In his writings, speeches and interviews, Hume's focus on the rights of innocent people was unremitting. The leaders of paramilitary organisations, and the voice of those like Paisley whose words implied violent acts ('If they don't behave themselves in the South, it will be shots across the border!'), sustained their political platform through the instrumentality of young and innocent people.

Miscarriage of Justice: The Cases of the Birmingham Six and Guildford Four

In 1975, English courts found two groups of Irish people guilty of IRA bombings in England. In infamous cases, known as the Birmingham Six and the Guildford Four, the Irish defendants were sentenced to life imprisonment even though they were actually innocent of the crimes. Their convictions were based on false evidence and brutal interrogation and their imprisonment came to represent a scandal in the English judiciary and policing systems.

The subject of their imprisonment came under discussion on 17 May 2016, when the Edward M. Kennedy Institute hosted a debate on the Northern Irish conflict. Its panellists were former Senate Majority Leader and US Special Envoy to Northern Ireland, George Mitchell, Ambassador Nancy Soderberg, newspaper publisher Niall O'Dowd, Congressman Peter King (R-NY), and Congressman Richard Neal (D-MA). During the course of the discussion Niall O'Dowd stated:

> This is probably sacrilegious: Hume had missed some opportunities in the 80s and 70s, I certainly think so. I think the Irish government was very remiss in the cases of the Birmingham Six and the Guildford Four, which were huge human rights abuses that for some reason the Irish government at the time, led by Garret FitzGerald – and John Hume – told the Friends of Ireland in Congress: 'Do not compete on this issue; do not say that this is a travesty, a terrible miscarriage'. And the Irish-Americans got very upset about that ... There was a certain view at that point that it had to be the Irish and British government against Irish-America.[8]

When challenged on this by Nancy Soderberg: 'Although Ted Kennedy didn't listen to that. He pushed very hard for the Guildford Four and the Birmingham Six,' O'Dowd continued:

> It didn't come across like that, Nancy, it really didn't. I hate to tell you that. It didn't come across. Other than the fact that there was an Irish-America in competition with the Irish government, John Hume and the British government. Whereas I always believed that Irish-America

and the Irish government together – which eventually happened, thanks to Albert Reynolds – made a huge difference.

There is no evidence for O'Dowd's version of events. Remembering Hume's passionate defence for the people in the North of Ireland, it is implausible that Hume should be challenged for fudging on human rights issues. The evidence is to the contrary, as Mark Durkan MP, Hume's close associate who was an intern in Senator Kennedy's office in 1985, remembers: 'Throughout their period in jail, John Hume was involved in efforts to establish an affirmation of the unambiguous innocence of the Guildford Four and the Birmingham Six. Hume informed British Home Secretaries directly of his belief in their innocence. He raised the cases with Prime Minister Thatcher, as did the Irish government, including Taoiseach Garret FitzGerald.' When Mark Durkan spent a period as a junior staffer in Kennedy's office in 1985, he recalls that Hume never discouraged representations on those cases; rather he supported them, and spoke to other congressional offices about the injustices. He encouraged US Congress members to raise the cases with the British Embassy in Washington, with visiting British ministers, and with the State Department.

O'Dowd's allegation is further contradicted by Gerry Conlon, a member of the Guildford Four, who served fifteen years in prison on a wrongful conviction. When Gerry Conlon addressed an SDLP Party Conference in February 2005, he paid tribute to John Hume, Seamus Mallon and Mark Durkan, among others. Conlon credited their role in securing a personal and written apology for the injustice from then Prime Minister Tony Blair, and praised:

Séamus Mallon [who] came to see me in prison. We knew that Séamus Mallon's voice was a voice in the wilderness. He put in place a liaison between the prisoners and the Irish embassy. He told us of the obstacles we faced. Some of them appeared insurmountable ... That's why I am indebted to Séamus Mallon and to John Hume and, later, to Mark Durkan ... My mother said – 'you go down and thank those people in the SDLP because they were the people who were there for you. These are the people you must support, these are the people you have to stand with'.[9]

Moreover, Congressman Brian Donnelly recalled that during a trip to Ireland in the 1980s, Hume urged him and Congressman Bernard Dwyer, also part of the delegation, to visit the Guildford Four in prison. They did so and Congressman Donnelly remembers that Hume never attempted to play down the injustice of such cases; on the contrary, he routinely discussed their cases with US politicians. Some members of Irish-America featured those travesty cases in their lobbying of American politicians, while also supporting the violent campaign of those who actually committed the crimes in Birmingham and Guildford. Hume differentiated his own position from theirs and advised American politicians to do likewise. Hume identified this differentiation as a necessary point of principle, and a necessary context in confronting the cases.

The Irish government lobbied on a number of occasions to re-open the case, but the British dismissed all representations with the argument that new evidence was necessary. This was a double-bind, since the IRA volunteers who carried out the attack in Birmingham could not find a way to provide necessary new evidence to have the case re-opened. There was a difference in approaches in Irish-America, to which O'Dowd's comments allude. In reference to the same discussion at the Edward M. Kennedy Institute, Nancy Soderberg remembers:

> We weren't as public as Niall would like it to be. I think that was the difference. The House caucus is much more linked to the grassroots and those are the grassroots issues – the hunger strike or the political prisoners, the MacBride Principles – basically prohibiting investment in Northern Ireland, were all very passionate issues for that side. Our side took it a different route. We did raise the political prisoners regularly. We certainly were working at it behind the scenes (as evidence for that they came to thank Ted Kennedy for his support). The purpose of the Friends of Ireland statement was a little bit broader in trying to shape a peace, not hit the current issues. I think that that was very much John Hume's vision, but it also melded with Ted Kennedy's.

O'Dowd's argument is akin to criticising a Minister of Justice for not sitting nightly in a police patrol car and notching up arrests. Hume did not wholly dedicate himself to every human rights abuse – such abuses occurred on a daily basis in Northern Ireland – since his vocation was to implement a multilateral political strategy. Besides, within the SDLP, it was Seamus Mallon who was more the 'case worker'.

The Birmingham Six case returned to the spotlight from 1985 onwards, when Chris Mullin showed through forensic television documentaries the baselessness of their guilt. Previously, public interest in their case rose and fell as appeal procedures were examined in England; the cases were partially overshadowed by the Dirty Protest and the hunger strikes in the early 1980s. For Hume, the imprisonment of innocent Irish people in English prisons was symptomatic of an overarching problem of injustice, which had to be addressed through a political process rather than through grassroots activism and rhetoric. Inasmuch as the rule of law was circumspect in England vis-à-vis Irish people, the remedy was a justice and policing system that was accountable for its actions, which is where oversight from the United States could play a role.

The rule of law was all the more deficient in the British security forces' operations in Northern Ireland, where the army had comprehensively destroyed its reputation through massacres such as Bloody Sunday, through torture of innocent people interned without trial and through its collusion with loyalist terrorism. Hume's agenda was to establish a democratic political structure in Northern Ireland which would prevent human rights abuses which included, but was not limited to, the scandal of wrongfully imprisoned Irish people in English jails. The human rights abuses visited upon innocent civilians through bombing town centres, for example the victims of the Enniskillen bomb, were completely lacking in legitimacy, and yet they did not receive the same amplification, if any, in NORAID circles. IRA violence against the Nationalist community as a technique to intimidate 'its' community received a similarly soft-spoken reception. Critics who claim that Hume should have done more about specific human rights abuses in the North of Ireland might also concede that NORAID/ IRA should have done less to create them in the first place. Is it anything more than fair-minded for such critics to amplify their criticism of the damage that NORAID and its tacit supporters in Washington did, and reduce slurs on Hume's record accordingly?

Hume and the Friends of Ireland routinely faced criticism that they could have done more on certain issues and cases. The Ancient Order of Hibernians was unhappy with criticism of the IRA from the Friends of Ireland. The Irish Ambassador to the US (1981–5), Tadhg O'Sullivan, tried to reach an understanding with the AOH (through its then President, Joseph A. Roche) in which there could be a common position of support for Irish unity and reconciliation; a defence of human rights in conjunction with a rejection of violence and of NORAID. This culminated in a 'Uniting Ireland' resolution, sponsored by Senator Kennedy and over thirty senators and the Friends of Ireland in the House of Representatives. But the AOH ultimately could not reject NORAID and violence and division in Irish-America endured.

A tacit alliance between the Friends of Ireland and the Ad Hoc Committee, as well as the AOH, was later made possible by the IRA Ceasefire, when Albert Reynolds became Taoiseach (1992–4). Alongside Hume, Reynolds was instrumental in securing a non-violent approach to politics in the North of Ireland. The absence of violence enabled that to happen. As far as Irish-America being 'in competition' with John Hume goes, that Hume adopted one approach and others espoused another is no grounds to doubt his motives or commitment to justice. Hume and the Friends of Ireland had simply operated at another plane of engagement. Tom Melia elaborates:

I think that they were focused more on trying to encourage and enable a structural solution for Northern Ireland, a diplomatic engagement of bringing the two governments together, bringing the two major communities in Northern Ireland together. Human rights activists focus on case work, on people unjustly imprisoned or otherwise mistreated by their governments or their systems. Then there is another family of organisations and people that approach the question from a systems approach, the reform option for a country's justice system, political system and social system. The latter I would call the 'democracy promotion' community. You have to have a democratically founded system where the judiciary and the prosecutors and the police have some accountability to the voters before you can get to their better treatment of individual citizens.

The first essential step towards a peace settlement is establishing the rule of law to which the vast majority of people subscribe: a police force, a judiciary and a government to which people can give assent. From that basis many other democratic rights can flow. That basis was lacking in

Northern Ireland during the Troubles, given a clearly biased security force in favour of one section of the people. Hume continually advocated reform of that system (or lack of proper system) as the first step to establishing peace in the North of Ireland. If Hume and the Friends of Ireland were to have focused solely on specific human rights cases, they would not have been able to give the requisite attention to inter-governmental negotiation and pressure, at which they had acquitted themselves so well. The annual statement of the Four Horsemen and the tenor of the Friends of Ireland always retained that focus. John A. Farrell elaborates this point:

> The Four Horsemen statement was not without controversy, because it went against the grain of the Irish romanticism and the support for the IRA. When it first came out there was a lot of Irish-Americans who said, 'why are they going soft on Northern Ireland – Brits Out, Bloody Sunday, why are you counselling something else?' So it was a risk for them. In Boston, where you had all these jars on the bars collecting money for the IRA, it was a risk for Tip O'Neill and Ted Kennedy and it was also a political danger to them because they could be outflanked by this emotionalism which supported NORAID. The IRA had a strong emotional grip within Tip O'Neill's neighbourhoods in North Cambridge, which it did in many working class neighbourhoods in Boston. That is how he first got introduced to the whole notion of Irish independence and being on the side of the Irish Catholics in the North.

In North Cambridge, Tip O'Neill encountered a great deal of abuse for his stance. Supporting Hume's approach did not increase O'Neill's political capital; rather, it cost him a lot. Inside Congress, however, there were clear consequences for Congressmen who defied Tip O'Neill on the Irish Question. Is it fair to say that swing voters who might have veered towards the Biaggi group supported the Friends of Ireland instead simply because they did not want to get on the wrong side of Tip O'Neill? Christine Sullivan Daly, who served as Tip O'Neill's appointments secretary, responds:

> Could be. There were some people who may have felt that way. But the position that the Speaker took was a very difficult position to take

because so many of the Irish members of Congress were from districts with huge Irish populations and many of those people disagreed with them. The Speaker had protests wherever he went when he first took this position and Ted Kennedy did as well.

Leader of the SDLP

By 1983, Hume was party leader of the SDLP, had been elected to the European Parliament as an MEP, and represented the Foyle Constituency in Britain's Westminster Parliament. In addition to his official political roles in these three capacities, Hume's unofficial activities in Washington all combined into a workload that would overwhelm most politicians. His travels, and what some colleagues perceived as his lack of transparency, disturbed his deputy leader, Seamus Mallon. Mallon was attempting to guide the Party in Hume's absence, following up on constituents who had been imprisoned on specious grounds and on the security forces' abuses of power. To some extent, Hume's travels may have even been preferable for Mallon, a brilliant politician in his own right, as he could proceed autonomously on domestic matters. Still, Mallon remembers that Hume's absences were unsettling:

He went on solo runs which was sometimes very disturbing for other members. He could not take criticism well; he wouldn't take it at all. He always preferred to be on his own. Here was this man who had enjoyed company, but much preferred working alone. That caused difficulties. The other side of the coin was the way in which he conceived and acted upon the needs as he saw them with the Irish government and worked very closely with the American powers that be – the White House, people in the Capitol – and within Europe.

It was almost impossible for people to do the things in organisational terms required of a political party. For example, branch meetings: my branch met in the living room of my house because nobody would rent us a room because if they rented us a room, it was certain that a bomb would be planted in it. We had no resources, no money, no back-up. And Hume was busy with other things like the American process, like dealing with Dublin, and London, and Europe.

Peter Barry, then Irish Minister for Foreign Affairs, once took Hume aside after Hume had returned from America and spoke to him about the need to shore up his party's standing in Northern Ireland. Hume heeded Barry's counsel. Even so, it was not always the case that Hume's constituency work for the party and his forays to the US were in conflict, as Christine Sullivan Daly relates:

> We had this fabulous trip to Los Angeles all laid out for John and he was going to meet with a lot of influential people. We had a breakfast at the Beverly Hills Hotel with Ed Asner and Shelley Fabares and some other Hollywood types. Jane Fonda was involved and Tom Hayden and some political people. In the middle of all the celebrity lavishness, John pulled my brother, who lived in LA, aside and said, 'could you do me a favour and drive me out to the Central Valley to such and such a town?' My brother said, 'sure, I'll try my best to find it'. So they drive out into the Valley for hours and hours. John wants to find this school bus company that is located in the middle of nowhere, in some industrial complex, because one of his constituents in Derry has a daughter who has just moved to LA and he wants to go out and say hello so he can go back to the parents and say I checked on your daughter. So he spends hours going out to this place in the middle of nowhere to find this 19-year-old young woman who's working as a receptionist in this bus company. He goes in and he says 'hello, your parents want to make sure you're OK'.

The big picture was that Hume's American dimension was an extension of his policy and strategic planning and a necessary component of its success. When this dimension was stymied in the mid-1980s, it was time, once again, to mobilise the support of the President of the United States to help to balance out Anglo-Irish relations.

6

From Rejection to Acceptance

The New Ireland Forum

Over the course of a few years, 1983–5, Anglo-Irish relations went from a state of apparent hopeless collapse to a breakthrough – in the form of an international agreement which would have far-reaching consequences for peace in the North of Ireland. Hume was central to the 1983–4 initiative for a New Ireland Forum to re-examine approaches to the Northern Ireland problem and find new ways to confront it. The New Ireland Forum had the unexpected consequence of exposing the degree of British Prime Minister Margaret Thatcher's unwillingness to properly acknowledge an Irish dimension to resolution of the Northern Irish crisis. Hume was also instrumental, principally through his Washington connections, in successfully pressing Thatcher to accept the need for a new start in negotiations with Dublin which ultimately produced the 1985 Anglo-Irish Agreement (during which Thatcher's earlier emphatic rejection was ironically to work against her).

The New Ireland Forum had been convened as a platform for discussion with the later possibility of constitutional reform. Taoiseach Garret FitzGerald was, while a Constitutional Nationalist albeit open and pluralist, interested in the core demands for policing and human rights in a shared Northern Ireland as part of a New Ireland. Additionally, FitzGerald was one of the few in Ireland at the time who seemed to understand the scale and importance of Hume's work in America and that the British would only act on the question of the North under duress; and that the only stimulus to which they would respond was US pressure. This key insight led to the solid foundations of support he built in Washington. A mutual understanding and appreciation between Hume and Taoiseach Garret FitzGerald became the catalyst for more effective coordination with Washington, and for the breakthrough leading to the New Ireland Forum.

The Forum's premise was a recognition that from 1922 onwards, the Southern Irish ruling class had, by turns consciously and unconsciously, abandoned the North of Ireland. A good deal of the Report that emerged from the Forum deliberations is 'Humespeak', traceable to the SDLP's 1972 pamphlet of proposals, *Towards a New Ireland*.[1] The New Ireland narrative, while always present in the background, had in the early 1980s been somewhat usurped by the nihilism of IRA activities. The Forum succeeded in reasserting the central role of debate and agreement towards a new polity in Ireland. As Hume put it in a speech entitled 'The Way Forward as I See It':

> One of the tests of leadership in this community is to accept the discipline of trying to reach both sides of the community simultaneously. It is not difficult to gratify one side by encouraging its prejudices about the other. It is difficult to bring to each side a sense of the dilemma felt by the other. Yet until our leaders and our people manage that breakthrough, we will not make progress in Northern Ireland.[2]

The Forum was resolutely ecumenical in its make-up and its programme, drawing its attendance from most strands of Irish political, civic and religious life. Most, but not all: Seamus Deane, in an interview with Hume in 1980, had asked him if he would exclude organisations such as the UDA and the IRA from a general conference to settle the Northern Irish problem (what became the New Ireland Forum in 1983–4). Deane added, 'even though their exclusion might lead to a continuation of the violence the conference was designed to bring to an end?' Hume affirmed that he would exclude them since, in that case, their presence would be 'just blackmail. All they want then is power'.[3] Hume's clear demand was that at a democratic forum only people and parties which were unambiguous in their support for exclusively constitutional means of solving political problems were welcome. Hume was to evolve from this position, and in the 1980s took the decision to privately speak to Sinn Féin–IRA to persuade them to join peace talks on the condition that they discontinue their armed campaign.

The symbolism of one early meeting associated with the Forum illustrates the challenge of maintaining an inclusive and cross-party approach. On 2 April 1983, a meeting was scheduled between Taoiseach Garret FitzGerald, Tánaiste Dick Spring, Hume and the Leader of the Opposition, Charlie Haughey, to discuss the Forum. When Haughey arrived he made it clear that he did not want to sit at a square table across from Hume and FitzGerald. Consequently, a senior official was given ten minutes to provide a round table for the meeting and he did.

Despite the self-evident constructive nature of the Forum – central proposals of the Forum included parity of esteem and a federal/confederal model of State, recognising the identity of all strands of Irish life – Thatcher rejected its findings out of hand, with her famous 'Out, Out, Out' speech (indicative of her frustration that the initiative on Northern Ireland had moved from London to Dublin). During a press conference on 19 November 1984, Thatcher, in response to a question from an Irish television reporter, made the following remark about the Report: 'I have made it quite clear – and so did Mr Prior when he was Secretary of State for Northern Ireland – that a unified Ireland was one solution that is out. A second solution was confederation of two states. That is out. A third solution was joint authority. That is out.'[4] Thatcher's ill-judged comments on the New Ireland Forum Report have since become something of a self-parody. Hume was in Washington when she made her rebuff, as Paul Quinn remembers: 'He was absolutely disconsolate and extremely depressed. He was quite an emotional fellow and he just thought that Thatcher's vehemence was the end of the line.' Hume made his fury known to the British press the following week:

There is now no credible, political force on the Unionist side in Northern Ireland which will accept anything short of majority rule or which will agree to any form of political recognition of the Irish identity of the minority. We may yet be driven to the conclusion that no serious business can be done with this particular British government. *The Nationalist minority in the North has outgrown the Northern State* [author's emphasis]. The British Government may still prevail over us. But they should bear this in mind: You do not have our consent. You have never had our consent. All your military might cannot force our consent.[5]

From that point onwards, Hume redoubled his efforts to marshal American influence to condition British engagement in the New Ireland Forum's principles. He asked Tip O'Neill to stress to President Reagan that Thatcher should be more sensitive to Irish perspectives and give more credence to the Forum. O'Neill agreed and dealt directly with Reagan on the matter (as Speaker O'Neill had the status to leapfrog over the State Department). Reagan by now had a good relationship with FitzGerald. Earlier that year, on 15 March 1984, FitzGerald had addressed a Joint Session of the US Congress and, in turn, on his visit to Ireland a few months later, President Reagan gave an address before a Joint Session of the Irish National Parliament (Dáil Éireann) on 4 June 1984. A combination of pressure from O'Neill and a respect for the Irish government made it almost impossible for Reagan not to intervene with Thatcher and impress upon her the need for a more equitable approach.

The US media was equally aghast at Thatcher's insensitivity in her response to proposals to heal a bitter conflict, one in desperate need of a fresh initiative. When she rejected the Forum Report so comprehensively, US opinion tended to look less favourably both on Thatcher and her dogmatism. An editorial in *The New York Times*, 'The Ins and Outs of Ireland', was accurate in all its assertions, and it also showed the degree to which Irish efforts to convey the full background and complexity of the Northern conflict had succeeded with members of the US press:

In diplomatic reports, 'full and frank' talks are those that fail to reach an agreement. Britain's Prime Minister Thatcher went even further in describing her recent meeting with Ireland's Prime Minister Garret FitzGerald. 'That is out' is how she dealt with his Government's three ideas for ending the agony of Northern Ireland.

Mrs. Thatcher may be in no mood for concessions to Irish nationalism so soon after she was nearly killed by the bomb of its violent fringe. But if Britain persists in rejecting every peaceful change, the hit squads of the Irish Republican Army will be the beneficiaries. This is doubly true if Britain also fails to address the legitimate grievances about criminal justice in Northern Ireland.

Britain bears a heavy responsibility for its Irish troubles. It partitioned the island in 1922, granting independence to the south while turning the north into a sectarian stockade under its own flag. It then tied its hands by granting Northern Ireland's one million Protestants a veto over any changes in sovereignty. This veto has been misused to block concessions to the North's half-million Catholics.

In bitter despair, a minority of this minority has turned to violence. Prime Minister FitzGerald voiced the hopes of the non-violent majorities, North and South. His Irish Forum report broke new ground by proposing not only North–South union or confederation but acknowledging Protestant claims to British identity. It offered a third-choice compromise of 'joint authority' – letting both Britain's and Ireland's flags fly in Northern Ireland.

If Mrs. Thatcher sweeps that aside, she reinforces the inflexibility of her most highhanded citizens. No one doubts her courage in opposing the demonic fanaticism of the IRA. But she has yet to show the same resolve in dealing with Northern Ireland's Protestants, who refuse to share power or even symbols with an oppressed minority.

That oppression is shamefully evident in the criminal justice system. Ninety-five percent of Northern Ireland's police are Protestant and a single judge can convict without jury. And nowhere else in Great Britain do the police aim plastic bullets against demonstrators. Eliminating these anomalies requires no change in flags. Doing at least that would dispel the futility that results from Mrs. Thatcher's annual meetings with Ireland's leader.[6]

In the US Congress, too, Thatcher's dismissal immediately triggered vigorous efforts by the Speaker, Tip O'Neill, to bring her to heel. On 20 April 1979 in Dublin Castle, the Speaker had insisted that the British government 'get serious negotiations moving quickly towards a just, realistic and workable solution' to the Northern crisis. Having thus insisted, it was not in the Speaker's nature to fail to defend such an initiative when it was under attack. Thatcher avoided properly confronting O'Neill's demand for reasonable engagement on the Irish Question in 1979; it was a considerable misjudgement to think that she could continue to avoid it after denouncing the Forum's Report in the manner in which she had. O'Neill wrote to Reagan raising the matter of the future of the New Ireland Forum in advance of President Reagan's meeting with Prime Minister Thatcher. O'Neill expressed concern that Thatcher's comments about the Forum would put the bid to create peace in Ireland in jeopardy.[7] Reagan replied, indicating that he would raise the subject with Thatcher.

On 2 May 1984, the Speaker had helped to steer a Concurrent Resolution of the US House of Representatives and the US Senate welcoming the New Ireland Forum initiative, and the Report resulting from it (the Concurrent Resolution was issued on 17 May 1984). James Sharkey remembers:

> Taoiseach Garret FitzGerald had gone to Washington and had spoken very convincingly on the New Ireland Forum initiative. His appearance before the Joint Session of Congress was met with rapturous applause. Shortly after the Forum's Report, Congressman Brian Donnelly brought a resolution forward to both houses of Congress, to the Senate and the House, commending the work of the Forum and recommending that it be studied and advanced. It was not much understood and appreciated in Ireland, but it was an important breakthrough to have such a Resolution passed. You may take it that it was fully appreciated by the White House and by British observers in the United States.

The unanimous passage of a motion commending the conclusions of the New Ireland Forum in the US Congress was a major occurrence. It was perhaps unprecedented in the history of Congress up to that point (the degree of change which occurred can accurately be measured in contrast to Congress' shut down of the Fogarty Resolution three decades earlier). Thatcher had misjudged the measure of American elected representatives' determination to aid the Forum. Moreover, there was an onus on US presidential consolidation of Irish peace initiatives too, since a precedent had been set and a framework for US presidential support for Irish peace had been established by former US president, Jimmy Carter. When the proposals contained in the New Ireland Forum Report were publicly rejected by Thatcher, her rejection was not enough to prevent the substance of those proposals being ultimately championed with US support.

Thatcher had underestimated the sea change which had occurred in the US in relation to the Irish Question. She had taken insufficient account of Tip O'Neill's capacity to challenge Reagan, should the President adopt as inflexible a line on brokering an Irish settlement as Thatcher herself. In truth, though, Reagan was naturally inclined to consolidate peaceful initiatives in the North of Ireland. When the well-intentioned New Ireland Forum Report, seeking to foster greater understanding and dialogue between Britain and Ireland, was vehemently rejected by the 'Iron Lady', Reagan was then much more open-minded about putting down a marker of US support. This is borne out by correspondence between the Speaker and the President. In a letter issued by O'Neill from the Speaker's Office:

> Dear Mr. President,
> I understand that you will be meeting with Prime Minister Thatcher next week … I want personally share with you my deep concern that the Forum, which is the best hope for a peaceful, lawful and constitutional resolution to the tragedy of Northern Ireland may be in serious jeopardy as a result of Mrs. Thatcher's public statements about the Forum's Report.[8]

President Reagan wrote in response:

> Dear Mr. Speaker,
> During my meeting with Mrs. Thatcher at Camp David I made a special effort to bring your letter to her personal attention and to convey your message of concern. I also personally emphasized the need for progress in resolving the complex situation in Northern Ireland, and the desirability for flexibility on the part of all the involved parties.[9]

Furthermore, Reagan had visited Ireland earlier that year, in June 1984, and been welcomed as a son of Ballyporeen (predictably the British attempted to prevent that visit). Reagan's own Irish dimension was by now important to him.

The 'Greening' of President Reagan

The background to the 'greening' of Reagan is rather complex. Seán Donlon recounts how the US president with the most Irish name since JFK became aware of his Irish ancestry:

I had met Ronald Reagan when he was running for president and I asked him, as I would ask any person with a name like that, how far back his Irish connections went. To my surprise, he said: 'I have often looked into it, I am not sure that we have an Irish connection. We have traced our ancestry back to England'. So we got with a lot of help, particularly from the Mormon Church in Salt Lake City, who at that time had the best records from all over Europe – they had collected shipping records, birth records, baptismal records – and they had created an extraordinary archive of family information. We discovered that the ancestor, the relevant Reagan, had left Ballyporeen in County Tipperary, and [we] eventually arranged to get the President to visit there a few years later.

He had said to me during the election campaign: 'if you find that I am Irish I do not want you to announce it during the election campaign because people will think that I am simply using it. But if I am Irish I will mark it on the first St Patrick's Day when I am in the White House'. So, as soon as he arrived in Washington in January of 1981, I got in touch with him and invited him to lunch at the embassy on St. Patrick's Day. Among my many guests, I had Tip O'Neill, Ted Kennedy, Hugh Carey, Pat Moynihan. During the lunch, Tip O'Neill said to President Reagan, 'next year I'll do the lunch if you would come to it?' (There was a tradition in Washington that the president never came to the Hill except to give the State of the Union address once a year.) But immediately he said, 'oh yeah I'll come, if you give a lunch on St Patrick's Day I'll come'. So, ever since then on St Patrick's Day the Speaker has given a lunch and so far every President has attended.

The Speaker's St Patrick's Day Lunch on Capitol Hill became an institution from 1982 onwards. Tip O'Neill's biographer, John A. Farrell, notes that the Speaker was careful to ensure that John Hume's agenda received optimal scope: 'Tip decides he's going to have this big luncheon and he has Hume come over and he seats Hume next to Ronald Reagan'. Senator Chris Dodd elaborates further the role that the Speaker's Lunch played in the US Congress on St Patrick's Day:

> Those luncheons on St Patrick's Day, or around St Patrick's Day, really created great opportunities. Not the luncheon itself – that is the public

event. It was the meetings that happened all around that – a lot of meetings in what they call a 'hideaway office'. John [Hume] would be present, certainly, the Taoiseach, the foreign ministers, the aides – like Seán Donlon – people like that who are really knowledgeable and deeply involved. So you could really have some very serious conversations about the problem and how to frame it.

Until the late 1970s, St Patrick's Day in Washington was a muted affair. That changed with President Reagan and it has endured to this day. In the larger context, however, it was crucial that the occasion become an instrument to advance policy. Hence, on receiving the bowl of shamrocks on St Patrick's Day and then travelling across town to Capitol Hill for the Speaker's lunch, the President would make an annual statement in support of peace in Ireland. The political chaos in the North of Ireland made the construction of careful cooperation all the more pressing. Reagan began to be influenced not only by the Friends of Ireland but by his Deputy Secretary of State (later National Security Advisor), William Clark. Clark was a close personal friend of the president, who had automatic and immediate access to him (he had worked closely with Reagan in California) and he was not shy to express his sympathy for Irish Nationalism, which was vilified in the British press. In this, Clark was counter-cultural: not only vis-à-vis the institution of the State Department but also for his divergence of views on this issue with the White House Chief of Staff, James Baker, and with the president's counsellor, Edwin Meese.

The Road Back to Constructive Politics

In the immediate aftermath of Thatcher's rejection of the New Ireland Forum Report, the repair work initiated by Thatcher's counterpart, Taoiseach FitzGerald, was crucially important. That is not to unduly emphasise the personalities of leaders: 'Nations have no permanent friends and no permanent enemies. Only permanent interests,' as Lord Palmerston said. Thatcher saw herself, along with Reagan, as co-regent of the Free World; for her, that role was restricted to the West's face off with the Soviet Union and did not extend to US interference in her 'domestic' issues, such as running the Northern Irish State. (The perception that Thatcher and Reagan were soul-mates could be qualified with a series of instances in which they differed – Northern Ireland was only one source of dissonance between them – they also differed on issues such as Reagan's invasion of Grenada, a former British colony, and on the Falklands war.) Thatcher had not yet grasped that the US was truly interested in Irish peace. Interest in Ireland had risen and fallen in Washington, but since a peace agenda was established it had moved powerfully to the fore and was unleashed. Tony Blair conceded that:

> People in Westminster tended to take a very one-sided view of the Troubles and the struggle (there were people on the left that didn't and took a different perspective). There wasn't much middle ground and one of the things that John Hume did was actually find the middle ground upon which people could congregate. And this was part of his unique insight and contribution.

Yet, in November 1984 the reception for that middle ground in Westminster could not have been more hostile.

The Anglo-Irish Agreement

While the New Ireland Forum meetings were taking place, the foundations of the Anglo-Irish Agreement, which derived in many ways from the new thinking involved in the New Ireland Forum, were being negotiated by officials from the Irish and British governments. The Forum and the Anglo-Irish Agreement had much in common in that the objectives of the Forum were to generate a discussion about a New Ireland and an Agreed Ireland. Thus Anglo-Irish Agreement negotiations explicitly acknowledged that pre-existing political structures were inadequate: the administration of neither of the two States on the island of Ireland could resolve the conflict; nor had those States brokered peace in a framework that excluded Britain. The Irish dimension was fundamental to the discussion. As Paul Quinn remembers, 'the New Ireland Forum … laid the predicate for what became the Anglo-Irish Agreement, which in turn created, for the first time, an official role for the Irish Government to play vis-à-vis the British with respect to Northern Ireland'. As Seán Donlon explains:

> Margaret Thatcher then became Prime Minister [she was re-elected] in 1983 and she was persuaded, I suspect, mainly by two officials in

her own system – Robert Armstrong and David Goodall – both of them had knowledge of and interest in Ireland. I suspect it was mainly through their influence that she was persuaded that the security situation in Northern Ireland could not be dealt with mainly by counter security measures.

Michael Lillis, who had been posted in Brussels while Haughey was Taoiseach, was recalled by FitzGerald (who became Taoiseach in 1982) to head the Northern Ireland Division of the Irish Department of Foreign Affairs. He was a key negotiator from the Dublin side during the Anglo-Irish Agreement negotiations; Robert Armstrong and David Goodall, the two most senior officials in Thatcher's cabinet, were his principal British counterparts. The prospects of reaching an agreement did not always seem good throughout 1984. However, it was clear that if an agreement could be reached, it would receive practical support from the US in the form of the International Fund for Ireland, making good on Jimmy Carter's 1977 Statement.

Lillis and Goodall were Joint Chairmen of a coordinating committee on routine matters between the two governments. In September 1983, Lillis invited Goodall for a pre-lunch stroll along the Grand Canal in Dublin. He proposed, on FitzGerald's instructions, which had been cleared by Hume, that only the involvement of the Irish State in the governing of Northern Ireland would provide the hope of reconciling the extreme alienation of the nationalist community. He was addressing Thatcher's only concern: security. But he was also proposing a new regime that would change politics. Goodall reported the proposals to Thatcher and came back to probe further. Anglo-Irish negotiations then began in earnest and continued until November 1985.

FitzGerald populated the team with a number of very talented officials, including Seán Donlon, Michael Lillis, Dermot Nally, Noel Dorr from the Department of Foreign Affairs; Head of the Department of Justice, Andy Ward, and Declan Quigley of the Attorney General's office were added later. They consulted regularly with Garret FitzGerald, Dick Spring and Peter Barry – the Taoiseach, the Tánaiste and the Minister for Foreign Affairs. No Northern Irish party or politician was involved in negotiating the Anglo-Irish Agreement, yet the Irish government opted to involve Hume confidentially and Lillis would travel to Derry every other weekend for two years to brief him on a confidential basis.

As noted, Robert Armstrong and Sir David Goodall were the prominent officials on Thatcher's team. Goodall was a man of considerable intellectual ability, with Catholic roots. He was sympathetic without having a particular sympathy for Ireland. Armstrong was highly esteemed by Thatcher. The officials worked hard and drank hard together, and both were ultimately crucial in persuading Thatcher of the agreement. Throughout the negotiations, intellectual navigation came from the Republic; the British assumed a managerial role; the North and its citizens were seen as the main subject of the debate. Diplomats used to personally transport written documents relating to Anglo-Irish negotiations, at risk to their lives in some circumstances, lest secret intelligence forces intercept the material.

They met thirty-six times in total, their meetings sometimes lasting several days. They would relay the substance of their discussions very closely to their Prime Minister and Taoiseach. They agreed, first, that Northern Ireland could not go back to Stormont's *ancien régime* and that therefore power-sharing was the core issue; since Stormont had been part of the problem before, Stormont also needed to be part of the solution. The British and Irish would not agree to a government unless it was based on partnership. Secondly, the two governments were in accord that any agreement could not be pulled down as the Sunningdale Executive had been. It could not depend, as Sunningdale had depended, on a capricious Northern Irish prime minister. Thirdly, it was clear that no Dublin–London agreement could provide for something that Unionist councillors could reject.

Michael Lillis's first priority was negotiating the best agreement for the Irish government, but any such development was closely linked with the Irish Question in Washington. He met Mark Durkan in 1985, then Hume's junior associate, before Durkan left for the US to intern with Ted Kennedy. The pair discussed how the Agreement should be communicated there and Lillis briefed Mark Durkan on the International Fund for Ireland, which was expected to come into existence once an agreement was reached. Lillis gave Durkan a focus on what he should do and say to build support for it on the Hill. One priority was how to talk about it to the American political class, since a fund stemming from taxpayers' dollars took more persuasion than simply tugging entrepreneurial strings. The Irish embassy, and any SDLP delegate, needed to be clear both about what the fund would be used for and what it would *not* be used for. The fund was to be distinctive and exclusive to Northern Ireland, and they stressed that it would not go to Britain to relieve its Exchequer. Durkan elaborates:

> I spoke to Michael Lillis who gave me a brilliant orientation in relation to the politics of Washington and how the Irish Question played in Washington, and the different versions of the Irish lobby in Washington. He was very clear in relation to where they were in terms of the negotiations with the British government, which had ups and downs, some of them public, some of them not public. He was very clear that, as far as they could see, they were in with a real chance of securing an agreement. He wanted to make sure the US dimension could come in very strongly behind that. It left me feeling a bit daunted as to what was expected of me. I was going out for a great work experience, but here I was given a mission as well. My job in the summer and autumn of 1985 was to use my base in Teddy Kennedy's office to lobby other congressional offices in and around the idea that there may be an agreement. What we were trying to do in 1985 was to work in anticipation of what we hoped would be an agreement between the British and Irish governments, and subsequently we did get the Anglo-Irish Agreement in November 1985.

Although the talks were conducted in complete secrecy, there were still leaks. For instance, Michael Lillis recalls being alarmed when Rosemary O'Neill (a political officer at the State Department and daughter of Tip O'Neill) mentioned to him that she knew Hume was involved with the Anglo-Irish Agreement. If that information were to have filtered to the British it would have caused consternation, to say the least. That an MP was working behind the scenes with Britain's formidable ally, the US, on the basis of information provided by Dublin could have troubled the negotiations.

The Americans and the Anglo-Irish Agreement

The importance of the Thatcher–Reagan dynamic became fully apparent during the Anglo-Irish Agreement negotiations. O'Neill had placed Reagan next to Hume at the Speaker's lunch in 1982, and both he and Senator

Kennedy continually endorsed the Hume approach to the Northern crisis. Since that approach was effectively being dismissed by Thatcher, with her embarrassingly emphatic rejection of the New Ireland Forum Report, O'Neill – especially during his regular meetings with Reagan – could reference the reasonableness of the Hume approach. Thatcher had overplayed her hand and underestimated the way in which Reagan was 'channelling Tip who in turn was channelling Hume', as Sean O'hUiginn put it. It was this channelling that enabled compromise and the re-establishment of Anglo-Irish cooperation.

Thatcher visited Washington for Camp David in December 1984, a month after her 'Out, Out, Out' speech. She visited Washington again in February 1985 to address Congress. On these occasions Reagan, prompted by O'Neill, put Ireland on the agenda and urged her to give a fair hearing to any reasonable proposals. If Reagan was the carrot, O'Neill was the stick, as Thatcher was to find out. On 20 February 1985, before addressing the Joint Houses of Congress, Thatcher visited O'Neill at the Speaker's Office in the House of Representatives, as is customary before addressing Congress. This time her encounter with Tip O'Neill left Thatcher reeling. Tom O Neill, remembers:

> I think Margaret Thatcher went to her grave having great disdain for one American politician, and that was my dad. He told her in no uncertain terms where he was from, where his family was from, showed her a picture of Donegal. He reminded her about the importance of peace in Ireland. She was being put down by an American politician whom she considered to be her junior and she did not like it for one moment.

Her public face, when she was addressing Congress, showed that she was the picture of cooperation and fully supportive of the New Ireland Forum Report, as reflected in what Thatcher said to Congress about Northern Ireland during her address:

> Garret FitzGerald and I – and our respective governments – are united in condemning terrorism (applause). We recognise the differing traditions and identities of the two parts of the community of Northern Ireland – the Nationalist and the Unionist. We seek a

political way forward acceptable to them both, which respects them both. So long as the majority of people of Northern Ireland wish to remain part of the United Kingdom, their wishes will be respected. If ever there were to be a majority in favour of change, then I believe that our Parliament would respond accordingly, for that is the principle of consent enshrined in your Constitution and in an essential part of ours.[10]

There is no disagreement on this principle between the United Kingdom Government and the Government of the Republic of Ireland. Indeed, the four constitutional nationalist parties of Ireland, north and south, who came together to issue the New Ireland Forum Report, made clear that any new arrangements could only come about by consent, and I welcome too their outright condemnation and total rejection of terrorism and all its works.

Be under no illusions about the Provisional IRA. They terrorise their own communities. They are the enemies of democracy and of freedom too. Don't just take my word for it. Ask the Government of the Irish Republic, where it is an offence even to belong to that organisation – as indeed it also is in Northern Ireland.

I recognise and appreciate the efforts which have been made by the Administration and Congress alike to bring home this message to American citizens who may be misled into making contributions to seemingly innocuous groups. The fact is that money is used to buy the deaths of Irishmen north and south of the border; and 70% of those killed by the IRA are Irishmen – and that money buys the killing and wounding even of American citizens visiting our country.

Garret FitzGerald – and I salute him for the very brave thing he did yesterday in passing a special law to see that money did not get to the IRA – Garret FitzGerald and I will continue to consult together in the quest for stability and peace in Northern Ireland and we hope we will have your continued support for our joint efforts to find a way forward.[11]

Thatcher restricted her acknowledgement of White House and US Congress engagement in the search for Irish peace merely to attempts to reduce the flow from the US of money to buy weapons. A fuller acknowledgement would have included the constructive cycle of US engagement. Her indication that she would continue to work with her Irish counterpart was a concession under duress that she would have to abandon her dismissive mode.

Supporters of NORAID were outraged that O'Neill had agreed to allow Thatcher, who in their eyes was the personification of British malevolence, to address Congress. (Disengagement from the political process remained NORAID's central idea for the way forward.) More perspicacious observers understood that it was no concession at all: O'Neill's welcoming of Thatcher into Congress was a springe to catch a woodcock. That the key political incumbents in 1985 were an Irish US president and an Irish Speaker of the House of Representatives proved to be essential to the American influence on the Irish Question. Reagan depended on O'Neill's cooperation and goodwill to pass his legislative programme through the House of Representatives, which O'Neill dominated. O'Neill, determined to secure Hume's programme, traded parts of his own American priorities to get Reagan to pressurise Thatcher. O'Neill, connoisseur of power that he was, exploited that position of strength to its fullest. To his staffers, observing him horse trade, he was like an ancient Irish Chieftain in that he put his hand on the shoulder of his interlocutors and he was warm, but it was always clear who was Boss.

O'Neill knew that Reagan was persuadable in taking an active stance on Ireland, so he cultivated a warm personal relationship with him. O'Neill told him Irish stories and Reagan told him Hollywood stories and then they would argue over which of them had been more deprived when they were growing up. Seán Donlon remembers that both the Speaker and the President were great storytellers:

> One of Reagan's techniques, which I have seen him use with visitors, is that if he does not want to discuss something when you arrive in his office – and you are told beforehand that it's a twenty minute meeting or fifteen minute meeting – he starts to tell you a story and it takes fifteen or twenty minutes to tell the story. He then shakes your hand warmly, with a photograph taken, and you are out the door before you realise that the meeting is now over. But he and Tip would trade stories, particularly Irish stories. I would frequently get phone calls in the Embassy from both sides. They would phone me from the White House and say 'any new Irish stories', the President is meeting

the Speaker this evening. I would also get a call from Kirk O'Donnell saying 'any new Irish stories', the Speaker is meeting the President.

The two men fought bitterly over wider issues: the O'Neill and Reagan clash was a broad collision of ideology which manifested itself in their divergence on Medicare, the New Deal and Reaganomics; O'Neill had Democratic intuitions on Democratic issues and pushed Reagan very hard on the working class. On issues that mattered to O'Neill, he knew how to turn the screws on the President, though there were limits to which Reagan could be pushed. As Ted Kennedy remembered: 'We tried a number of different interventions with Reagan to get him to appoint a special envoy for peace [in Ireland], but he was not interested in that.'[12] While O'Neill's role was enormous, he needed a policy and traction on the ground in Northern Ireland to hinge it to; concern for Northern Ireland could not be implemented without a vehicle. That programme was Hume's strategy, without it the effect of O'Neill's engagement would have been nil. The credit due to O'Neill for progress on the Irish issue comes from the symbiosis between him and Hume.

In May 1985, Taoiseach Garret FitzGerald visited Senator Kennedy in Cape Cod to discuss the details and strategies of the Anglo-Irish Agreement, which was then under negotiation. Kennedy remembers that the role of the sovereign government in Dublin was central to both Hume and FitzGerald's strategy to create new political structures: 'There was the agreement between Hume's SDLP [Social Democratic and Labour Party] and the Irish government ... I remember Garret had spent a lot of time thinking through all of these multidimensional aspects of it and having a very good grasp of the interrelationships of these issues and what was possible. He had backup positions and a very comprehensive view.'[13]

There was a wobble from the British side in the lead-up to the signing of the Anglo-Irish Agreement. The British Embassy pressured George Schultz, then the US Secretary of State, to move Reagan to reverse his support for the Agreement. When Tip O'Neill heard of this, he telephoned President Reagan and warned him that if he reneged on backing the Anglo-Irish Agreement he would shame him from the well of the House. Thus, Hume was vindicated in his strategic belief that bringing American influence to bear on Anglo-Irish relations was the only path to resolution; Thatcher's acceptance was an exercise in saving as much face as possible.

Vehement denunciation in America of the IRA's atrocities, such as the attack on Hyde Park (in which four Americans died) and the Brighton bomb which targeted the British cabinet and Prime Minister Thatcher, generated sympathy in America towards those in Britain who stood against terrorism. However, it also strengthened the cause of those advancing a constitutional approach. Thatcher had yet to feel the full force of that judgement, though it came in 1985. A year after her rebuff of the New Ireland Forum Report, Thatcher backed down completely from her rejection of an alternative political settlement for Northern Ireland, partly because London was, and is, so solicitous of its relationship with Washington. As Michael Lillis states: 'Afterwards she said to one of her closest associates, Lord McAlpine, who was the Treasurer of the Tory Party (and this is where it ties into John Hume in America) … "It was the Americans who made me do it".'[14]

Karl Meyer, speaking of the role of *The New York Times* in helping to bring Thatcher to a more judicious position, recalls:

> In the 1980s, the Irish debate was seen by many people in apocalyptic terms – as a fight between good and evil. If you take it as a 'good and evil' fight it is hard to find a middle ground. I am proud of the fact that my paper – and I have to say that my views had to find collective agreement from the editor and the other members of our editorial board, so I was not just speaking for myself in this – tried vigorously to take a reasoned path on the Irish debate. I am very proud of our role. Mrs Thatcher at that time was very much in her black and white phase, everything was good and evil and so on. She changed over time and I would like to think that our editorials, admonishing her not to throw in the sponge on this, played some small part in showing that there were other voices in the room; that it was not just the hardliners on both sides dictating the terms of debate.

Ratification of the Anglo-Irish Agreement

The Agreement was signed and registered in international law at the United Nations, and as such it was rock solid. At Sunningdale, the Irish and British governments could not agree on terminology, for example regarding the United Kingdom (was it the United Kingdom or all of Great Britain and

Northern Ireland?) and formalising the Agreement in international law, thus it went into abeyance. Moreover, with the Sunningdale Agreement, the only focus of change was in Northern Ireland, and it did not extend to the broader Dublin–London involvement. It remained contentious to define the status of Northern Ireland, given that it opened questions about the Irish Government's constitutional claim to the North of Ireland; to remove that claim would have required a referendum. The governments needed a deep agreement, and a substantial settlement on most of the substance of the conflict, and with the Agreement in place there would arise the necessity for a referendum on Articles 2 and 3. Hume understood this and never lost sight of the need for such a referendum.

The Agreement between Britain and Ireland was endorsed in the US with a television appearance of O'Neill and Reagan welcoming the Anglo-Irish Agreement: the US interest was intended to preempt the Unionist antipathy likely to arise from it. Once in place, the Anglo-Irish Agreement triggered the International Fund for Ireland, envisaged by Hume during the drafting of the Carter Statement, and enabled the US to exercise a role in Anglo-Irish relations through soft power. US federal dollars started to flow to Northern Ireland as a result of the Agreement, and with funds Irish-America achieved the full status of an effective and persuasive lobby in Washington. After Charles Brett and John McGuckian, Willie McCarter became President of the International Fund for Ireland and brought his credibility to it. To date, 904 million euros have been sent to Ireland to fund over 5,800 projects.[15] The setting up of the International Fund for Ireland was crucial. Congress agreed that 22 million dollars be disbursed in 1985 (in the first year), to tie in with the Anglo-Irish Agreement, and between 20 and 30 million dollars per annum thereafter. Once Congress had shown leadership by sowing in seed funds, New Zealand and Canada followed suit. In tandem with the fund, Madeleine Albright established an advisory team to go to the North and campaign for peace.

Backlash to the Anglo-Irish Agreement

Opposition to the Anglo-Irish Agreement was manifold in Northern Ireland. The DUP opposed what it saw as an aggressive Irish-American lobbying effort built into the Agreement. On the other hand, Sinn Féin could not accept an agreement which in their eyes seemed to ratify partition. Sinn Féin therefore wholly rejected the Anglo-Irish Agreement. The architects of the Agreement were accused of being quislings and it was also widely portrayed as a stunt to prop up the SDLP's electoral prospects. As historian Andrew Wilson put it:

> The Anglo-Irish Agreement was very much a consequence of the political changes in Ulster after the hunger strike. Sinn Féin electoral victories, during and after the prison dispute, created intense pressure on the SDLP. John Hume realized that his party needed a major political achievement if it was to resist the challenge from Republicanism. He hoped to secure concessions from the British government through direct Anglo-Irish negotiations.[16]

While there was truth to the suggestion that the Anglo-Irish Agreement was a reaction to the politicisation and rise of Sinn Féin, to characterise it as a political stunt is to ignore two decades of Hume's reconciliation efforts, as reflected in the Agreement.

In Britain, too, the Anglo-Irish Agreement, though approved by a huge majority in the House of Commons (a painful illustration of Unionism's lack of allies), encountered passionate hostility, particularly from Enoch Powell MP. During the debate in Parliament that followed the signing of the Agreement, the right-wing of the Tory Party and Unionists vehemently challenged Thatcher. Observing the debate, Irish diplomat Richard Ryan recalls that 'Enoch Powell accused the Prime Minister of having been coerced by US interests. I was watching closely at that moment: something snapped in her face because that you cannot get away with.' Meanwhile, in Dublin the Leader of the Opposition and of Fianna Fáil, Charlie Haughey, made out that he was held back from accepting the Anglo-Irish Agreement by hardliners in his party such as Ray MacSharry. He rejected the Anglo-Irish Agreement – it had been negotiated by Haughey's rival for the office of Taoiseach, Garret FitzGerald – and he sent a close colleague, Brian Lenihan, to Washington to denounce it. Hume was livid, but allowed events to take their course. Seamus Mallon remembers:

> I spoke to the Fianna Fáil people and said that I was standing with the Agreement. I told them they were going to be out of step with history if they did not. Despite that, Charlie sent Brian Lenihan out

to Washington. I think Brian discovered very quickly that they were on infertile ground. I knew he had been clobbered, to put it gently. I know Tip O'Neill: he could cut you off at the legs very quickly, as he obviously did that time. I knew it was a misjudgement. I said to them, 'do not go down that road'.

Lenihan had found, through his foredoomed petitioning of Tip O'Neill and his Friends of Ireland colleagues for rejection of the Agreement, that they took their lead on Irish affairs from John Hume. Seamus Mallon, Hume's SDLP Deputy Leader, had also been for a time a senator appointed by Haughey. Mallon stood with his party and against Haughey's line, and Mallon still feels that Haughey never forgave him for ultimately backing the Anglo-Irish Agreement:

I do not think he ever really did. I think it became a barrier. Not so much maybe for Charlie but members of his party. I became somewhat of a pariah. But I had to make my choice. My choice was not to please anybody in power. My choice was to try and protect people in the North of Ireland from the abuses in security.

Ultimately, Haughey was to reverse and agree to accept the Anglo-Irish Agreement before becoming Taoiseach in 1987. Thatcher sent Robert Armstrong to Dublin to see Haughey and tell him that he should have no qualms about accepting the Agreement; 'the Anglo-Irish Agreement was the best deal Ireland ever got', according to one source.[17]

Unionists held that US interests were served by the Agreement and hence it could be neither benevolent nor balanced; that it was laden with Irish-American baggage, which Unionists widely perceived as necessarily anti-Unionist (one Unionist source bemoaned the lack of a 'Friends of the Union' grouping in the US Congress to counter the 'Friends of Ireland'). That was paranoid; serious American engagement had a much more nuanced agenda, and it was a genuine sponsoring of peace, as evidenced by the fact that when Unionist politicians began to visit Washington in the years after the Anglo-Irish Agreement they were warmly received. Hume took the view that while Unionists would be suspicious about the stated political agenda, they would be pragmatic about the collateral consequence to the deal. The Anglo-Irish Agreement called on all to reject violence, but equally it stressed the need for political settlement with an accent on economic development as a means of copper-fastening its political gains. The International Fund for Ireland was also supplemented by Europe (European Union money was to have a similar effect a decade later, under President of the European Commission, Jacques Delors, in supporting the Northern Ireland peace talks after the Cessation of Hostilities).

In the wake of the Anglo-Irish Agreement, 100,000 Unionist protesters gathered in Belfast to denounce it. The thundering 'Lundy' response from Ian Paisley and company on the signing of the Agreement was fervid; Dr Paisley, in front of the City Hall bellowing 'Never, Never, Never', is an iconic image of that moment. Hardline Unionism felt after the Anglo-Irish Agreement that their birthright was being violated. But, unlike the Sunningdale Agreement, the Anglo-Irish Agreement could not be undermined by protest and demonstration. Unionists gradually started to see that the Agreement was irreversible, and that it marked a watershed in the political evolution of Northern Ireland. It is axiomatic that the first necessity of conflict resolution is to take the protagonists out of denial, and the Anglo-Irish Agreement provided just that awakening for many Unionists. Jeffrey Donaldson's retrospective reaction to the agreement is revealing:

> Unionists were excluded from the dialogue that led to the Anglo-Irish Agreement, and they put their trust in Margaret Thatcher, who they perceived to be a Unionist Prime Minister. When she signed the Agreement with Garret FitzGerald, I think Unionists were initially shocked, almost disbelieving, that someone like Margaret Thatcher could do this. On reflection I think that the Anglo-Irish Agreement was the catalyst within Unionism for a realisation that in the end we were going to have to sit down and negotiate with Nationalists to find a way forward; that if we wanted to get rid of what we described as this diktat in the form of the Anglo-Irish Agreement imposed upon us then there was only one way we were going to move it and it wasn't by protest, it was by negotiation.

While Unionists were excluded from the process of negotiating the Anglo-Irish Agreement, so too were Nationalists. John Hume, while not formally part of it, was seen by Donaldson and other Unionists as covertly involved. Hume was indeed consulted, as we have seen, as the Agreement evolved towards a final document. How did a young Unionist politician like Donaldson at the time (Donaldson was elected at the age of 22 in 1985) perceive John Hume, given that he had an inside track in DC and an inside track in Dublin?

> Initially there was very little outreach on the part of John Hume towards Unionism. I think John Hume's view at that time was that he was not ready to engage with Unionism. He needed first of all to create the framework within which a future negotiation could take place; John Hume disengaged from the Assembly, wasn't involved in a dialogue with Unionism, and instead was dealing at a more international level and dealing with the British and Irish governments. I think that it was a mistake that Unionism did not recognise earlier the importance of that influence, the significance of that influence, the way in which Hume would use the pressure point of Washington to apply pressure on London to do business with Dublin, almost to the exclusion of the Unionists. So I do not think that we really caught on to that soon enough. It was only in the latter years that we began to recognise that there was no point howling at the moon for John Hume and his influence in Washington. We needed to be on the Hill. We needed to be in Washington giving the counterbalance to that influence and saying, 'any solution in Northern Ireland has to be one which both sides can endorse'.

David McKittrick, who covered this period as a journalist, explains that other Unionists politicians were quite unnerved not only by the Agreement but by what they saw as the creeping 'Hume factor' in the North of Ireland:

> There was something about him [Hume] that Unionists did not like. Part of it (a number of Unionist politicians will say this in private) was that he was better than them, smarter than them. He was doing these political manoeuvres like going to America, which had not occurred to them. They did not really think in those ways. You will hear a number of people around here in Belfast who still say, 'if only we had a John Hume'.

The reaction to the Anglo-Irish Agreement was visceral. There were various attempts to sabotage the Agreement, above all through widespread protest, which led nowhere. The feeling of the people on the street who had witnessed Thatcher's 'betrayal' was mixed. In the South, the Agreement was broadly welcomed, yet Hume had his critics, particularly on the question of not being fully accommodating or sensitive enough to a Unionist perspective? David McKittrick explains:

> Hume satisfied himself long years before that he was not getting anywhere with Unionism, that he had to go to America and Dublin and so on. You could tell with the Anglo-Irish Agreement of 1985 just about everybody in the South approved of that and very warmly approved of that. Oddly enough the person who did not at the time was Mary Robinson, who disapproved of it and said Unionists should have a better voice and more input. In fact, I think she withdrew from that in the years that followed.

To this day, some Unionists remain implacably against the Agreement, and resent their exclusion from its negotiations. Michael Lillis's perspective on their exclusion from negotiations is pithy: 'Most unionists at that time were so immured in their veto-proofed immunity from any other reality that they would have wrecked the negotiation process.'Lillis also argued that that veto served the Provisional IRA well since it provided 'proof that only their violence and not the political efforts of the SDLP and Dublin could wring concessions from Britain.'[18] From the point of view of Unionists, the Anglo-Irish Agreement was something close to a disaster that delayed peace, as David Trimble contends:

> It did delay things by ten years and it was really very foolish for the British and Irish governments to go behind our backs and impose something on us which they knew rightly we would have strong views about. To say 'we didn't consult you because we thought you wouldn't agree' is not a good enough reason in a democracy for not talking to people.

Yet the fact remains that Margaret Thatcher, perhaps the most de facto pro-Unionist Tory leader in modern times – 'Northern Ireland was as

British as Finchley' – did a deal over the heads of Ulster Unionists without consulting them. One of the legacies of that fact was that Ulster Unionism was significantly unhinged and its guarantee from London felt suddenly less *guaranteed*. Given the Unionist structure, such a form of guarantee depends on the continuing steadfastness of the guarantor: that London continually affirms its guarantee. As Brendan O'Leary argues:

> The ultimate significance of the Anglo-Irish Agreement for Unionists was straightforward. The Union would continue but they had lost veto power over how the Union would be run and they faced the problem that unless they chose to accept a power-sharing government, which was open to them under Article 4 of the Anglo-Irish Agreement of 1985, then British and Irish cooperation would deepen and in effect they would face the joint government of Dublin and London over the North. That institutional structure, which Unionists tried to break with strikes, with demonstrations and with violent terrorism on the part of Loyalists, held. The only way out of the trap was negotiation and that was eventually the path taken.

The Anglo-Irish Agreement therefore acted as a spur to incentivise Unionists to be creative and to propose alternatives. Whereas John Hume's critics would bemoan him for his 'single transferable speech' (his continual reference to the need for agreement and the primary division in Ireland being its people rather than its territory), Unionist leaders just said 'No' and 'Never, Never, Never', but to be credible they ultimately had to propose alternative policies. As David McKittrick mordantly observed: 'Jim Molyneaux was the leader of the Ulster Unionist Party from 1979 to 1995, and the only idea he came up with was "let's do nothing".'

The more hardline Unionists stayed on the street. After three years of futile agitation, when they saw that the Agreement could not be overturned, they tried to replace it with the Mayhew Talks; the new Secretary of State, Patrick Mayhew, had started to meet with DUP member, Peter Robinson, and the stated purpose of those talks was to look for an alternative to the 1985 Agreement. The post-Anglo-Irish Agreement protest is a good study of political leaders who in fact are more adept as followers of trends. Those Unionist politicians who continually chanted 'Never' and 'No' learned to do a complete reversal: While Peter Robinson had routinely refused to be involved in discussions, once the Mayhew Talks began he was enthusiastic to be sown into developments in the North.

Hume's work after the agreement was paramount. Though he risked shedding support from within his party as well as outside it, he argued that all strands of the Northern crisis needed to be involved in a settlement. He was anxious that the genuine progress of the Anglo-Irish Agreement should not be seen as an encroachment or an assault on Unionist identity. Steadfast in his faith of 'spilling our sweat not our blood', Hume was just as enthusiastic to broker the progressive settlement to Unionists as he was to incorporate Nationalist identity in an Agreed Ireland.

The signing of the Anglo-Irish Agreement, while a huge breakthrough in helping to secure agreement from the political middle out, did not ultimately succeed in bringing about a Cessation of Hostilities. It failed to weave all strands – above all, violent organisations – into its framework of activity. Nevertheless, despite its flaws, and the Unionists' reactionary manoeuvres in its aftermath, the Agreement stands as a watershed moment which laid the groundwork for the peace process to come. The Agreement gave Dublin a powerful voice in Northern Ireland and provided a platform for the peace process; it dealt with most inter-governmental issues, except policing and the decommissioning of arms. Crucially, the Anglo-Irish Agreement entailed devolved power and Westminster upheld the Agreement in the teeth of fierce Unionist opposition. Moreover, while the Anglo-Irish Agreement, like the Sunningdale Agreement before it, instated the principle of consent, it proved stronger and more durable than its predecessor.

The economic investment heralded by the Anglo-Irish Agreement materialised almost immediately. James Baker, a Reagan staffer trying to persuade his President, plaintively asked 'why should we slit our throats over 22 million dollars?' And Hume, referring to US investment, observed: 'When the Anglo-Irish Agreement was signed by Margaret Thatcher and Garret FitzGerald, what was the result? Full support from the United States. As Tip O'Neill said to me and Ted Kennedy said to me on the telephone, "We keep our promises [The Carter Statement had promised investment]. We're setting up the International Fund for Ireland".'[19] Part of the rationale for the International Fund for Ireland was to support counties on both sides of the Irish border, which had been economically hurt by partition.

Tip O'Neill had also assisted the Irish who lived in America as well. In 1985, he was named Distinguished Freeman of Cork, and visited Ireland again to receive the award. The drafting of what became known as the 'Donnelly Visa', named after Brian Donnelly, Congressman from South Boston and Chairman of the Friends of Ireland (1984–92), also happened in Ireland. The resolution for the visa was written in County Wicklow, after a failed attempt to visit Glendalough due to a snowstorm.

The Maryfield Secretariat

A core legacy of the Anglo-Irish Agreement was that the Irish government, through its representatives posted to Northern Ireland, could haul RUC officers who were abusing their power over the coals. The establishment of the Maryfield Secretariat, the location where Irish diplomats posted to Northern Ireland under the Anglo-Irish Agreement's provisions lived and worked, was a triumph, although some felt that it had all the hallmarks of an embassy and therefore could be perceived as being partitionist. The Secretariat sparked outrage among some Unionists, who felt that the British had betrayed them by instituting a Dublin contingency within Northern Ireland which could make recommendations to London. Thatcher had realised neither the symbolic nor actual effect of having civil servants from Dublin in Belfast. The Unionist reception to those Dublin representatives was short of hospitable. Seán Donlon, then Head of the Department of Foreign Affairs, recounts that those posted to the North were under lethal threat:

> Before they went up, they had to have things like their fingerprints, their dental records and particularly their feet on record. I couldn't figure out: why are they going through all of this? People pointed out to us that in a bomb situation, if you're blown to bits we want to have a record of as many of your bits as possible to identify you. But that's what they did. They never complained.

Inside 'the bunker', as the Maryfield Secretariat was known, Irish diplomats dealt with the British government on issues such as the civil service. Michael Lillis and Daíthí O'Ceallaigh, who were assigned to the bunker, were forbidden to travel within Northern Ireland. The latter recorded a total of thirty-nine trips to Northern Ireland from Dublin. Sean O'hUiginn, known as the 'Prince of Darkness' because of his very dark hair and his rapier tongue, was also posted to the bunker. Their framework was simple: what worked for Hume was okay by them. Hume kept in touch with them and they remember that he never spoke down to civil servants and was devoid of any baronial manner. Usually people from the North were not assigned to the Anglo-Irish Department of Foreign Affairs Anglo-Irish Division because of the risk that their families could be threatened (Hume himself never accepted police protection; he refused to give in to any form of violence).

The mechanisms of the Agreement were radical. The Irish Government could make proposals on any and all issues involving Northern Ireland and both governments had a treaty obligation to 'make determined efforts to resolve differences'. The process worked continuously. A few examples from the first fifteen months of its operation include: the repeal of the flags and emblems act; the strengthening of the law on incitement of hatred; a huge increase in minority representation on public bodies; demolition and replacement of three notorious Northern Irish ghettos – Divis and Unity in Belfast, the Rossville Flats in Derry; a new police complaints commission; better rules for routing controversial parades; full investigation into and reporting of incidents, including logged responses from security forces; the improvement of habeas corpus rules and procedures; better policy and management of prisoners and incidents; tighter rules on the admissibility of evidence, most notably 'coerced evidence'; the strengthening of rules for fair employment; discussion on budgetary concerns on infrastructure, education and health. The Anglo-Irish Agreement had demonstrated the determination of senior British foreign policy strategists to prioritise relations with the Irish Republic, and to ensure that future cooperation was insulated from the caprice of individual politicians and immune from the considerable force of Unionist resistance.

Hume's work in building an awareness in Washington had made it a great deal easier for politicians there to engage on the Irish Question, because he represented a clear-headed, constitutional approach which they could adopt. This was an anxiety from Whitehall's point of view, because the Friends of Ireland were defying British policy in the North of Ireland. However, Tony Blair acknowledged the need for this work:

> The contribution of John Hume to this whole process is immeasurable in this sense: he really cleared the ground for the seeds of peace to be planted and to bloom in the end. He did that by offering a sense that there could be a constitutional way forward, there could be a way that was non-violent towards achieving the aims of justice and peace. That was a kind of revelation; and he also helped get rid of all the weeds and the undergrowth that had prevented people from seeing that maybe there is a different way forward altogether and that was incredibly influential in America ... So this was the move that really created the ground in which we were able to plant and get busy. Those years that John toiled on ... those years that were productive for the future, beyond any doubt at all.
>
> When he was doing this clearing exercise within American politics, he was engaging with the American policymakers in a way that got them to understand how this thing might be resolved differently, so when Bill Clinton then came to power there was something for him to work on and he did it in this way. He did it, not by describing the IRA and Sinn Féin as terrorists, but describing how the goals of Nationalism and Republicanism could be met differently and could be met by a process of engagement – if the Americans were to use their influence with the British – not to say 'concede to their demands' but say to them 'think differently about how this can be resolved'.

The Irish Times, recognising Hume's work for the Anglo-Irish Agreement, called him the 'uncrowned King of Northern Ireland'.[20] Even so, given the prevailing opposition, Hume was conscious of the need to 'communicate' the Agreement. Michael Lillis remembers having lunch with Hume at Doherty's Hotel, Greencastle, when Lillis was writing a speech for him. They had a few drinks but Hume was totally silent and pensive and the worst possible companion during those sessions. At the end of the day, he would start to speak about the contents of the speech, but he would then work over it again and again to make it completely satisfactory, and by the time Hume had finished it would be his speech and his alone.

The unique originality of his US strategy was the result of this thinking process. It was his thinking about the subject and this need to communicate that was central to what was to come next. There was now a solid agreement in place between London and Dublin. The Unionist veto on change had been, for the first time in history, firmly faced down by the British. The IRA's campaign was not an inch closer to realising its objectives and its leaders were getting older. Moreover, the IRA's political wing, Sinn Féin, had registered significant success at elections. Had the time come to fully persuade them of the validity of the political process?

Hume–Adams, 1985–8

John Hume described the disaffection with politics in the North of Ireland during the Troubles thus:

> 'Will it never end?' is the jaded reaction to the latest atrocity. 'What is it all about?' is the rhetorical question to which people would prefer not to hear a reply. This has been the disastrous attitude which generated the political vacuum. Not alone is this attitude irresponsible and immoral: it is also dangerous to us all because it has encouraged the killers.[1]

The practical benefits that the Anglo-Irish Agreement brought to the people of Northern Ireland, particularly the Catholic minority, were important in helping them to see that politics could, in fact, work and that it required their support. Hume tried to sway the people as much as possible towards political engagement and away from any form of endorsement of violent acts, thereby isolating the IRA still further from the community (never more than a minority following at any given time). As Mark Durkan relates:

> John Hume was trying to communicate two things to people about the Anglo-Irish Agreement: firstly, it will bring a catharsis within Unionism, when Unionism realises that for the first time they are not able to use sectarian solidarity to mobilise their numbers to veto anything, which might make them disposed to a different negotiation in the future. Secondly, it also creates a challenge for those Irish nationalists who do not believe in physical force to challenge those who still do.

Simultaneously, Hume embarked on a high-risk tactic of speaking to the IRA to urge them to cease their violent campaign. As Kevin Cullen of the *Boston Globe* suggested: 'If a date can be ascribed to the birth of the peace process in Northern Ireland, it was Jan. 11, 1988, when Adams and Hume met at Father Reid's urging and shook hands.'[2] Cullen is correct that setting a date for the beginning of the process of bringing the Republican movement in from the cold is open to debate. That is partly because Hume's dialogue with Gerry Adams had a series of false starts. Seamus Mallon remembers:

> The Catholic Church and one, if not two, of the Protestant denominations' representatives, the British Government and the Irish Government and John Hume responded to the Sinn Féin request for meetings with us [the SDLP]. We had a meeting, I think I was at two. It became very obvious very quickly that both Adams and Hume were going to do solo runs in this. That's what happened.

The impetus to facilitate dialogue from political and religious leaders would not have had any impact unless a sea change had occurred within the Republican movement. Gerry Adams admits: 'We wasted years, you know … not through any foolishness on our part but I suppose through naïveté,' and he elaborates:

> By this time, Sinn Féin and the SDLP were political rivals, so in the course of a radio debate with him, I said, 'well, look, sure why don't we meet?' Just before John had met with me, he said something like, 'sure, there's no point in meeting Sinn Féin, the IRA runs the show. I'll meet the IRA. Why meet the monkey, when you can meet the organ grinder?' So the IRA said 'OK, we'll meet'.

Hume had agreed, in 1985, to meet Republican leaders and the encounter went as follows: He met Gerry Adams in Ballybofey in County Donegal. There he was blindfolded, bundled into a van and taken to Louisburgh, in County Mayo, to speak to the IRA. The IRA insisted that the conversation be videotaped. When Hume refused to grant permission to be videotaped the meeting was over. The IRA kept him another few days before releasing him. Gerry Adams relates:

Garret FitzGerald intervened and said if he came across any such meeting he would break it up, that anybody at the meeting from the IRA would be liable for arrest and so on. So the meeting proceeded. The IRA had said that they wanted to video part of the exchange because John would be out explaining his version of the meeting, but they would not have that ability. John disagreed with that, as far as I understand, and John told me that the engagement was friendly and so on.

After failed attempts to meet along with party colleagues, and after a meeting with the IRA that led nowhere, what became known as the Hume–Adams dialogue began in earnest. Gerry Adams explains:

I think what stood by us and the peace process was that we probably met privately without anybody knowing for about eighteen months. So we developed a sense of each other and he believed – and I believed – that we were both serious and sincere. I think his motivation was to stop the killing and he thinks – at least this is my view of it – that I was sincere in trying to develop some alternative to what was happening. I think that stood by us and that's what got us through all the difficulties.

Given that the Hume–Adams dialogue was a complete secret, it is almost impossible to recreate a clear view of the substance of their conversations. Hume was very tight-lipped about his contacts with Adams. Tellingly, however, he opened up to Ted Kennedy, who related:

Towards '88, that's when Hume told me he had been meeting secretly with the new head of Sinn Féin, Gerry Adams. He was making the argument that the violence wasn't working, and even if the British would get forced out, the Catholic community would be at the mercy of the Royal Ulster Constabulary and the 8,000 members of the [Ian] Paisley Unionist Party. So he proposed that the IRA 'give up the campaign of violence and agree to meet with all parties, hosted by the Irish Government, and if the settlement could be agreed upon, it would be put to a vote in both parts of Ireland, with Britain agreeing to abide by it.' John's proposal, in broad terms, would eventually happen a decade later.[3]

It appears that Kennedy's memory likely served him well. While few documents exist from the time, a letter Hume sent to Adams to establish the framework of their dialogue corroborates Kennedy's impression of Hume's proposals. Hume argued that since the Irish had a right to self-determination, and since they were divided about how to exercise that self-determination, then only agreement on how to exercise it could possibly resolve the conflict. To create the possibilities for agreement he therefore urged Adams to agree to participate in all-party peace talks, on the condition that the IRA ceased their violent campaign. As Kennedy noted above, that is what 'in broad terms, would eventually happen a decade later'. However, the IRA was not ready to lay down its arms. As Nancy Soderberg, then of the Ted Kennedy Office, stated: 'I asked Adams one time, had you had an American President like Clinton in the '80s, could we have done this earlier? And he said, "No, it would not have worked. They weren't ready".'[4]

Hume urged Adams to view the Anglo-Irish Agreement as a great opportunity for Irish Nationalists because, if agreement were reached on the exercise of self-determination, then the British government would respect that agreement:

> Does that challenge not also remove all justification for the use of violence, because does not the British declaration on endorsing and accepting agreement among the people of Ireland on Irish unity not make clear that Britain is now saying that she has no interest of her own in being there and that her only interest is to see agreement among the people who share the island of Ireland?[5]

Once the IRA could accede to this argument, they could no longer refuse to come to the conference table, which is why Hume pushed it very hard. He was, in future years, to provide still more evidence and pressure to show Britain's lack of selfish, strategic or economic interest in remaining in Northern Ireland. But the principle was already there in the Anglo-Irish Agreement. Developing this concept, Sean O'hUiginn argued:

> Hume devised the approach that the right of the Irish people's self-determination was unquestioned, but that they were divided about how to exercise it. Now that seems almost hair-splitting to the average

person, but when you reflect on the practical implications it was an enormously fruitful definition because it meant that the reality of partition reflected a difference in the Irish people about how their undoubted collective right to self-determination was to be exercised. Then the solution to the problem lay in persuasion of the people who did not want a unified approach by people who did.

Hume understood that the issue of self-determination was at the very nub of Sinn Féin's gripe with the way in which the country had been partitioned and how the legitimacy of an all-Ireland system of government and elections had been disregarded. From Hume's point of view, however, they were sawing off the branch they were sitting on by not driving that issue wholly into the political realm and forcing referenda on the matter, North and South, the first such election since 1918. Brendan O'Leary elaborates:

The deep animating grievance of Irish Republicans was that there had never been an act of self-determination on the island of Ireland, a comprehensive act applied to the island as a whole. So what Hume argued was that if the Irish people as a whole comprehensively endorsed the same settlement on the same day in a referendum, which asked fundamentally the same question in both jurisdictions, [then] that was the secret to creating a political settlement.

As the Hume–Adams dialogue continued in secret, where did Sinn Féin–IRA stand on the continuation of a violent campaign? As late as 1985, Martin McGuinness said in a BBC documentary: 'We don't believe that winning elections and any amount of votes will bring freedom in Ireland … At the end of the day, it will be the cutting edge of the IRA that will bring freedom.'[6] Just three years later, in 1988, Sinn Féin, while it was not prepared to renounce violence, acknowledged the role of dialogue too. *The Los Angeles Times* reported that 'Sinn Fein Vice President Martin McGuinness stressed that the IRA has gone on record as saying there will be no more ceasefires. "Talk (can) take place, but the war will go on", he said.'[7] Five years further along, in February 1993, the Army Council of the Provisional IRA sent a message through their back channels to then British Prime Minister, John Major: 'The conflict is over but we need your advice on how to bring it to a close … We cannot announce such a move as it will lead to confusion for the volunteers, because the press will misinterpret it as a surrender.'[8] Thus there was a long but steady declension towards Sinn Féin publicly stating that the armed struggle needed to be replaced entirely with the political process.

During the 1980s, however, the refusal to admit the futility of violence continued, and it was accompanied by a war of words which extended to systematic slurs on Hume's integrity. Hume was being harassed by the IRA, as Derry-based journalist Eamonn McCann witnessed:

> Even when the so called Hume–Adams talks were underway there were ferocious attacks made by Republicans on John, denouncing him as a traitor and as pro-Brit. There is something really objectionable about the way in which the man who was providing a respectable context for the Provos to work in, was simultaneously being denounced by them as a traitor.

America was to feature heavily in the cleansing of Sinn Féin's reputation as a purely political party. The man who became Sinn Féin go-between in New York, Niall O'Dowd, recounts that Adams saw that the campaign of violence was ultimately futile:

> The question I put to Adams was, 'Tell me, how are you're [sic] going to win this war? How many Brits are you going to kill?' ... I was quite surprised and glad to find out that Adams shared that perspective, not directly, but the idea that, 'Yes, of course this is running into the sand, I know that we have to find a different way.'[9]

Hume's reputation in Ireland – as noted previously in the *Irish Times* reference to him as the 'Uncrowned King of Northern Ireland' – had never been widely questioned and his critics, from predictable sources, had failed to significantly influence the mainstream. However, for one brief period, that did change: when a news story broke that Hume had been secretly meeting the man who was widely believed to be the leader of the IRA. As Eamonn McCann, who was the conduit of the story, remembers:

> I was approached on Shipquay Street in Derry by a person who lives very near to John and he said, 'You'll never guess what I've just seen'.

He said he wasn't sure, but he thought that he had seen Gerry Adams knocking on Hume's door and then going in. At the time I was doing freelance work for *The Sunday Tribune* and, on a regular basis, I would talk to Ed Maloney, particularly on Saturdays because that is when news for Sunday newspapers was generated, and I said to him that I had just talked to a fellow who says that he thinks he saw Gerry Adams going into John Hume's house. Ed Maloney phoned John and asked was this true and very interestingly John said, 'No it's not true,' and he put down the phone. About two minutes later John phoned back and said, 'Look I don't want to be telling you lies, yes it is true'. That is how the story came out.

This was thunderclap news. Mark Durkan explains:

The fact of talks became public again in early 1993, people just felt that John had lost his way, lost his judgement and was throwing away his reputation and was throwing away his long pedigree of non-violence and his claims to statesmanship. There was very strident and very negative criticism and a lot of friends shrank back from him in that time.

People shrank away from 'Jester Hume', who was now being portrayed as a partner 'under camouflage' of the IRA. For Conor Cruise O'Brien, the Hume–Adams talks revealed Hume as the IRA's accomplice and he welcomed, 'developments indicating that some significant sections, both north and south of the border, are tired of the IRA and its accomplices and are willing to say so publicly.'[10]. Yet Hume's actions were not at variance with his publicly stated position, as Mark Durkan explains: 'When the talks between Sinn Féin and the SDLP concluded in 1988, John Hume said at the time that the debate would continue in private and in public – nobody seemed to hear that.'

The vitriol Hume endured resulted in a minor health breakdown. He had reached a level of exhaustion with his campaign to bring peace to the North and the continual criticism affected him deeply. On 23 October 1993, Gerry Adams, his partner in dialogue, was a pallbearer for an IRA assassin who had killed eight civilians in the Shankill Road bombing. Being tainted through association, Hume was under huge pressure which culminated, finally, on 30 October 1993, in an emotional public breakdown while attending the funeral of eight people murdered by the UDA at Greysteel. The backdrop to this was, as Gerry Adams recalls, based on a particularly personalised attack on Hume from one source:

> It's very, very important to say this: he was vilified by The Independent News & Media group. He came from being, if you like, the darling of the Southern establishment, to just being demonised, for doing what? For talking? He subsequently, when the cessation [of hostilities] was in trouble years later, met the IRA with me, again in a very engaging and friendly manner – the guy was very down to earth.

Hume's line remained that if he could save one life by talking he would continue to do so. Congressman Bruce Morrison (who at this stage had broken with the Friends of Ireland and joined the Ad Hoc Committee in the US Congress) agrees with the need to do so, arguing: 'You cannot make peace if you do not talk to the warriors. And you do not have to approve of what they are doing and you certainly do not, by talking to them, approve of what they're doing.'

Within his own party, and in the opinion of the Irish public, Hume's approach (and even his integrity) was suddenly doubted. A strain of Unionism had long held that Hume was a respectable front for a sinister terrorist campaign. Sinn Féin had declared its intent to gain power with the ballot box in one hand and an Armalite rifle in the other. Therefore, secret talks – or at least private talks – with the leader of Sinn Féin seemed to many, including Hume supporters, that he was lending credibility to a murder campaign. In reality, Hume's absolute policy of non-violence was unchanged. What was actually starting to change was Sinn Féin's view of the ultimate efficacy of the Armalite approach; that brought a modification in turn in Hume's reflections on the sequence of events required to deliver peace. More absolutist positions – surrender all weapons upfront and then talks can ensue – are, as Congressman Bruce Morrison argues, politically impractical: 'My response to the ballot box in one hand and the Armalite in the other is let's find a way to lose the Armalite, but keep the ballot box and keep the faith of the people that the ballot box can be the answer.'

Whether it is defensible to enter dialogue with paramilitaries is moot if considered in general; in this specific case, Hume saw that decommissioning needed to be a result but not a precondition of dialogue. Is the critique that absolute clarity is necessary that violence is now off the table and politics is the only thing on the table a morally defensible one? 'I think it does not work,' says Bruce Morrison:

> It is a nice idea and if you can get it great, but show me an example where it has ever worked. Peace is made through a process, not an event. And the process starts with stopping the violence, but not saying that it could never happen again because if you say it could never happen again then you never get to the first step which is the ceasefire step. The ceasefire step comes first and after that comes the weaning process away from the gun and toward the politics. You have to build credibility with the groups of people, both the leaders and the people at the grassroots, that this politics is not a sham. We all know that violence is wrong, unfortunately sometimes it is effective. Politics is right but it is often ineffective.

Despite the chaos in the streets, the murders and bombings, the persistent attacks and vilification, Hume never wavered from the view that there needed to be a dialogue about a constitutional settlement. There also needed to be a means for the Dublin and London governments to consolidate things, and he never ceased trying to accomplish that. In Derry he had strong electoral support, but he also encountered a lot of opposition. When he took his seat in Westminster, his house was shot at and even fire-bombed. What did Martin McGuinness think of the fact that, despite what Hume was trying to do for the people of Derry, he was targeted by the IRA in such a manner? 'That was totally and absolutely wrong,' recalls McGuinness, 'and I think I said so at the time. I was totally opposed to those people who thought that that was something that would be productive. How could it be productive?'

Similarly unproductive attacks in the media on Hume's integrity happened in tandem with the targeting of his home and family. For instance, Sinn Féin's newspaper *An Phoblacht* had once described Hume (and his colleague, Paddy Devlin) as 'slavish and slobbering … discredited political hulks lying shipwrecked on the treacherous sands of the collaboration in the 1974 "power-sharing" Assembly'.[11] Levelling the charge of treachery against Hume for participating in the power-sharing

Sunningdale Executive in 1974 is ironic given Sinn Féin's full participation in a power-sharing assembly from 2007–17. McGuinness stopped short of condemning *An Phoblacht*, a newspaper reflective of the IRA's politics, for the vicious slanders on Hume:

> I may have disagreed politically with what the SDLP represented at that time but that was a democratic right I had to disagree. Where I absolutely drew the line was giving no support whatsoever to anybody who felt that they had a right to attack his home. If there were things said in the *An Phoblacht*, many things were said in many political organs of many newspapers.

Moreover, there were attacks on the SDLP office in Derry. While there is a logic to someone who has been targeted by the British Army feeling justified in retaliating against them, and exclusively against them, attacking non-combatants or peace campaigners was both contrary to the ideals of authentic, inclusive Republicanism and politically inept. It was absolutely repugnant to attack a centrist politician from Derry, trying to uphold democratic values and to generate jobs in the city. What prompted such persistent attacks? What was it about Hume that the IRA so despised and what drove their refusal to acknowledge him? Eamonn McCann argues:

> John contradicted their narrative (now they have adapted their narrative). The Provos recruited people to fight because they said that they would not stop an inch short of a United Ireland. That intransigence went down very well with angry young people. The Provos retained, and still retain, a notion of themselves as being the official authentic representatives of the Nationalist people of Ireland. When the Provos started a campaign, they didn't say 'we are launching a campaign'; they declared war. To this day, conventional parties approach the electorate seeking their support. Sinn Féin comes into areas like this [the Bogside in Derry] and claims your allegiance. It is a different approach altogether. It makes them very bitter when people say to them, 'no, you're just like any other party', or 'you have to debate with us just as any party would'. They do not like that at all. The Provos crave respect from the people they purport to represent. They do not always get it and they are not too happy about that.

A recurring theme of the IRA's critique of Hume was his putative treachery, which presents another fine irony. The ideals that the IRA held up to disaffected young men in impoverished housing estates in Northern Ireland were their ideals, not Hume's. That Hume pursued other objectives did not constitute any form of a betrayal. That Sinn Féin decided to considerably modify their goals and change their means may indeed expose them to the charge of betrayal among their supporters. Of the slogans emblazoned in Derry today, 'Hume Traitor' is completely absent whereas the 'Sinn Féin Touts' slogans endure. Hume's consistency stood in contrast to his interlocutors. As Sean O'hUiginn put it: 'The starting shift that happened at the time of Hume–Adams was not in contradiction to what Hume had been advocating before, it was rather that the last recalcitrant constituency had been recruited to it.'

While Hume was portrayed as a traitor, he was nevertheless seen by Sinn Féin as a credible usher to bring them in from the cold. That was possible only because Hume occupied a very particular position in the psychology of Irish voters. As Bertie Ahern, former Fianna Fáil politician and Taoiseach (1997–2008), explains:

John got a huge Nationalist vote. John got a huge Republican vote. Many people who were supporters of the armed struggle equally were supporting John Hume. I think John had that innate understanding that he was representing all of these people. Maybe he thought some of them were misguided, maybe he thought they were all misguided, but he still realised that someday and in some way, he had to pull all of this together.

Now that Gerry Adams had said, 'sure, why don't we meet', Hume took that invitation as a signal that Sinn Féin no longer believed that the armed struggle could succeed. The political weather vane had unmistakably changed direction. As Robert Fisk explains:

Long Kesh was [holding] a large number of men who were growing old, certainly dark into middle age. I think John realised that that pugnacity was wearing down, that it wasn't worth it anymore. I think that by bringing in the Irish-Americans and by constantly thinking ahead he was able to open the window and say 'look, there is a future beyond Long Kesh, beyond walls and barricades'. He could look forward as well as back. And that's what made him a statesman rather than a politician. Statesmen effectively are people who live outside their own countries as well as inside.

With Sinn Féin edging towards public peace talks, Hume's main agenda was to accelerate that process. His central strategy, to persuade people of all political stripes in Ireland to embrace constitutional politics, remained, as ever, bringing wider influence to bear – including in the US and Europe.

8

Washington and Europe, 1988–93

John Hume was elected and re-elected a European Member of Parliament for twenty-five consecutive years (1979–2004). During this time, he continually referred to an early epiphany during a visit to Strasbourg, located just on the Franco-German border, when he walked across a bridge from French Strasbourg into German Kehl. He surmised that these two European nations had slaughtered each other for centuries until finally, through building post-war European institutions, they had found a way to make common cause: to 'spill their sweat not their blood' as Hume put it. Through that partnership, crossing from France to Germany had become as simple as walking across a bridge. France and Germany had come to respect each other's culture, language and identity and agreed that they shared an overarching European identity which did not in the least impinge upon their regional or national identities. Indeed, it was not lost on Hume that the native language of the Strasbourgians is a cognate of German and not French: ancestrally, they have far more in common with their neighbours immediately across the Rhine in Germany than they had with Paris. Moreover, Strasbourg–Kehl operates as an economic area and bilingual schools are popular. In the shape of this successful bi-cultural environment, Hume found inspiration for the divided people of Northern Ireland.

Such economic cooperation between former adversaries had for Hume an almost transcendental significance: through a process of mutual gain they had become bound to each other, and the impulse to go to war became much less imaginable. Senator Paul Kirk noted earlier that in the 1970s in Washington: 'John Hume advocated that the difference between a mutually destructive cycle [which] could be replaced with a mutually constructive cycle.' With its connotation of being renewable, 'cycle' is the operative word. Thus the theory that drove European construction was an inspiration to Hume. In Padraig O'Malley's words, Hume had a 'masterful propensity to conceptualization'[1] and he conceptualised the European Community as a process through which the North of Ireland could reconfigure itself.

The international perspectives Hume gained during his service in the European Parliament proved an asset in his efforts to bring American influence to bear on the Irish Question. Mark Durkan suggests that:

> One of the reasons why the American politicians really engaged with John Hume was that he was not just able to talk to them about his own issue, the Northern Irish issue, he was also able to give them a read as a prominent international figure. John Hume had a very good sense as to what the European project was. He [told] them [that] 'this strange project in Europe is not that different from what you thought you were doing in the days of your Founding Fathers. Maybe there are different languages, maybe you are talking about territories that have historically been at war. But the fact is in essence it is not very different. We are trying to create a situation where people with their own identities and sense of wholeness are able to cooperate, and are able to do something bigger for each other. It can work and it can develop politically'. Thus Hume continually presented the Northern Irish problem to American politicians as potentially having a European solution.

Washington listened keenly to Hume's European perspective, and looked on Hume as a 'point man' to interpret Europe, particularly during the Cold War. At dinner conversations in Washington the subject would move from the North of Ireland to wider matters, and Hume would illustrate contemporary happenings in Europe. (Similarly, as a Westminster MP, he also communicated to Washington aspects of British policy: in the 1980s, people heard from him of Thatcherite policies, for example copycat Workfare ideas, which were then starting in the US. He had been elected to Westminster from 1983, and the misgivings he voiced about Thatcher's policies chimed with Americans who had similar reservations about Reagan's economic policies.) In Washington, Hume's addresses on Europe broadened his support base, particularly among US Senators. For example,

January 9, 1985

Dear Mr. Speaker:

Thank you for your letter of December 13
setting forth your concerns about the present
state of the Anglo-Irish dialogue on Northern
Ireland and asking that I discuss Northern
Ireland with Prime Minister Thatcher during her
December visit to Washington.

During my meeting with Mrs. Thatcher at Camp
David on December 22, I made a special effort
to bring your letter to her personal attention
and to convey your message of concern. I also
personally emphasized the need for progress in
resolving the complex situation in Northern
Ireland, and the desirability for flexibility
on the part of all the involved parties.

I fully share your view that the way forward in
Northern Ireland must be peaceful, and that it
must involve not only the two communities in
Northern Ireland, but also the governments of
Ireland and the United Kingdom. Please be
assured that my Administration will continue to
urge our Irish and British friends to follow a
path of reconciliation and accommodation
through democratic means.

While emphasizing the complexity of the situation, Mrs. Thatcher made a point of stressing
to me that press reports of her alleged

differences with Prime Minister FitzGerald were
exaggerated. She also noted that she would be
continuing her discussions with Prime Minister
FitzGerald early in the new year.

I greatly appreciate your personal interest in
this matter and look forward to your continuing
advice.

Sincerely,

Ronald Reagan

Adversaries in London, allies in Europe: John Hume and Ian Paisley. (Courtesy of the Hume Family Collection)

John Hume, Speaker Tom Foley and President Clinton, 1990s. (Courtesy of the Hume Family Collection)

John Hume and Governor Hugh Carey, 1990s. (Courtesy of the Hume Family Collection)

John Hume, Senator Chris Dodd shaking hands; Senator Pat Leahy looking on, 1990s. (Courtesy of the Hume Family Collection)

John Hume seated with President Clinton at the St Patrick's Day Speaker's luncheon in the Capitol. The host of the luncheon, Speaker Tom Foley, is to President Clinton's right beside Taoiseach Albert Reynolds. (Courtesy of the Hume Family Collection)

John Hume and President Clinton, 1990s. (Courtesy of the Hume Family Collection)

John Hume and President Clinton, 1990s. (Cou of the Hume Family Collection)

John Hume and President Clinton in the Oval Office, 1990s. (Courtesy of the Hume Family Collection)

President Clinton, Pat Hume and John Hume, 1990s. (Courtesy of the Hume Family Collection)

John Hume and President Clinton in front of the Guildhall in Derry, 1995. (Courtesy of the Hume Family Collection)

President Clinton and John Hume in front of the Guildhall in Derry in November 1995. Hilary Clinton and Pat Hume also present. (Courtesy of the Hume Family Collection)

John Hume and President Clinton in front of the Guildhall in Derry, 1995. (Courtesy of the Hume Family Collection)

Hume delivering his Nobel ure, 1998. (Courtesy of the ne Family Collection)

John Hume, Jacques Chirac and Romano Prodi, 1990s. (Courtesy of the Hume Family Collection)

John Hume and fellow Europeanist, Willy Brandt, 1980s. (Courtesy of the Hume Family Collection)

Nobelists John Hume and Nelson Mandela, 1990s. (Courtesy of the Hume Family Collection)

Senator Joe Biden, who became US Vice-President in 2008, came to know John Hume through his speeches on Europe during the 1980s. During the Cold War years, America had a particular political interest in European construction and wanted Ireland to be part of it. The geopolitical aspect of the Northern Irish Troubles and Hume's role in positioning it within the European debate, past and present, became the dominant aspects of speeches Hume made on the future of Ireland in Europe.

After the end of the Cold War, Hume's European dimension remained of interest to President Bill Clinton when he was elected. Clinton recounts that he viewed the Northern Irish conflict in the wider sphere of Europe:

> Keep in mind when I started working on this, the conflict in Northern Ireland and the conflict in the Balkans, then confined to Bosnia, later getting into Kosovo, were the two things that were preventing Europe from becoming united, free and at peace for the first time since nation states arose on the continent. So I thought it was a big deal for the emerging European Union idea and for the necessity to fight for a democratic model in the aftermath of the Cold War. So I thought the ramifications of success or failure would go far beyond the borders of Northern Ireland and the Irish Republic.

Just as Hume had educated prominent journalists and editors on the Irish Question in the United States (who in turn demanded high standards from politicians and public figures), so he did in Europe. Robert Fisk gives this snapshot of Hume wielding influence through third parties:

> The most provocative interviews with British army officers were almost always with French television and radio. I think there probably is a John Hume connection there because John could explain in good French what was going on. The French would come across [to Northern Ireland] and they would see Northern Ireland through John's eyes. John would be very outspoken, direct, and he didn't go waffling on too long. He knew there'd be a cut in the tape. He was a very intelligent media performer.

Hume always made clear that he considered the European Parliament to be an important forum for disparate European nations to interact. It was, as this vignette reveals, a place where important encounters could take place and declarations could be made. As Robert Fisk explains:

> Arafat was given – I think 1988 would have been the date – his first opportunity to address the European Parliament in Strasbourg. Lots of Israeli supporters, or so-called Israeli supporters, [were] outside with placards: 'Why are you inviting this terrorist to Strasbourg?' Arafat realised that he could not say 'the partition of Palestine'. He could not use these words. I sat at the back of the European Parliament looking very dejected, and suddenly John Hume walks up: 'Hello, Bob, how are you? What are you doing? Spoken to Arafat?' I said, 'no, nobody can get to him'. [Hume asked] 'You want to speak to Arafat?' I said, 'yes', and he said: 'Come with me'. So he grabs me by the arm and I chase down corridors full of these boring Eurocrats, down many corridors, and I see he goes into a little room and there's Arafat. And John comes up and walks up behind him and in a way which Arabs do a lot, he sort of leant over and he's facing this way, Arafat, and John spoke into his ear. And he came over to me and said: 'He'll see you for about six minutes'. I thought scoop! Every journalist wants this kind of exclusive. I sat down opposite Arafat and I said you're accepting the partition of Palestine. 'I am accepting two states', he said it. If I look through a list of twenty stories I remember really cracking something, that would be among them, and it was John Hume who did it. I grabbed him in the corridor and I said, 'John, John, thank you'.

Hume had always been interested in seeing Northern Ireland's dilemmas through the lens of the burgeoning European project. Even as a school teacher in his early twenties (his subjects were French and History) Hume advocated Ireland's entry into the nascent European Community. Hume's wife, Pat Hume, remembers:

> The first speech I heard John make was in 1959; it was a speech about why Ireland should join the common market, which was six countries at the time. One of the reasons why he supported Ireland's joining the common market was: here were people who had slaughtered each other during the war, and yet they had come together to work their common ground – roof over their head, food on the table.

Having been convinced of such a theory from his early twenties, it is unsurprising that as an elected representative he put it into practice with a will. Bertie Ahern observed that Ian Paisley and John Hume, political adversaries since the 1960s in the Parliament of Northern Ireland through to their heated Westminster exchanges in the 1980s, were nevertheless capable of working together for their constituencies in Europe:

> When it came to a Northern Ireland issue that was important to the people of Northern Ireland across the community divide, the first two guys to get together to go to an EU president or commissioner or delegation were John Hume and Ian Paisley. They could have their differences over the domestic political situation, but, particularly on the common agricultural policy and the fishing policy, I know of several times when they gathered together. They were two formidable guys to have marching into your office in a united front. I think probably the shock that the commissioners would get, that they were there together and that they were supporting a cause, would probably win 51% of the argument before they said anything.

Economic betterment was always a central priority for Hume. He wished at every turn to provide a reason for people to feel vested in Northern Ireland, a corollary of the political engagement which he also encouraged. A favoured technique to accomplish this was developing practical initiatives to generate jobs in Northern Ireland. From his very first days as a businessman through to his time as Minister for Commerce in the short-lived power-sharing Assembly established by the Sunningdale Agreement (1973–4), Hume put huge store in the role of employment as a means of uniting the disparate elements of Northern Ireland in a common purpose for their mutual benefit. He believed it necessary to fuse economic prosperity and political regeneration into his agenda for a New Ireland. President Bill Clinton adds that at the national level of US government, and particularly in Congress, the Irish bloc was heavily involved in adding economic aid to political support:

> They always hoped for a resolution of the disparate treatment of Catholics and Protestants in Northern Ireland, hoped for a resolution of the tensions between the North and the Republic, but they could

never figure out a path forward. John Hume's path could be easily embraced, or at least more easily embraced, by interested Irish-Americans whether they were Catholic or Protestant. Whether their sympathies lay with the idea of union with the Republic or maintain[ing] the United Kingdom ... they just wanted to somehow open up the prospect that the Irish should be free to make this decision for themselves first. And secondly that in the process of moving the politics they could either eliminate, or at least drastically reduce, the discrimination in economics, in education, in law enforcement right across the board.

Boston–Derry Ventures

Through his contacts in the US, Hume encouraged the establishment of an entity known as 'Boston–Derry Ventures' in October 1987. As the then Mayor of Boston, Ray Flynn, stated, Hume was:

> Replacing the gun in Northern Ireland politics with a job: that was his solution to dealing with peace and justice in Northern Ireland. He knew words alone wouldn't do it. He knew that he had to bring some industry, some jobs into Northern Ireland so people could work together. His was a novel voice, you would call it like a real liberal voice in America today. When we would be on this campaign to bring industry to Northern Ireland: different shopping centres, hotels, automobile plants, companies, John would show up, he'd take the trip across the Atlantic and he'd encourage that and he'd praise the businesses for coming in. It was almost like he was the Prime Minister of Ireland.

Instances are legion of Hume dropping everything (sometimes at a politically sensitive time) to travel to the US to encourage investment: how he gave the keys of his Donegal weekend home to a captain of industry and told him to come and see the beauty of Donegal and Derry for himself; how, on learning that a factory behind his home was to close, he immediately left for Detroit to speak to a potential investor and was back within forty-eight hours to continue with his political work. The structural support of the Boston–Derry ventures, and the clear incentive of the International

Fund for Ireland for would-be investors, helped to offset misgivings about investing in a conflict zone. Hume sought a platform for people who wanted to contribute to the International Fund for Ireland. Those people began to work with Ray Flynn during his mayoralty (1983–90) and they organised Derry–Boston trade shows. Derry was a hard sell at trade shows because of the ongoing conflict, but Bostonian investors kept an open-mind about investing in the North of Ireland and money sourced in Boston became important seed capital for new businesses, which was then supplemented by the International Fund for Ireland.

Boston–Derry Ventures became Boston–Ireland Ventures, as it wished to serve a cross-border base (Galway, Mayo, Sligo, Donegal and Derry) without being self-conscious about it. There was regular interaction between the counties and it was genuinely ecumenical in its make-up, involving Unionists as well. 'Ventures' also brought people from Galway and Derry to Boston and from 1988–91 they tried to market their furniture, crafts and products and show the best of the cities. Aside from the work of the US Consulate in Belfast and Invest Northern Ireland, also in Belfast, it was almost solely Hume who brought investors to the North of Ireland. That perhaps explains why the founding of a similar mission, 'The Friends of Belfast', rankled Hume, who felt that Derry merited the inward investment more. Hume also met key people in 'proper' Boston too, through Mayor Flynn and others. They became very supportive of Hume at a key time, since the Irish in Boston were taking substantial power in the city in terms of political positions and boardroom control of major companies. Working through Irish CEOs, Hume's circles were small but effective.

Hume's focus on people rather than territory always won in his proposals to potential investors. One investor recalls visiting Hume in Belfast: he would walk into an Orange pub with them and start telling stories. The regulars in the pub, in turn, had stories of their own of how they built the Titanic and the Victoria Hospital. Hume would mimic Paisley and chasten people for singing rebel songs ('don't be singing that') and five minutes later he would be singing 'Kevin Barry' himself. Investors admired Hume's ability to win a crowd: he got them to like him first by telling stories, and then broached more conceptual issues. He concentrated on the fact that everyone has got a family and economic needs: he had an instinct to unite people and it seemed to many that he would have rather lost an election than make a divisive or polarising comment. He always strived for common ground: treat your neighbours with respect; political ideology does not buy bread and milk.

The political boon associated with economic prosperity was clear to all of the advocates of inward investment. As Frank Costello, who worked with the Boston–Derry Ventures, relates: 'This was trying to get people out of poverty. If you give people hope and opportunity in being part of an economy, part of a society, things will get better. It will also change the politics – if people are involved – feeling they're participating. And that tied to democratic politics and economic justice.'

Costello also gives the political context to US investment in Northern Ireland: 'It became very apparent that in the 70s and 80s, when you had systematic discrimination directed at the Nationalist community … [that it] was forcing people out of the place. It was making people who were still living there not realise their full potential. And it took, from one standpoint, a MacBride Principles campaign.'

The MacBride Principles

Throughout his political life, Hume instinctively advocated the broadening of economic areas of cooperation as a remedy for political dilemmas. He argued that this approach was particularly apt in a place such as the North of Ireland, where the narrowness of the state's make-up was a contributory factor in breeding problems of further splintering and protectionism. Since the 1960s, measures such as the establishment of a 'new city' in the east part of the state, while cutting off infrastructure and denying Derry the right to a university, led to the emergence of the Civil Rights Movement and Hume's own political activism.

Hume's qualifications as a civil rights advocate were unquestionable, and he extended that advocacy as an elected representative through sponsorship of the economic rights of the people of Northern Ireland. He further channelled that advocacy as an elected representative in Europe, obtaining financial support to succour his underinvested constituency, and as a respected political figure in the United States, through his encouragement of investment in Northern Ireland. Yet Hume opposed an affirmative action programme of fair employment principles, known as the MacBride Principles, adopted by American companies investing in Northern Ireland to even out the bias in employment allocation. To some commentators such opposition was tantamount to opposing a civil rights principle, and therefore it was in contradiction to the civil rights agenda he had always advanced. Quite the contrary, however, since Hume threaded a consistent path in seeking economic investment from Europe and America while at the same time implacably opposing the MacBride Principles.

The MacBride Principles resembled the Sullivan Principles, formulated by Rev. Leon Sullivan in 1977 to counteract the injustices of apartheid in South Africa. The Sullivan Principles encouraged corporations to push for an end to apartheid and the establishment of transparent elections in South Africa through disinvesting in the country. As noted earlier, Hume had been, from his first involvement in politics in the 1960s, a passionate advocate of shoring up the most discriminated region of Northern Ireland: 'Indian territory' as he called the western parts of the Northern Ireland such as Derry. Therefore his implacable stance against the MacBride Principles puzzled some and angered more.

Hume believed the Principles were neither enforceable nor were they desirable. There were clear problems in enforcing them. For instance, in the case of Principle Number 2, which demanded that employers provide 'Adequate security for the protection of minority employees both at the work place and while travelling to and from work.'[2] While, on the face of it, such a proposal is very reasonable, making such guarantees was impossible in the North of Ireland. But why would a civil rights leader dispute that the Principles were desirable? Given that Hume was a thoroughgoing advocate of civil rights, why then did he give such short shrift to the Principles?

Hume associated the Principles far more with disinvestment than with investment (for holding the investor to account in a foreign country). Hume was convinced that the best way to heal the wounds of the past for the people was through positive-sum initiatives and that the Principles were unavoidably a zero-sum game. Arousing a sense of dispossession in the minds of Protestant workers, even if it came with the boon of instilling a sense of possession in Catholic workers, did not fulfil Hume's ambitions for a divided people working together. Furthermore, any programme that further identified the people of the North of Ireland according to their sectarian lineage was anathema to Hume. Thirdly, the proponents of the Principles awoke a deep suspicion in Hume about the Principles themselves.

The MacBride Principles were launched in November 1984 by Seán McManus and the Irish National Caucus, and Hume had gone to considerable lengths in the first part of the 1980s to ensure that the Irish government did not back the INC line on Northern Ireland. The Friends of Ireland were similarly in complete opposition to cooperation with the INC. At the very least Hume doubted the motivations of those advocating the Principles. For example, one time Hume was speaking in front of seventy-five people at Kennedy's restaurant in New York when an elected representative from the Bronx spoke up about the Principles, saying: 'Would you mind if I ask John Hume publicly if, after ten years, you think the MacBrides did any good?' Hume's riposte was blunt: 'I'll tell you what the MacBride Principles are. They are not about jobs in the North of Ireland. They are about votes in the Bronx.'

Congressmen who supported the Sullivan Principles also tended to sign off on the MacBride Principles. Nancy Soderberg remembers that it was Hume who convinced Ted Kennedy not to back the MacBride Principles. Kennedy had supported the Sullivan Principles and it was widely expected that he would take the same view of the MacBride Principles, but Hume was adamant that the two circumstances were not analogous. He argued that the problem in Derry, and elsewhere in the North, was how to bring the existing workforce into compliance with the Principles – in the case of a company that wanted to invest but did not want to be anyone's political football, he felt that the Principles would be a deterrent. His argument, as Nancy Soderberg recounts was, 'the MacBride Principles would have contracted the economy and not given anybody a decent job, that's what John Hume's point was … the MacBride Principles were seen at the time as a deterrent to investment and people would not invest under those conditions. And actually I think that was probably right'. There were back alley spats between Boston and New York investors: some were MacBride Principle people and Hume held that the Principles were counterproductive. Hume also criticised newspaper editors who were in their favour.

Always working in tandem on economics and politics, Hume was working to build a sense of social inclusion, and a sense of commercial ownership, which the IRA had damaged so badly with their 'economic targets', for example the sectarian bombing of Unionist-owned businesses in Derry.

Hume understood that it is easy to exploit social deprivation when there is no hope, whereas the IRA had argued about discrimination in jobs and then blew up places of employment. (Yet it must be acknowledged that during the IDB trial into investment in Carrickfergus and Coleraine there was almost no access for Catholics, whereas in the 1980s UVF members could leave jail and walk straight into a shipyard job.) What finally helped to ease the situation was when Hume went to a local man nicknamed Paddy 'Bogside' Doherty, a dynamo of civic involvement in Derry, to tell the IRA to stop bombing the so-called 'economic targets' – power plants, bridges and railway lines – that were relentlessly blown up throughout the Troubles.

In brief, Hume's stance on the MacBride Principles was 'we need jobs, not principles'. Ultimately, the Boston Executive passed the fiat of the MacBride Principles, minus two of the principles regarding workers' rights, which were held to be unenforceable from overseas. It was extremely difficult for many of his supporters when Hume opposed the MacBride Principles *in toto*: he simply could not countenance the threat of disinvestment. The Irish government also opposed the MacBride Principles, for many of the same reasons as John Hume. Many of their most outspoken advocates did not endear the Principles to the Irish government either. They may well have been admirable in a well-ordered society, but they transferred to Northern Ireland with great difficulty. As Brendan O'Leary argues:

John Hume reacted to the MacBride Principles in a very hostile way. He had early on adopted the view that what Northern Ireland required was an increase in foreign direct investment, economic growth as a way of solving all local conflicts, and he feared that the MacBride Principles, if applied, would lead to the flight of foreign capital from Northern Ireland. It is one of the few major strategic errors that John Hume made in the course of his political career. Not only because he was in effect opposing the logical consequences of a civil rights principle, but because in effect by opposing it, he left this political space open for Sinn Féin to capture. He failed to institutionalise his advantages. He failed to build the party internationally. He was an internationalist but he wasn't good at building the party internationally. I think historians will conclude he was too individualist for the good of his own party.

Whether it is attributable to his opposition to the MacBride Principles, or to Hume's individualism, it certainly was the case that Sinn Féin would ultimately capture Hume's political space, both in the North of Ireland and even more comprehensively in the United States. Before that happened, however, it fell on Hume and others to address the lingering issues in Northern Ireland and to finally broker peace. He was immeasurably assisted in this by the election of the US president most committed to resolution of the Irish Question: William Jefferson Clinton.

The Political Process and the Peace Process, 1993–8

Three issues predisposed Bill Clinton, the Democratic candidate for US President, to commit to seeking peace in Northern Ireland. First, during his election campaign, Clinton had been approached by a combination of Irish-American business leaders, particularly in New York, coordinated by the newspaper publisher, Niall O'Dowd. In essence, they assured him that they could deliver the Irish vote in the 1992 presidential election in return for his full engagement on the Irish Question, which would include the sending of a peace envoy and issuing a visa to Gerry Adams. That would involve staring down his State Department. Tom Foley, who became Speaker of the House of Representatives in 1989 (Tip O'Neill had retired as Speaker in 1987 and Jim Wright had served as Speaker in the interim), remembered that prior to the election he was among a gathering invited to Arkansas to discuss the Ireland Question in the forthcoming election. Tom Foley, who became Speaker of the House of Representatives in 1989, was among a gathering invited to Arkansas to discuss the Ireland Question; when he arrived it was clear to Speaker Foley that Clinton, if elected, would fully engage in the Irish Question to bring peace. It was clear to Speaker Foley when he arrived in Arkansas that President Clinton would, under the right circumstance, authorise a visa for Gerry Adams and send a Special Envoy to Northern Ireland. Clinton had accepted the deal and it helped him to be elected President of the United States. Secondly, Clinton's British counterpart, John Major, and his administration in Britain had been publicly supportive of George Bush Senior's re-election, which for a time caused Clinton to see Anglo-Irish relations through a greener lens than might otherwise have been the case. Thirdly, as noted earlier, the great geopolitical shifts brought about by the end of the Cold War prompted American leaders to view the pacification of Northern Ireland as an essential cog in the wheel of European construction.

The fulfilment of electoral promises, a slight tilt towards a special relationship with Ireland, and a vision of an ancient conflict neutralised through reconciliation made for a potent temptation to exert considerable diplomatic skill and ingenuity. Once inaugurated, in January 1993, Clinton undertook from the very start of his presidency to build on decades of work by the US Congress and the White House to finally broker peace in Northern Ireland, and Clinton identified Hume as the touchstone for his involvement. Clinton remembers that aligning himself to Hume's view of the conflict was a natural choice from any perspective:

> I naturally gravitated to John because he was widely trusted across the board in our Congress and I needed some support in Congress to do this. [Hume] tended to legitimise the notion that America should do more because there was a huge bloc in America, including a fair number of Irish-Americans, who didn't want us to do this. Didn't want us to put our relationship with the UK at risk. The so-called 'special relationship' had been used to basically freeze us out, even though America had the largest diaspora and the largest Northern Irish diaspora in the world by a large margin.
>
> And because there was John, with his sane voice always coming here at St Patrick's Day for the Speaker's lunch and always being present on the side of peace, it helped. It made it immeasurably easier for me to justify what I was doing.

Jack Roney, a prominent Washington businessman, recalls meeting John Hume at a function in Washington shortly after Clinton had been inaugurated in 1993. In the course of the conversation, Hume told Roney that he had just spoken to Clinton and he had been greatly impressed by the President's depth of knowledge of Northern Ireland – for example, he had read all of Hume's speeches. Clinton was beginning to acquire a reputation for being his own 'driver' on Ireland, and committed himself personally to the details of the Irish Question. Thus he started, and in that vein he continued: Clinton's detailed and dedicated involvement on the Irish issue over both of his terms (1993–2001) was without parallel in history for a US President.

The sheer breadth of Clinton's engagement is worth recounting. On his first St Patrick's Day in office, 17 March 1993, he nominated Senator Ted Kennedy's sister, Jean Kennedy Smith, as Ambassador to Ireland, and she was to prove an able and dexterous promoter of the peace agenda. The visiting Irish Taoiseach, Albert Reynolds, expressed his enthusiasm at travelling across Washington to Congress to be hosted by 'another great Irishman', Speaker Tom Foley. On that occasion, Clinton commended the dialogue between the British and Irish governments which provided 'the real chance' of producing a framework within which peace could occur'.[1] That dialogue resulted in the December 1993 Reynolds–Major Joint Declaration and Clinton undertook to 'continue to stay on top of the situation'.

A few months later, during a visit by the President of Ireland, Mary Robinson, he was asked about a visa for Gerry Adams. He indicated that the State Department had 'unanimously recommended that the visa not be granted. I have no grounds to overrule them'.[2] Yet, with the British government at that stage in direct talks with Gerry Adams, he was soon to identify grounds to overrule them. Clinton deemed it to be the correct time to move on the issue of a visa for Adams to enter the United States, which he awarded in January 1994. There was above all a need to involve the pro-IRA supporters in the peace process. (On St Patrick's Day, 17 March 1995, Clinton made clear that a decision on the visa issue the previous January was helped by Adams's 'prompt statement about the willingness of Sinn Féin to discuss arms decommissioning [which] had an influence on my decision'.[3])

The Adams Visa

In January 1994, Gerry Adams entered the United States on a temporary visa. The decision to grant him this permission, given the widely held suspicions about his IRA connections, was highly controversial, causing a furore in the US, Britain and beyond. The decision exposed the shifting sands of the political dynamic between Britain and America, and the shifting perception of the IRA both in Ireland and the United States. Speaking about the period leading up to the first IRA ceasefire, Nancy Soderberg, formerly of Ted Kennedy's office, who was by now Deputy Assistant to the President for National Security Affairs, recalls that she detected that change was afoot:

> I could tell something was going on in the fall of 1993 because I was hearing from the Irish National Caucus people, where I had a pretty open-door policy. Bruce Morrison, Richie Neal, Peter King certainly, all were telling us something was happening and I kept hearing it over and over and over again. Then I would pulse the US government, the British government, the FBI, the CIA ... our Justice Department, all of whom uniformly came back and said 'no, there is no difference ... there's no division in the IRA, there's no one who's seriously pushing for a ceasefire, including Adams. Don't believe them'. But because I was listening to the grassroots, the NGOs, the women, the caucus, the people who spent all this time on the ground there, it was clear to me something was going on. But the person I kept asking was John Hume, who in the spring and summer of 1993 said, 'not ready yet, don't get involved, don't give Adams a visa yet'. By the fall, the two had 'married' and Hume saw that Adams needed the support of coming here to the United States to talk to the IRA supporters [and] get support for the ceasefire. He could not deliver the ceasefire without the support of the US. Then the joint declaration came, which essentially took away the political reason for the violence of the IRA because now they had a democratic way to get an independent Ireland.

The Downing Street Declaration, on 15 December 1993, provided a cogent argument for the IRA to cease their violent campaign. Hume and Adams had already made several joint statements (and they were to make several more). However, the fact that the heads of state of Britain and Ireland both supported the principle of constitutional change based on consent reduced the IRA's sense of its own *raison d'être* very considerably and strengthened the hand of those within Sinn Féin and the IRA seeking a new beginning. Hume was determined to exclusively channel this new openness to change through the political process, and one of the ways in which he chose to do this was to back calls for a visa for Gerry Adams to enter the United States. In so controversial a proposal, Hume had to act as full guarantor. Ted Kennedy recounted:

An awful lot of the information I was getting was coming from my sister Jean, who talked to John a good deal and represented what he had said to her. When I returned in very early January we got the sad news that Tip O'Neill had died [on 5 January 1994]. I knew that John Hume would be coming [to the funeral] and I'd have an opportunity to talk with him at some length, which I did. After the funeral, John and I spent about three hours at Locke-Ober's in Boston talking about this issue.[4]

Kennedy asked detailed questions about the rationale for the visa, and when he stood up from that dinner with Hume it was clear that he was about to make a series of calls to build initiative for granting the visa. However, not everyone acknowledges that the initiative to issue a visa to Adams came from Hume. In Niall O'Dowd's opinion: 'I think it came down to Tip [Thomas P.] O'Neill's funeral, where Kennedy asked Hume the question, and Jean had worked on Hume and a lot of other people like Sean O'Huiginn [sic] had worked on him, and Hume said okay.'[5] The reality was just the opposite. Hume was the persuader rather than the persuaded as Ted Kennedy himself related:

> The issue had come to a head due to the invitation that had been issued to Adams by Bill Flynn and Niall O'Dowd's organization to address a meeting in New York at the end of the month. John [Hume] told us there was a split in the IRA of whether to accept the joint declaration and that a visa for Adams would help carry the internal debate. He made a very powerful case about the importance of moving the peace process forward, and said this was a great opportunity to do that. I found that he was as convincing as Reynolds had been.[6]

Hume's determination became Ted Kennedy's and Kennedy began by asking three prominent Irish-American senators to form a coterie to petition President Clinton. George Mitchell relates how Ted Kennedy got him involved in Irish issues:

> One of the areas in which I got to know Ted some was with respect to Irish issues ... there was a dispute over a visa for Gerry Adams. I recall Ted and Pat Moynihan and Chris Dodd speaking to me about

joining on a letter, to try to get the President to grant a visa, which was very controversial at the time. The U.S. Ambassador in London was adamantly opposed to it … It was granted and it helped move the process forward, and so I gradually began to become acquainted with [the Irish issue] … [I] spent two days in Ireland, the only time I had ever spent there before now, just to become acquainted with it, and I began to develop an interest in it.[7]

Like President Carter in 1977, Bill Clinton was confronted with the choice of upsetting his State Department and his British friends, or of opting to take a risk on something that could move peace closer. The group of senators' efforts occurred in tandem with Hume personally assuring President Clinton that this was a unique moment and it needed to be grasped. Bill Clinton relates:

I knew when I became president, because of what happened in December of '92, that I would have a political opportunity if I were willing to assume the risks. And it wasn't just the risk of alienating the British, there was also the risk that I would stick my neck out, for example in the visa for Gerry Adams, and IRA violence would continue. Innocent civilians would continue to die and I would look like I'd been played for a fool. And that, over the long run, had a bigger downside. But I trusted Hume's instincts, and he among others encouraged the visa. He said, 'you know, I can only take this so far. Someone with credibility, with the harder-line Republicans has got to be there'.

The British had always assumed that they had a special relationship with the US, and yet suddenly it seemed that John Hume was taking the lead and perhaps had an even more special relationship. Bill Clinton recalls:

Well, of the group of people in Congress, and among people who were interested in Northern Ireland, who were most opposed to what I was doing, there were basically two arguments raised. The one was there's no way America could get in here without doing irreparable harm to the relationship with Britain, and if we did that we couldn't do any good in Northern Ireland anyway. The other argument was: this thing can't be resolved with the intransigence of the IRA, so that if you get involved in a way that weakens the UK's hand it will look like you're giving aid and comfort to terrorism, no matter how much you hug John Hume. That was basically the argument – that it was a no-win deal, I shouldn't do it – the US State Department took that decision. The then ambassador … from the United States to the UK, Admiral Crowe, took that view and he was a man I very much admired. He'd been chairman of the Joint Chiefs of Staff, he endorsed me when I ran for president at some hazard to himself and to my great benefit. There were a lot of people I deeply respected who felt that way but I believed, particularly after the declaration at Downing Street … that we could get there and that it was highly unlikely that the British and Irish Governments alone could get there without our support.

Moreover, pressure came from the House of Representatives. Congressman Richie Neal, later Chairman of the Friends of Ireland, relates that he and a group of Congressmen met Clinton's National Security Advisor, Tony Lake, to argue that the visa must be granted:

It was one of the most incendiary meetings that I have participated in during my twenty-eight years in Congress, and there was a lot of recrimination in that room and harsh words were expressed at the President's National Security Advisor. Remember that the National Security Advisor is actually in the White House, unlike the Secretary of State who is at the State Department. So the National Security Advisor in many ways has the President's ear. And the meeting was so bad that Tony Lake, in a moment of exasperation, looked at us and said, 'I want to tell you something,' he said, 'after this meeting, I promise you, I will elevate this issue to the same position of the Middle East at the White House'.

And he did.

Granting the Visa

Nancy Soderberg relates the moment when the White House decided to issue Gerry Adams with a visa:

Jean Kennedy was instrumental, the Irish Government was instrumental, but had John Hume not recommended it, we would not have done it. When we actually decided to do it, it was a Sunday morning and Warren Christopher spent about a half an hour on the phone with the President about how cooperation with the British would end, and it was the wrong thing to do, and terrorism, and the first World Trade Tower attack had just happened. And then he hung up, and Tony Lake and I were in his office in the White House. The President was on the phone and we didn't believe the British would stop cooperating with us. The entire US Government was opposed to it, I'll never forget the feeling of Janet Reno literally yelling at me on the phone; Louis Freeh, the head of the FBI, was opposed to it.

The issue leaked quite quickly and we hadn't had time to tell the British, and I have never seen angrier British in my life. That was probably the most dramatic thing. John Major did not take our call for a week.

Bill Clinton also remembers the moment vividly:

There was some broken china there, you know. I had a lot of trouble with the British for a brief period when I got involved, but I think the fact that John [Hume] was there saying there is a way out of this, there is a peaceful way out of this, there is an inclusive way out of this. There's a way for a role for the UK to continue and a role for the Irish Republic and a shared power situation in Northern Ireland. It made it a whole lot easier.

During a 29 November 1995 press conference in the company of Bill Clinton, British prime minister, John Major, was pressed on whether he agreed with this view, having been asked: 'Do you think ... the President has been too accommodating to Mr. Adams, or do you think it's now – his efforts have been worthwhile?' Major replied: 'I don't think it's a question of being accommodating at all. American support in this process has always been immensely helpful, and the President has always taken a very great interest in that process.'[8] If you can't beat them, join them.

The impact of Adams's trip to the US was immediate and far-reaching. With his arrival, the focus on Hume transferred considerably to Adams.

Loretta Brennan Glucksman recalls a reception for Adams at The Waldorf Astoria in New York, during which Hume was ignored: 'We were in a big room at the Waldorf and I looked around and there was this feeding frenzy among the media trying to get to Gerry Adams and John's in the back corner standing by himself.' Within a few months, on 13 March 1994, the IRA issued a statement: 'the IRA wish to publicly note that our positive and flexible attitude to the peace process is an abiding and enduring one'.[9] Two days later, Hume told *The Boston Globe* that he would use his direct access to President Clinton to induce the British to pay attention to this development:

> Given that the British government would talk to [the IRA] secretly when peace wasn't on the table, I am asking, why not talk to them publicly when peace is, in fact, on the table ... If the British government believes the IRA is bluffing, they should call their bluff ... The people who are dismissing this statement do not have a historical appreciation. They do not appreciate the tone of the words.[10]

Brokering the Ceasefire

Hume flew the kite further, that he would make his views known to the US Congress, to White House officials, and to the President himself later that week in Washington during the St Patrick's Day celebrations. When Hume got to Washington a few days later for St Patrick's Day on 17 March 1994, he drove his point home to Clinton, who put great store in Hume's judgements and political instincts. Hume saw a chance to reinforce a shift in attitude within the IRA toward ceasing their violent campaign, which culminated in a series of fundamental breakthroughs later that year, when the IRA and the Combined Loyalist Military Command issued ceasefire statements, on 31 August 1994 and 13 October 1994, respectively.

Albert Reynolds in particular, in the role of Taoiseach, was also important in consolidating the IRA ceasefire. Iconic footage of Adams, Hume and Reynolds in front of the Department of the Taoiseach was intended to symbolise a new cooperation both across different strands of nationalism and across the border. But, as Eamonn McCann argued at the time, it was necessary to include Hume in that photo, from a Republican point of view, since Sinn Féin was particularly sensitive to being seen to recognise the Taoiseach at the expense of their own claims to legitimacy: 'the occasion might too easily have been seen as the Republican leadership formally relinquishing something which the Movement had always regarded as a core belief. The inclusion of Hume made the picture presentable as three nationalist leaders conferring together, rather than one conceding legitimacy of leadership to another'.[11]

These ceasefires also prompted Clinton to make good on his promise to send a special envoy to Northern Ireland. On 1 December 1994, Clinton announced the appointment of George Mitchell as Special Adviser for Economic Initiatives in Ireland. While critics of Hume denounced his conferral of 'legitimacy' on Adams, he was also sharply aware of how important it was to properly handle that claim to legitimacy on the part of Sinn Féin; in a meeting with *Boston Globe* journalists and editors, Hume referred to the need for a referendum as the best way to address it:

> John Hume, Northern Ireland's leading moderate nationalist politician, renewed yesterday his call for a referendum of all Irish people on an end to violence and a commitment to multiparty peace talks ... 'An unambiguous statement by the Irish people could have some sway over IRA extremists ... given one of the IRA's theological foundations, that the last time the Irish people spoke was in 1918,' Hume said in a meeting yesterday with Globe reporters and editors.[12]

Hume, speaking on the *Charlie Rose* show on 21 March 1996, said:

> The fact that [Adams] came to the United States was a very crucial and important step in the peace process and was one of the major factors that led to the cessation of violence ... and as a result of that cessation of violence, up to 400 people in Northern Ireland now [are] walking around alive who would otherwise have been dead ... [Given that] 20,000 soldiers in my streets and 12,000 armed policemen and the toughest security laws in Western Europe hadn't stopped the killing throughout the 25 years, I felt that if I could save a single human life by direct dialogue, it is my duty to do so.[13]

What had prompted Hume to move from characterising the IRA's approach in the early 1980s of a continued armed campaign in tandem with an openness to the political process as being 'just blackmail. All they want then is power',[14] through to ushering their way into politics? Sinn Féin members had gained mandates; the Anglo-Irish Agreement, the Hume–Adams dialogue had culminated in the joint Hume–Adams Statements, and the Downing Street Declaration. All were building towards a moment when the IRA could no longer refute the validity of the political process and abandon their military campaign. However, that discussion on arms decommissioning turned out to be an interminably long one, staggering on into the next millennium. The issue of decommissioning hung as the Sword of Damocles over both the peace talks' participants and those acting as guarantors that those negotiators with a history of violence would exclusively embrace constitutional means.

While the decommissioning debacle continued, Bill Clinton made the decision to become the first sitting US president in history to visit Northern Ireland. (Clinton first visited London and in his public statements championed the need for courage and taking risks in good faith. Poignantly he referred to the former Prime Minister of Israel, Yitzhak Rabin, who had been assassinated for taking such risks.) During his historic trip to Derry, on 30 November 1995 Clinton put down a marker for Hume's work dating from the 1960s:

> Hillary and I are proud to be here in the home of Ireland's most tireless champion for civil rights and its most eloquent voice of non-violence, John Hume. I know that at least twice already I have had the honor of hosting John and Pat in Washington. And the last time I saw him I said, 'You can't come back to Washington one more time until you let me come to Derry'. And here I am.[15]

After the euphoric scenes in Derry, a winter of discontent was marked and marred by the IRA breaking their ceasefire. The Irish, British and American governments sustained their efforts to secure peace. On the following St Patrick's Day, in 1996 in the White House, Taoiseach John Bruton affirmed, in both language and strategy deriving from Hume's formulations, that the goal remained 'a comprehensive agreement, not an internal settlement within Northern Ireland, a comprehensive settlement dealing with the relations between Britain and Ireland, dealing with relations between Northern Ireland and the rest of Ireland. What we're aiming at in that three-stranded approach is a system of government for the people of Northern Ireland to which both communities can give equal allegiance'.[16] Bruton maintained that the issue of decommissioning should not be allowed to derail the peace process, which to some observers meant that it had been deprioritised. Decommissioning was therefore becoming hugely symbolic of anxieties on both sides: the IRA feared to be seen as surrendering, while those on the opposite side of the conference table feared conceding anything to the political wing of a still armed terrorist organisation.

While Clinton's commitment to a tiny pocket of the earth was dramatic, his engagement was not always welcomed. There were elements of Clinton's involvement with Northern Ireland that Ulster Unionists found unpalatable, particularly at the outset. In an adept act of diplomacy on Bill Clinton's part, he invited all strands of Northern Irish political life to the White House and encouraged them to think of it as a space where Northern Ireland's cultural pluralism could co-exist. David Trimble recalls dressing in tartan and singing Ulster Unionists songs in the White House, which helped to create a new view of Bill Clinton among Unionists:

> The Unionist community viewed Clinton with a great reserve, which Clinton was aware of, and in his very first visit here, in the speech that he delivered early in the morning in which he told Republicans 'you're the past, not the future', and addressed them in very unequivocal terms. That actually changed the Unionist outlook on him, and is the reason why that evening at the City Hall in Belfast he had a huge crowd.

Decommissioning remained a very complex issue and had deep implications for the sovereignty of both Britain and Ireland. The sovereign governments of Britain and Ireland were fully committed to peace negotiations, now chaired by Senator George Mitchell, but they were led by political parties. In the revolving doors of political leadership, the representatives of the two governments were anxious to stamp their seal on history by negotiating the deal. This urgency unwittingly lent Sinn Féin a time advantage, and strengthened their hand when they procrastinated on decommissioning. Seamus Mallon remembers:

> The reality is that the two sovereign governments, Irish and British, had a responsibility for forty years to protect the people of this island from

those who held illegal arms for subversive reasons. They did not get those arms. Why, with all the intelligence that exists nowadays, were those arms dumps not dealt with? Way before the arms becoming an issue in a political process, they were a governmental problem. Only the two governments had the authority to deal with them [illegal arms], but here you had a situation where the governments were actually using the developing political process to solve problems which were not a remit of the new Assembly or the new political process, almost where the governments actually use the creation of a political system to solve the problems for which they are responsible.

Mallon's argument is that the peace process elevated former terrorists to the status of legitimate mainstream politicians. He suggests that the process made Sinn Féin almost as a legitimate governmental entity in its own right, rather than as a subsidiary agent within a negotiating process in which two sovereign governments granted them an opportunity to leave behind their violent and illegal past actions and fully participate in politics. Mallon implies that in the course of the peace process, the two sovereign governments should have seized the IRA arms to demonstrate their own primacy and sovereign authority. From 1997 to 2001, Canadian diplomat John de Chastelain was Chair of the Independent International Commission on Decommissioning (IIDC) and in 2000, two high profile international figures, Martti Ahtisaari, former president of Finland (1994– 2000), and Cyril Ramaphosa, South African businessman and politician, inspected IRA arms dumps and reported to the IIDC. This ritual of decommissioning, overseen by international observers, gave a degree of legitimacy to Sinn Féin–IRA, allowing them progressively to rewrite the narrative of the Troubles, which still continues apace. One source concedes that there was an element of bilateralism in official dealings with Sinn Féin and the IRA, who had arguably been the decisive and primary motor of instability in Northern Ireland over thirty years. They thus became *primus inter pares* among the groups with whom Senator Mitchell had the responsibility to consult. On a number of occasions, the two governments directly negotiated with Sinn Féin. However, the IRA, impatient with the British government and indignant that the decommissioning of weapons was a precondition for their entry into talks, resumed their violent campaign on 9 February 1996.

Speaking at a news conference on 29 May 1997, Clinton's impatience with the violent campaign was beginning to form into an ultimatum to the IRA: 'Obviously, I think that Sinn Féin should participate in the talks. And I think the IRA should meet what I think has to be the precondition. You can't say, "We'll talk and shoot; we'll talk when we're happy and shoot when we're not".'[17] The thinly veiled threat to Sinn Féin was clear; their charmed position as the political wing of an organisation carrying out bomb attacks was becoming less and less tenable, and the parameters within which it could operate were contracting. Clinton's pressure worked. Six weeks later, the IRA met the condition Clinton had made, and on 19 July 1997, Clinton welcomed the second IRA ceasefire 'on behalf of the American people'. Now the conditions precedent had been fulfilled, it was time for the most gruelling part of the journey to begin: the all-party talks in Northern Ireland, chaired by George Mitchell, overseen by the Irish and British governments, and supported at every turn by the US President.

Negotiations towards the Good Friday Agreement

In 1868, British Prime Minister William Gladstone said: 'My mission is to pacify Ireland', yet Ireland was to become known as the graveyard of many a British political career. In becoming engaged on the Irish Question, Prime Minister Tony Blair had studied the careers of British liberal prime ministers from Gladstone to Lloyd George and Harold Wilson. What was his impression of the prospect of trying to negotiate a peace settlement?

> This historical struggle was a leftover from a bygone age that should be capable of resolution. The Republic of Ireland had become a confident nation. We were in the European Union. They were in the European Union. This was a struggle in the North that neither side in the end could win by force – not the British, not Irish Republican – so surely in the interests of the people there should be a rational way through it.

In recognising that the history had changed and so therefore must the political response, Blair was completely aligned with John Hume, who said:

> The Plantation of Ulster was England's reaction to the [Irish] links with Spain. The Act of Union was England's reaction to the links with

France. Ireland was the back door for England's European enemies. That is all gone in the new Europe of today. So the basis of the problem, in traditional Nationalist terms – in my opinion – has changed, but the legacy remains.[18]

John Hume had the respect of President Clinton and of the most influential US Senator, Ted Kennedy, who at crucial times during the negotiations looked to him for an indication of the direction the talks were taking. Was the fact that Hume could bring the power and influence of the White House and the US Senate to bear decisive from Tony Blair's point of view?

> The thing about John is he was really persuasive with Ted Kennedy, with President Clinton and with others who were major players in this on the American side. [He was], I think, the only person who could literally go into every single point and position within the spectrum of British and Irish politics and get a hearing as someone credible. Bill Clinton was prepared to use the presidency in a very – in the right sense of the word – calculating way to bring about the maximum benefit to the process. That was just very rare that you get into that situation with the President of the United States of America. When you do, it's of enormous assistance because you can deploy that asset, if you like, at strategically important moments.

During the talks, it was important to acknowledge the asymmetry between Dublin and London; London was inevitably the stronger power and American involvement counteracted any tendency to abuse that power. Hume saw to it that if the British government forgot that point, the Americans would exact a penalty (Tip O'Neill's intervention after Thatcher's recalcitrance remained a cautionary tale). Therefore, one of the consequences of the American dimension in the peace process was to equalise the balance of power and thus fortify the foundations of the Agreement. Some Unionists also suspected that Clinton (who enjoyed a very warm relationship with Tony Blair) was exercising influence vicariously through Blair. Unionists had had a more comfortable relationship with Blair's predecessor, John Major, who instinctively protected their interests. Predictably, since Major gravitated towards the traditional Unionist position and welcomed their support at Westminster, Hume was considerably at odds with him. On one occasion, as David McKittrick relates, Hume 'grabbed Major's lapels and said, "Look Gladstone didn't do this, Parnell didn't do this, you're the man who could do this. Lloyd George didn't bring peace to Ireland, Gladstone didn't bring peace to Ireland, but you have a chance, if you act on this now, to actually do that".'

Senator Mitchell, in chairing the talks, started with the complexity of the Northern Ireland problem and resolved to work through it based on Hume's analysis. As Mitchell put it:

> How do you compose a government that shares power, that reflects the realities of political and economic life in Northern Ireland in which all could participate? But John had the vision to understand that it could not be viewed solely in that context, that it had to be viewed in the larger context. So a second strand was the relationship between Northern Ireland and the Republic of Ireland for very obvious reasons. The Nationalists are a minority in Northern Ireland, but of course in the entire island of Ireland it is the Unionists who are a minority and that difficulty kept cropping up. And so you couldn't really solve the issue of Northern Ireland without establishing a new and firmer basis for the relationship between Northern Ireland and the Republic of Ireland. That was a second strand or portion of the discussion. Going further, you couldn't take out of the discussion the reality that Northern Ireland is part of the United Kingdom, in union with England, Scotland and Wales, and so they had to be included in the discussion to get a full context [of] the relationship between Ireland and the United Kingdom. That was the third strand. So once that was understood and accepted by all, there was at least a possibility of moving forward, of devising a way to get an agreement that embraced all three strands. And that was the political genius of John Hume, because it was that architecture, that construct, that made possible getting an agreement.

John Hume's Legacy: The Good Friday Agreement

The Good Friday Agreement was the crowning achievement of John Hume's political life. It encapsulated the central tenets of his approach to addressing the Northern Irish conflict. The three sets of relations were fully part of the negotiations, as was the American dimension to ensure that those relationships remained reasonably balanced. It provided structures for economic dividends, to encourage the divided people to work together, and it enshrined the principle of consent to constitutional change, which Hume had advocated since 1964. The Agreement formally marked an end to the Northern Irish Troubles.

It was a crucial breakthrough, as was the common commitment to the 'Mitchell Principles' of dedication to non-violent methods, all of which was fortified by the oversight of the newly elected British Prime Minister, Tony Blair, and newly elected Taoiseach, Bertie Ahern. Both new leaders worked well together and were intensely committed to the search for peace in Northern Ireland. On Good Friday 1998, the peace agreement was signed by all parties. As Clinton rightly said at the time, the parties had 'fought too hard over the details to violate them. I expect the parties to honor the agreement. And then it's really up to the people. The people of Northern Ireland and the people of the Republic of Ireland are going to have a vote on it in May, in late May, and their judgment will prevail'.[19] Clinton stated that he was happy that the US had been in a position to help to secure the peace 'because of our historic ties to Great Britain and because of the enormous number of Irish-Americans we have'.

The Good Friday Agreement is a compromise in the most technical sense of the word, the notion of a promise to abide by an arbiter's decision. It showed that peace could be secured by the silver bullet of negotiation rather than the leaden bullet. As Congressman Richie Neal recalls:

At the British Embassy where we had been invited to say goodbye to Tony Blair, I was asked to speak, followed up by the Prime Minister, and I thanked him profusely in front of the audience. I said that he had taken great risks and that we felt that his willingness to engage us and his willingness to engage on the Irish Question was very important to advancing the cause of peace and reconciliation in the North. When [Blair] spoke, he said: 'There are many things in our common history that America and Great Britain have agreed upon. There was one thing we didn't agree upon: Ireland and the North of Ireland'. After all these years of incendiary comment back and forth and bickering and arguing here from Congress, where British Ambassadors were regularly summonsed to the Capitol Hill, he said, 'I want to thank you for helping to get us through this morass'.

Joint referenda on the Good Friday Agreement were essential to Hume, who saw the potency of Sinn Féin taking their mandate from 1918, when Sinn Féin displaced Redmond and set up the second Dáil. Hume therefore insisted on an All-Ireland referendum to seal the peace in the North, emphasising the need for simultaneous referenda, and his terminology went into the Agreement. The bones of Good Friday are very similar to Sunningdale: structures built on a partnership basis and the right of the Irish people to self-determination, and this is in both Agreements. Hume was anxious not to take sides; he was reasonable in his focus on parity and not partition. It was a decent settlement for the Catholic minority, which made him respected and entirely trusted in the European Union and the United States.

Five minutes before the vote for First Minister, Hume told Mallon he would not be standing: his health was in decline. For his part, Mallon, having been involved in all the fundamentals of the negotiation, was to prove a most able inaugural Deputy First Minister. A revealing, if minor, encounter in Paris demonstrated to Mallon the enduring commitment of the Clinton Administration to peace in the North. Deputy First Minister Seamus Mallon and First Minister David Trimble went to visit President Jacques Chirac in the Elysée Palace, to ask him to support the peace process. Towards the end of the conversation, Chirac switched from French to English, and Hugh Logue from the SDLP remembers that he said: 'You know, you have a friend in President Clinton. We have regular discussions on issues: world issues, Middle East, Russia, many things. But he never permits a conversation, a discussion, to close without raising Ireland with me, and the peace process in Ireland.'

Sean O'hUiginn once said that Hume had 'enabled the Nationalists to work honourably ... in Northern Ireland'.[20] He saw that a society in rejection of its framework is disastrous, so he set about creating a mutually acceptable framework. Hume was an apostle of the doctrine that it was impossible to force one million Protestants into a United Ireland by the bomb and the bullet. He had spent much of the 1970s and 80s in an effort to create a structure to minimise support for violence, so Hume's first objective was to create parity of esteem and to shift from violence to politics; to maximise support for a centrist approach. From that broad base came a cooperative impulse to tackle extreme prejudice. It is in that context that bringing Sinn Féin in from the cold was entirely consistent with Hume's political strategy. He argued that sectarianism in the North will die once tolerable structures are in place, which was the final phase of his life's work: his work to relax attitudes. Hume's huge legacy is the validity of the principles to which he committed himself throughout his political life and which underpin the Good Friday Agreement. There is a need to build on that; a need for the ideas, the logic, the tolerance and the creativity of a John Hume for a new generation.

In October 1998, John Hume was awarded the Nobel Prize for Peace (he shared the award with David Trimble). Reacting to the news that his former schoolmate had won the Nobel Prize, Seamus Heaney wrote in *The Irish Times*: 'When I knew John Hume at St. Columb's College, Derry, in the 1950s … you had the impression of somebody … reliable and consistent, who operated from a principled and definite mental centre.'[21] He continued to operate in that vein, for the rest of his life. As Heaney wrote in 'From the Canton of Expectation', a line often considered to refer to Hume:

> To know there is one among us who never swerved
> from all his instincts told him was right action,
> who stood his ground …

Hume's constant and indefatigable stand was always for democracy. Throughout all his efforts, he never swerved from the principles he outlined in 1964: 'Community activity, in which all sections play their part, can do nothing but create mutual respect and above all, build the country with our own hands.'[22] He matched that constancy with his achievements in wider political spheres and with the extraordinary ingenuity of inventing a role for America to support his objectives – not transitory political gains – but his objectives to unite people not territory in a new and Agreed Ireland. As Bill Clinton put it:

> He knew very well that he might be creating political circumstances in which his party could never be the majority party, in which the public could never reward him politically, because once there was a united government people would be tempted to vote for the people they

thought would most fiercely advocate their position. He did it anyway. He did it because the worst form of imperfect democracy is better than continued hatred and killing. That's his legacy.

Epilogue

Echoes Down the Years

When John Hume retired from politics in 2004 the power-sharing Assembly in Northern Ireland, one of the provisions of the Good Friday Agreement, was suspended. It was to be suspended frequently thereafter. Yet the political parties active in Northern Ireland had embraced political means to solve political problems. The principle of consent had replaced violent insurgency. As a result, there is a generation in Northern Ireland which is not exposed to the horrors of war and destruction. More than by anyone, peace in Ireland was established by John Hume.

The twentieth anniversary of the Good Friday Agreement and the fiftieth anniversary of the Civil Rights Movement in 2018 should serve to remind people of the struggle to achieve peace in Northern Ireland, and how the principles that secured a stable and peaceful society in the North are a necessary bolster to constructive politics today. That journey is not fully comprehensible without examining John Hume's political life and yet there is a tendency in the current political climate to shed not light but shade on his work. Hume continually highlighted the necessity of the principle of consent, the three sets of relationships (the communities within Northern Ireland, between North and South Ireland, between Ireland and Britain), an Agreed Ireland, and unity only by consent; many of these concepts, phrases and words became absorbed both by Republican and Unionist politicians in the power-sharing government established after the Good Friday Agreement, a principal way in which Hume's work endured when he ceased to have an active part in politics.

Hume's political outlook is reducible to his touchstone phrases that still resonate: equality of treatment for all sections of the people; agreement threatens nobody; it is people who have rights, not territory; we must have institutions that respect diversity; we'll spill our sweat, not our blood. His points of departure were always rooted in forming a new language to confront division in Ireland.

Language

Hume once said that, 'political leadership is … about changing the language of others'.[1] It was Hume's abiding belief that modifying the language of others would establish peace in Northern Ireland. When, for example, Hume was due to make his presentation at the 1975 Constitutional Convention in Belfast, Ulster Unionists boycotted the session. Even so, Hume addressed empty benches and stated, 'One day we will understand the words that we use.' The words that Hume used throughout the Northern Irish conflict – 'agreement threatens nobody', 'it is people who have rights, not territory' – formed the basis of his political approach to resolving the crisis. Hume retained an unshakeable belief that fully embracing the concept of agreement could be advanced through forging a new and simple idiom, which would act as a conceptual midwife to political realities. Such an approach is open to misuse. As George Orwell argued, if a person is induced into saying something over and over again, 'he may be almost unconscious of what he is saying, as one is when one utters the responses in church. And this reduced state of consciousness, if not indispensable, is at any rate favourable to political conformity'.[2] Yet, in the case of Hume's strategy, the conformity in question was to the premise of non-violent methods as the essential basis for politics to happen.

How important was Hume's language and what role did it play in driving political leaders to rethink their positions? Democratic Unionist Party MP Jeffrey Donaldson relates:

> John had what we called the single transferable speech. You would hear phrases like: 'My father once told me you can't eat a flag son", "an eye for an eye leaves everyone blind.' When you look at the narrative today, when you look at the political institutions, when you read the agreements, you can see a lot of the language that John Hume used in those years, the 1980s, the early 1990s when he was constructing, or involved in constructing, what became known as the peace process. A lot of that language survived and continues in the narrative today

in the new political dispensation ...We worked very hard in many of the negotiations, often hours and hours of endless discussion over one sentence, one paragraph, getting the language right, getting it in the right order, getting the nuances right. Some people criticise some of what became known as the constructive ambiguity in some of the language used, but you needed to have a language that both sides could attach themselves to, that both sides could identify with. That is important in a divided society because, in the end, you have two sides who want something that is mutually exclusive.

Hume's inculcation of a new language was not limited to politics. The divided culture of Northern Ireland, which caused so much of the political antagonism, needed, he argued, to be viewed in a new way. For Hume, the creation of a shared cultural State was the essence of political regeneration. These words, a perfect example of 'Humespeak', spoken by Jeffrey Donaldson in 2016, could have been spoken by John Hume decades earlier:

We should celebrate the fact that we live in a diverse society, but in mutual respect for our diversity, we can build that shared future that we want for Northern Ireland. I do not expect Nationalists to become Unionists. We are not going to get true reconciliation by whitewashing each other's culture or diluting it. What we are going to do is to open it up so that we experience it together, and we share in a way that promotes mutual respect and understanding.

When Brian Friel was rehearsing his play, *Translations*, in Derry's Guildhall in 1980 he stated to his co-producer (and dedicatee of the play), Stephen Rea, that the problem in the North of Ireland is about language. Friel believed that the different formulations to which the divided community adhered resulted in different attitudes to institutions of the State: security forces, depending on a person's background, may mean a source of security or the opposite. The need to reformulate the language used in the North was Friel's central concern as well, to find language that could encompass both identities or many identities. Sean O'hUiginn relates:

John Hume, like Brian Friel, had a belief that a lot of the problems up there were related to language. When one talks about identity, one talks about tribe, family, security, these things can mean one thing to you and something radically different to your neighbours across the valley. Hume knew the importance of words and these coinages that ultimately were a new definition of the situation. Everything that is agreed politically has to be reducible to language in some shape or form (it cannot be so nebulous that nobody can say what it is). So, on that definition, everything does come back to language. But Hume's contribution went beyond merely accepting the importance of that, it involved an active role in defining concepts, redefining concepts, in a way that made them capable of accommodating more elements than the traditional formulations: the three sets of relationships, the Irish dimension and so on were essentially either defined by Hume in those terms or related to a definition that Hume had put forward.

Slowly, Irish Republicans also started to adopt Hume's language. As journalist David McKittrick remembers: 'At a very early stage Sinn Féin started to use the word "peace" and "peace process" and I remember very well in those early days hearing Adams and McGuinness talking about peace here and it sounded so awful in their mouths. Yet the continued use of that actually established something in politics here.' In adopting it, they exhibited the zeal of converts, as Eamonn McCann relates: 'Martin [McGuinness] made a speech to the Sinn Féin Ard Fheis annual conference [in 2016] and three times referred to an "Agreed Ireland". That is John's phrase. Sinn Féin leaders are now echoing him. John wrote the Sinn Féin speeches 25 years ago. They haven't thought of a new one since.' Consider, for example, a policy document launched by Sinn Féin on 28 November 2016. The document states that 'social partners, civic stakeholders and popular opinion must concentrate on working together ... to build a New Ireland ... a new and unified Ireland will be pluralist, inclusive and accommodating to all our people in all their diversity ... The Orange tradition is an Irish tradition and the British identity of many people in the North must be accommodated in an agreed, united Ireland.'[3]

In a 1972 pamphlet, *Towards a New Ireland – Proposals by the Social Democratic and Labour Party*, a document that Hume had a considerable hand in formulating, almost identical language appears: 'the people of Ireland of all traditions, can come together on a basis of harmony and justice, ending for all time the unjust domination of any one Irish tradition by another'.[4] What exactly did Humespeak, and Sinn Féin's adoption of it, establish? Hume maintained that if he goes for a fish supper in Derry and people are echoing Humespeak back to him, then he has done his job. Eamonn McCann:

> Absolutely. John is a great man for saying the same thing over and over again. He is never embarrassed by it. 'What we want is agreement, agreement threatens nobody.' He kept saying it, over and over and over again. Such a banal little phrase, but it worked. It got into people's heads. Without being a fanatic, he was always very sure of what he was saying. People followed John because they knew that he was saying what he believed.

Revisionism

Predictably, the consistency of Hume and the inconsistency of some of his contemporaries has made Hume's portrayal in the history of the Troubles contentious. Hume's role is subject to a contest to shore up contemporary political support; the historical narrative is hewed to that purpose at the expense of a truthful account based on the historical evidence. Consequently, some commentators who do not know the evidence unconsciously disregard Hume's work. Others know the evidence and disregard it anyway.

How, for instance, are Hume's fundamental breakthroughs in Washington portrayed in Ireland today? By any standards, 1976 and 1977 were fundamentally important years in the development of a role for the United States in Irish politics. In such a short period, huge progress had been made in both the US Congress and in the White House – the formation of the Four Horsemen and the first statement by a US President promising economic aid and political support for peace in Northern Ireland. Yet, writing in *The Irish Times* on 20 January 1996, author of *The Greening of the White House*, Conor O'Clery, recounts in detail the way in which Fr Seán McManus co-opted Carter to wear an 'England Out of Ireland' button in the St Patrick's Day parade in New York on 17 March 1976, but O'Clery makes no mention of the unprecedented step that Carter made the following year as US president, on 30 August 1977, in issuing a statement of support for peace in Northern Ireland. In the same article, O'Clery also bemoans the 'disgraceful failure by Dublin to build up friends and contacts either in Washington or in Irish America'[5] during this period, despite the role of Irish diplomats in working with Hume to build the Four Horsemen and to secure the Carter statement.

The 1980s, when Speaker Tip O'Neill and the formidable Friends of Ireland caucus in the US Congress ensured that President Reagan supported the Anglo-Irish Agreement and forced Thatcher to sign it, has been characterised by journalist Bette Browne in *The Irish Examiner* on17 March 2015 as follows: 'The door of the White House was ajar for the Irish in previous decades. But it was essentially limited to sentimental leprechaun-loving events on St Patrick's Day, as typified under Ronald Reagan's presidency. That was until the Clintons came along and the Irish decided it was time to be taken seriously.'[6]

Yet the work accomplished during this period – fully acknowledged by Bill Clinton – was an achievement of extraordinary proportions, as even a side glance at the history of Anglo-American relations reveals. As Michael Lillis argues:

By 1870 Britain's position as the world's only real superpower was beginning to be overtaken by the US, a disparity of power that continued apace. Rather than resort to war, which nearly happened in 1895 over Venezuela's borders with British Guinea, Britain deliberately took the position of subservience to the world's most dynamic State and it has never wavered from that stance. The US provided victory for Britain in two World Wars. In return, Britain has been a reliable military ally to the US in most major conflicts ever since, most recently in Iraq, and a stalwart political supporter for the US in every multilateral forum. The US scrupulously avoided "interference" in internal British issues, notably in Anglo-Irish questions, despite agitation by Irish-American leaders in US cities and in Congress and despite repeated efforts of Irish nationalists in visits to America: Parnell, Pearse, de Valera among many others from 1880 to 1975. Hume realised that only US persuasion and influence, in the form of vigorous initiatives by the White House and the State Department (rather than State, City or even Congressional resolutions), would move the British Government from its unwillingness to confront the Unionist hegemony and political paralysis in Northern Ireland. The challenge was how to get beyond the settled unwillingness of US power to persuade the British to take a positive and active role for peace. The culmination was the critical role that President Clinton played with the British and the Unionists in creating the Good Friday Agreement of 1998. Successive British Governments resisted these efforts with varying degrees of diplomatic outrage, but Hume's vision prevailed.

Those interventions by the White House were the lynchpin of the peace negotiations in Northern Ireland. It is against this backdrop that Hume's achievement is fully revealed.

The tendency on the part of some to reduce the decade-long struggle to forge a new role for America in Irish affairs does not merely downplay Hume's historic breakthrough in forming an alliance with senior politicians in the US, it also denies that American participation in Northern Irish politics was an evolutionary process. By contrast, Senator Chris Dodd, a founding member of the Friends of Ireland caucus, sees in the protracted struggle for democracy in Poland something of Hume's struggle for peace in Northern Ireland. The Polish labour union movement, Solidarity, started with a workers' strike at the Gdańsk Shipyard. Within a year its membership had grown to 10 million and within a decade Poland had freed itself from the Soviet yoke. Senator Dodd relates:

> I was always motivated by Lech Wałęsa at the Gdańsk Shipyard where all alone one day he climbed over that wall and said we're going to do things differently. They beat the hell out of him and instead of just going home and never showing up again, he went back the next day. I think three or four people showed up and they beat them up. Then he showed up again at that wall and this time with twenty, twenty-five and they beat them all up. Then, in a matter of days, it was 500 to a thousand, and then ten thousand, but without him it never would have happened. In a sense, while Lech Wałęsa and John Hume are very different people, John Hume stood at that wall and offered a different idea. And then it is Ted Kennedy and it is President Clinton and it is George Mitchell. You get that critical mass that ultimately moves a government to change its mind.

Two motivations account for the *conscious* revision of the history of Hume's work in the 1970s and 1980s in America. Sinn Féin refuses to acknowledge this history and its importance because it would demonstrate that Hume's achievements were not theirs. Furthermore, this history asks the question, what did they actually accomplish during that period? Apart from the travesty of the most significant Irish political leader of modern times, such revisionism also poses risks to political stability on the island of Ireland today. As President Obama stated in a speech made at the St Patrick's Day Speaker's Lunch in March 2016: 'There are those here who fought long and hard to create peace in Northern Ireland and understand what happens when we start going into these dark places, the damage that can be done and how long it can take to unwind.'[7] Hume's political life, epitomising that long and hard struggle for peace, stands as a caution for Northern Ireland never to revert to violent schism to achieve political goals. Revising Hume's historical record is symptomatic of a turn away from a constructive cycle of politics.

Consider the following comments by Gerry Adams. Speaking about Unionists at a Sinn Féin meeting at Enniskillen, on 24 November 2014, Adams stated:

> The point is to actually break these bastards – that's the point. And what's going to break them is equality. That's what's going to break them: equality. Who could be afraid of equality? Who could be afraid of treating somebody the way you want to be treated. That's what we need to keep the focus on; that's the Trojan horse of the entire republican strategy.[8]

When Adams's comments caused fury, he tweeted, 'I shudn't [sic] call bigots, racists or homophobes bastards. Mea culpa', which suggested that the characterisation was restricted to Unionists who reject such legislation as extending full marriage rights to homosexuals. The emphasis on 'breaking' Unionists, given that Northern Ireland operates a political arrangement predicated on power-sharing, was highly questionable. What is most striking, however, about the comment is Adams's interest in equality merely as a tool to advance another agenda – a Trojan Horse is jettisoned the moment it has served its purposes in penetrating the ramparts of an enemy's political structure, whereas equality is a premise for any decent political structure, and particularly in a place which has had a history of failing to be egalitarian, a principle that Hume stood for since the early 1960s.

As Eamonn McCann argues:

> What has happened is that the Republicans, the Provos, very cleverly adapted to every change. There is an entirely false version of history being promulgated by the Provisional IRA in their political manifestation. The Republicans are promoting the idea that all they were ever fighting for was equality and that they were forced to bring out the gun in order to fight for equality. Not true. They were not fighting for equality. They were fighting to eject the British from Northern Ireland and to bring about a United Ireland. The Provisional IRA campaign failed miserably. There wasn't huge support for a war for a United Ireland, never had been among Catholics in the North. The Provo war was fought under a false flag. I think Hume knew that. People like Adams adapted to where their followers had been all along, and realised that what had fuelled support for the IRA was not a passionate dedication and an insistence on a United Ireland; it was resentment against the State. It was the day-to-day things and the fact that bigots were running Northern Ireland, and that the British jackboot was on the necks of the people.

McCann sees the attempt to devalue Hume's work happening in Derry today:

> John was enormously important in Derry. The reason why his importance is not fully recognised has to do with the fact that there are a considerable amount of people with a lot of influence who really do not want John's contribution acknowledged. The Bogside has become a tourist attraction. You get parties being led around by guides. I listened in to one of these guys giving school children from Southern Ireland an account of the history of the Bogside in which John Hume did not figure until the Hume-Adams talks. That is the level of the distortion of history which supporters of the IRA are involved in now because they have to – they can't tell the truth.

Hume's perspective was that the Troubles was entirely preventable; that there was a power-sharing arrangement, established by the Sunningdale Agreement in 1973, and its saboteurs wasted an invaluable opportunity. Is

Seamus Mallon's famous pronouncement that the Good Friday Agreement was 'Sunningdale for slow learners' accurate? Eamonn McCann:

> I would agree with quite a lot of what John Hume and Seamus Mallon have got to say about the Provo campaign. I do believe that it was a waste of time, most of all a waste of life and a waste of energy. I think it postponed any progressive development in the North. I think that John and Seamus Mallon are entitled to look back on the Sunningdale Agreement and say, 'why did 3,000 people die after this, to give us the Good Friday Agreement?'

The historical evolution towards a return to power-sharing gives the lie to the view that the political process shot up like a blade of grass in the 1990s. A credible new political process that could accommodate the divided people of Northern Ireland was happening from the 1960s; and it is a tragedy that it was sabotaged by a combination of British misrule and IRA and Loyalist terror. Hume said it well, after the fall of the Sunningdale Executive in 1974: 'Those who have attempted to bring down this Executive, and who in fact have succeeded, will in the long-term, in my view, be the losers. The only way to solve the problems of Northern Ireland is not through conflict of the different sections of our people, but through partnership. It would now appear that the representatives of a majority of people in Northern Ireland have rejected that concept. I think that is a tragedy. For the first time in the history of this country, a long and bitter history, at least for five months, Catholic and Protestant sat down to administer. And we would hope that the day will not be too long distant when they can do so again.'[9] The passage of time – the full twenty years that passed before the IRA and Loyalist Ceasefires – lend extraordinary poignancy to those words.

What does Seamus Mallon say to those people who bombed and killed, who rejected the power-sharing Executive established in 1973 and yet who now have taken power, recognising Dáil Éireann in Dublin, and the Northern Ireland Assembly? Mallon:

> You have sold out your principles for a mess of potage and a glass of wine. You have embarrassed a lot of your supporters. Mark my words, that is where a change will come, in their support base. I spoke to a man once in a pub whose son was in jail for 18 years for an IRA

offence. He said, "My son was sitting for 18 years in jail because of the induction by Adams and McGuinness and the lies they are now telling". They have obliterated the whole concept of violent Republicanism in the island of Ireland. They have destroyed it in a very fundamental way, because it was seen to be, at the end of the day, a war fought for their personal advantage.

Rather than elide the decades of careful construction that are the hallmark Hume's political life, there is a compelling rationale to visit his 1964 articles, his earliest analyses voiced in the media and his 1960s Stormont speeches. For a younger generation to do so would be for them to take a much fuller possession of recent Irish history. Hume's careful argumentation in the 1960s and thereafter is a vitally important illustration of the cause and nature of the Northern division and the policies required to confront it. A study of Hume's life provides an effective method of enabling a still unstable Northern Ireland to reach a clearer sense of its political identity. To diminish Hume, to sum up his work in the 1970s and 1980s as a political leader missing opportunities, is tantamount to diminishing the importance of that educational process. From the Civil Rights Movement (1968) to the Sunningdale Agreement (1973) to the Anglo-Irish Agreement (1985) to the ceasefires (1994) to the Good Friday Agreement (1998): recent Northern Ireland history was a process of education of all sides, a reduction of fear and tension and a process of bringing forward a power-sharing government.

From Political Figure to Historical Figure

Will Hume ultimately be acknowledged by history? Eamonn McCann:

> I think John will be –in any history of Ireland, not just of Derry – a major figure. The fact that I disagreed with John's perspective does not mean that I dismiss or attempt to marginalise the influence he has had. I may even regret the extent to which John had influence on politics in Northern Ireland, indeed I do, but the fact that he had that influence and he had that success in exerting his influence in the direction in which he wanted to go, is going to be acknowledged by history. There are some who will hold out and not acknowledge it, but history will acknowledge the importance of John Hume.

McCann elaborates further:

> I think John was far-seeing in the sense that he understood that the problem in the North would have to be resolved without changing the constitutional arrangements in any dramatic way. John would not have been disappointed to drop the calls for British withdrawal and a United Ireland because he had never made that demand in the first place. He did not think it was realistic. John's vision was absolutely central to the Northern Nationalist tradition: we want equality, we are not going to fight for a United Ireland because that is going to involve us in a civil war in the North. That is the way they saw it, and John articulated that. John used to say 'the things that they are looking for are not worth a drop of blood'. So, in the end, it has proven. What do we have now in this little patch of the world that would justify the cruelty, the misery, the pain, the grief and the bereavement that has attended the Troubles?

Hume's insistence on Irish people being the ultimate arbiters of self-determination and on the primacy of the rights of people is partly why the emergence of Hume as a political leader in the 1960s was a pivotal development in the history of Ireland. As David Trimble acknowledged:

> One really very important thing that John was saying, from a fairly early stage onwards, was that the problem about Ireland was not that the land is divided but that the people are divided and consequently what one had to do is to focus on the divisions between and among the people. That was hugely significant from our point of view. Beforehand, particularly de Valera's constitution [1937] declared that the whole island of Ireland was part of the Irish State; the Irish constitution is trying to be determinist through its form, Republicans were trying to be determinist by forcing people at the point of a gun. John is in a different position: that people would determine the outcome.

As a voice of 'the Northern Catholic' who helped to considerably reconfigure the identity of the 'the Northern Catholic' he became indispensable to Dublin and later to London too (though there his was often an unwelcome voice). He represented his constituency in Europe for twenty-five years.

Above all, he (almost single-handedly) redefined the relationship between Ireland and America to include a steady stream of political support for peace, justice and reconciliation in Ireland at the highest levels of political Washington. His work in Dublin, London, Brussels and Washington continually related back to the divided people of Northern Ireland.

The way in which Hume created a role for Washington – initially both houses of the US Congress, and then the White House – was crucial to advancing his objectives. However, it was equally important that Hume could channel his strategy through the sovereign government of Ireland to negotiate with the British, strengthened by the oversight of the United States. He used the vehicle of the Anglo-Irish Agreement to achieve this. In an article, which took the form of a political obituary of Hume, Hume's tireless critic and arch adversary, Conor Cruise O'Brien concedes the dramatic impact of that manoeuvre:

> John Hume has had more influence on the political life of this whole island, and on Anglo-Irish relations, than any of the six Taoisigh who have governed in the Republic since the premiership of Sean Lemass [1959–66]. For more than 20 years now John Hume has controlled the policy of every Dublin Government towards Northern Ireland … John Hume's most brilliant achievement in the politics of these islands was the breakthrough which led to the Anglo-Irish Agreement of 1985. Formally, neither John Hume nor any other Northern politician was a party to that Agreement. But that is precisely how John Hume wanted it to be. John Hume knew that any Government in Dublin would consult him about every step they might take in the consultative role they would be granted by the British under the Anglo-Irish Agreement, so that he would effectively control the Irish side of the working of the Agreement. The unionists, on the other hand, would be entirely shut out and in the dark. For the first time the minority in Northern Ireland would have more access to power and authority than the majority there. The insight that led to the upgrading of the nationalists and downgrading of the unionists was an exceptionally brilliant one. The insight was that nationalists could get more from the British by asking for the moment less than they had ever asked for before … Every informed person knew that the real architect of the modified nationalist claim was John Hume. Only he had the authority

to scale down the nationalist demand, and only he had the political genius to see that the scaling down was the key to the advancement of the nationalist cause. [10]

By bringing the United States into the frame, Hume achieved a very subtle but necessary change in Anglo-Irish relations. That step was like the process of changing a parallelogram by shifting its trapezoid rightwards and forming it into a rectangle: while the area of the rectangle is the same as the original parallelogram, its shape is visibly new. With the United States taking a seat at the negotiations, the negotiations were necessarily conducted at a higher level of seriousness and the British were much more bound to honour the agreement that resulted from them, a commitment which had been lacking in the past. That change was a precondition to the political progress required across the three sets of relationships.

If Hume is comparable in motivation, skill and determination to an historical figure, who might his analogue be? In May 1891, when Charles Stewart Parnell was politically defeated, socially ostracised and a few months from his death, he travelled to Belfast. There Parnell made an extraordinary plea to the people of the North. He urged the Protestant majority in the North 'to leave no stone unturned' to conciliate with the Catholic minority in the North and thereby to advance the cause of freedom throughout Ireland. Ireland could never, he argued, be free and independent 'until Ireland is *practically* united' [author's emphasis].[11] Parnell's stress on uniting people and making common cause between the different sections of the people on the island would hardly have changed if he were to have witnessed the partition of the country three decades later. The border became a convenient bugbear for irredentist Nationalists and a blockade behind which veto reliant Unionists could remain; it gave the question of territory infinitely more focus than it deserved, but it did not alter the nature of the problem in Ireland. The border became yet another symptom of an underlying problem, and the perspective that the removal of the border would solve all of Ireland's problems is at best ahistorical. It is also an abdication. Hume's earliest statement at the national level involved an urge to his fellow Nationalist-minded citizens to make a 'constructive contribution on either the social or economics plane to the development of Northern Ireland which is, after all, a substantial part of the United Ireland for which they strive'.[12]

In a notable circularity, Hume told the newspaper where he had nailed his theses in 1964 a full thirty-three years later: 'What I did was logical. To analyse the problem and on the basis of that analysis...to use every influence I had to try and solve that problem.'[13] The validity of his analysis was key to achieving the influence. His extraordinary political ability and dedication in using that influence to effect the requisite change in his country makes Hume a figure of rare stature in Irish history. Seamus Mallon puts this well: 'He was teaching in St Columb's, involved with the credit union, inside was a man who had something big to do and he did it. I was there, I could touch it, I saw it happening. There is a greatness about his political life, what he did and what he helped to change. I would put him in the same breath as Parnell and Daniel O'Connell.'

John Hume's Nobel Lecture

Oslo, 10 December 1998

Your Majesties, Members of the Norwegian Nobel Committee, Excellencies, Ladies and Gentlemen.

I would like to begin by expressing my deep appreciation and gratitude to the Nobel committee for bestowing this honour on me today. I am sure that they share with me the knowledge that, most profoundly of all, we owe this peace to the ordinary people of Ireland, particularly those of the North who have lived and suffered the reality of our conflict. I think that David Trimble would agree with me that this Nobel prize for peace which names us both is in the deepest sense a powerful recognition from the wider world of the tremendous qualities of compassion and humanity of all the people we represent between us.

In the past 30 years of our conflict there have been many moments of deep depression and outright horror. Many people wondered whether the words of W.B. Yeats might come true:

'Too long a sacrifice Can make a stone of the heart.'

Endlessly our people gathered their strength to face another day and they never stopped encouraging their leaders to find the courage to resolve this situation so that our children could look to the future with a smile of hope. This is indeed their prize and I am convinced that they understand it in that sense and would take strong encouragement from today's significance and it will powerfully strengthen our peace process.

Today also we commemorate and the world commemorates the adoption 50 years ago of the Universal declaration of Human Rights and it is right and proper that today is also a day that is associated internationally with the support of peace and work for peace because the basis of peace and stability, in any society, has to be the fullest respect for the human rights of all its people. It is right and proper that the European Convention of Human Rights is to be incorporated into the domestic law of our land as an element of the Good Friday Agreement.

In my own work for peace, I was very strongly inspired by my European experience. I always tell this story, and I do so because it is so simple yet so profound and so applicable to conflict resolution anywhere in the world. On my first visit to Strasbourg in 1979 as a member of the European Parliament. I went for a walk across the bridge from Strasbourg to Kehl. Strasbourg is in France. Kehl is in Germany. They are very close. I stopped in the middle of the bridge and I meditated. There is Germany. There is France. If I had stood on this bridge 30 years ago after the end of the second world war when 25 million people lay dead across our continent for the second time in this century and if I had said: 'Don't worry. In 30 years' time we will all be together in a new Europe, our conflicts and wars will be ended and we will be working together in our common interests', I would have been sent to a psychiatrist. But it has happened and it is now clear that European Union is the best example in the history of the world of conflict resolution and it is the duty of everyone, particularly those who live in areas of conflict to study how it was done and to apply its principles to their own conflict resolution.

All conflict is about difference, whether the difference is race, religion or nationality. The European visionaries decided that difference is not a threat, difference is natural. Difference is of the essence of humanity. Difference is an accident of birth and it should therefore never be the source of hatred or conflict. The answer to difference is to respect it. Therein lies a most fundamental principle of peace – respect for diversity.

The peoples of Europe then created institutions which respected their diversity – a Council of Ministers, the European Commission and the European Parliament – but allowed them to work together in their common and substantial economic interest. They spilt their sweat and not their blood and by doing so broke down the barriers of distrust of centuries and the new Europe has evolved and is still evolving, based on agreement and respect for difference.

That is precisely what we are now committed to doing in Northern Ireland. Our Agreement, which was overwhelmingly endorsed by the people, creates institutions which respect diversity but ensure that we work together in our common interest. Our Assembly is proportionately elected so that all sections of our people are represented. Any new administration or government will be proportionately elected by the members of the Assembly so that all sections will be working together. There will be also be institutions between both parts of Ireland and between Britain and Ireland that will also respect diversity and work the common ground.

Once these institutions are in place and we begin to work together in our very substantial common interests, the real healing process will begin and we will erode the distrust and prejudices of out past and our new society will evolve, based on agreement and respect for diversity. The identities of both sections of our people will be respected and there will be no victory for either side.

We have also had enormous solidarity and support from right across the world which has strengthened our peace process. We in Ireland appreciate this solidarity and support – from the United States, from the European Union, from friends around the world – more than we can say. The achievement of peace could not have been won without this goodwill and generosity of spirit. We should recall too on this formal occasion that our Springtime of peace and hope in Ireland owes an overwhelming debt to several others who devoted their passionate intensity and all of their skills to this enterprise: to the Prime Ministers, Tony Blair and Bertie Ahern, to the President of the United States of America Bill Clinton and the European President Jacques Delors and Jacques Santer and to the three men who so clearly facilitated the negotiation, Senator George Mitchell former Leader of the Senate of the United States of America, Harri Holkerri of Finland and General John de Chastelain of Canada. And, of course, to our outstanding Secretary of State, Mo Mowlam.

We in Ireland appreciate this solidarity and support – from the United States; from the European Union, from friends around the world – more than we can say. The achievement of peace could not have been won without this good will and generosity of spirit. Two major political traditions – share the Island of Ireland. We are destined by history to live side by side. Two representatives of these political traditions stand here today. We do so in shared fellowship and a shared determination to make Ireland, after the hardship and pain of many years, a true and enduring symbol of peace.

Too many lives have already been lost in Ireland in the pursuit of political goals. Bloodshed for political change prevents the only change that truly matter: in the human heart. We must now shape a future of change that will be truly radical and that will offer a focus for real unity of purpose: harnessing new forces of idealism and commitment for the benefit of Ireland and all its people.

Throughout my years in political life, I have seen extraordinary courage and fortitude by individual men and women, innocent victims of violence. Amid shattered lives, a quiet heroism has born silent rebuke to the evil that violence represents, to the carnage and waste of violence, to its ultimate futility.

I have seen a determination for peace become a shared bond that has brought together people of all political persuasions in Northern Ireland and throughout the island of Ireland.

I have seen the friendship of Irish and British people transcend, even in times of misunderstanding and tensions, all narrower political differences. We are two neighbouring islands whose destiny is to live in friendship and amity with each other. We are friends and the achievement of peace will further strengthen that friendship and, together, allow us to build on the countless ties that unite us in so many ways.

The Good Friday Agreement now opens a new future for all the people of Ireland. A future built on respect for diversity and for political difference. A future where all can rejoice in cherished aspirations and beliefs and where this can be a badge of honour, not a source of fear or division.

The Agreement represents an accommodation that diminishes the self-respect of no political tradition, no group, no individual. It allows all of us – in Northern Ireland and throughout the island of Ireland – to now come together and, jointly, to work together in shared endeavour for the good of all.

No-one is asked to yield their cherished convictions or beliefs. All of us are asked to respect the views and rights of others as equal of our own and, together, to forge a covenant of shared ideals based on commitment to the rights of all allied to a new generosity of purpose.

That is what a new, agreed Ireland will involve. That is what is demanded of each of us.

The people of Ireland, in both parts of the island, have joined together to passionately support peace. They have endorsed, by overwhelming numbers in the ballot box, the Good Friday Agreement. They have shown an absolute and unyielding determination that the achievement of peace must be set in granite and its possibilities grasped with resolute purpose.

It is now up to political leaders on all sides to move decisively to fulfil the mandate given by the Irish people: to safeguard and cherish peace by establishing agreed structures for peace that will forever remove the underlying causes of violence and division on our island. There is now, in Ireland, a passionate sense of moving to new beginnings.

I salute all those who made this possible: the leaders and members of all the political parties who worked together to shape a new future and to reach agreement; the Republican and Loyalist movements who turned to a different path with foresight and courage; people in all parts of Ireland who have led the way for peace and who have made it possible.

And so, the challenge now is to grasp and shape history: to show that past grievances and injustices can give way to a new generosity of spirit and action.

I want to see Ireland – North and South – the wounds of violence healed, play its rightful role in a Europe that will, for all Irish people, be a shared bond of patriotism and new endeavour.

I want to see Ireland as an example to men and women everywhere of what can be achieved by living for ideals, rather than fighting for them, and by viewing each and every person as worthy of respect and honour.

I want to see an Ireland of partnership where we wage war on want and poverty, where we reach out to the marginalised and dispossessed, where we build together a future that can be as great as our dreams allow.

The Irish poet, Louis MacNiece wrote words of affirmation and hope that seem to me to sum up the challenges now facing all of us – North and South, Unionist and Nationalist – in Ireland.

'By a high star our course is set, Our end is life. Put out to sea.'

That is the journey on which we in Ireland are now embarked.

Today, as I have said, the world also commemorates the adoption fifty years ago, of the Universal Declaration of Human Rights. To me there is a unique appropriateness, a sort of poetic fulfilment, in the coincidence that my fellow Laureate and I, representing a community long divided by the forces of a terrible history, should jointly be honoured on this day. I humbly accept this honour on behalf of a people who, after many years of strife, have finally made a commitment to a better future in harmony together. Our commitment is grounded in the very language and the very principles of the Universal Declaration itself. No greater honour could have been done me or the people I speak here for on no more fitting day.

I will now end with a quotation of total hope, the words of a former Laureate, one of my great heroes of this century, Martin Luther King Jr.

We shall overcome.

Thank you.

Endnotes

Chapter 1

1 John Hume, 'The Northern Catholic', *The Irish Times*, 18 May 1964.
2 John Hume, 'The Northern Catholic II', *The Irish Times*, 19 May 1964.
3 Seamus Deane, 'Why Bogside?', *Honest Ulsterman*, 27 (January–March 1971).
4 Unless otherwise annotated, all quotations from the major players in the life of John Hume are taken from the documentary, 'John Hume in America' that accompanies this book.
5 Jude Collins, *Tales out of School: St Columb's College Derry in the 1950s* (Dublin: The History Press, 2010), p. 206.
6 Parliamentary Papers, Proceedings: Parliament of Northern Ireland 1921–1972, *Hansard*, 72, p. 1801.
7 Maurice Fitzpatrick, *The Boys of St. Columb's* (Dublin: The Liffey Press, 2010), p. 159.
8 Conor Cruise O'Brien, 'Civil Rights: The Crossroads', *The Listener*, 24 October 1968.
9 See *The Autobiography of Terence O'Neill* passim.
10 P.J. McLoughlin, *John Hume and the Revision of Irish Nationalism* (Manchester: Manchester University Press, 2010), p. 16.
11 Parliamentary Papers, *Hansard*, 29 April 1969.
12 Parliamentary Papers, *Hansard*, 680, p. 72.
13 Parliamentary Papers, *Hansard*, 72, no. 914.
14 Parliamentary Papers, *Hansard*, 509, 28 June 1983.
15 Parliamentary Papers, *Hansard*, 72, pp. 511–12.
16 Parliamentary Papers, *Hansard*, 72, p. 1502.
17 Parliamentary Papers, *Hansard*, 73, p. 865.
18 Parliamentary Papers, *Hansard*, 76, p. 2006.
19 Parliamentary Papers, *Hansard*, 76, p. 2007.
20 Parliamentary Papers, *Hansard*, 77, p. 1247.
21 Eugene O'Connell (ed.), 'Interview with Eugene O'Connell', *Cork Literary Review (volume XIV)* (Cork: Bradshaw Books, 2011), p. 18.
22 Transcript of archival footage used in the documentary, 'John Hume in America'.
23 Maurice Fitzpatrick, *The Boys of St. Columb's* (Dublin: The Liffey Press, 2010), pp. 110–11.

Chapter 2

1 Joseph Lelyveld, 'Man in the News', *The New York Times*, 4 August 1972. Available at: http://www.nytimes.com/1972/08/04/archives/a-voice-for-peace-in-ulster-john-hume.html?mcubz=2&_r=0 (accessed on 7 June 2017).

2   Paul Routledge, *John Hume* (London: HarperCollins, 1997), p. 149.
3   Edward M. Kennedy Oral History, 'Interview with Carey Parker (10/20/2008)', Miller Center; University of Virginia, 20 October 2008. Available at: http://archive. millercenter.org/oralhistory/interview/carey_parker_10-20-2008 (accessed on 7 June 2017).
4   Edward M. Kennedy Oral History, 'Interview with Edward M. Kennedy (2/27/2006)', Miller Center; University of Virginia, 27 February 2006. Available at: http://archive. millercenter.org/oralhistory/interview/edward_m_kennedy_2-27-2006 (accessed on 7 June 2017).
5   Edward M. Kennedy Oral History, 'Interview with Carey Parker (10/20/2008)'.
6   Ibid.
7   John A. Farrell, *Tip O'Neill and the Democratic Century* (Boston: Little, Brown, 2001), p. 140.
8   Edward M. Kennedy Oral History, 'Interview with Edward M. Kennedy (4/3/2007)', Miller Center; University of Virginia, 3 April 2007. Available at: http://archive. millercenter.org/oralhistory/interview/edward-m.-kennedy-4-3-2007 (accessed on 7 June 2017).
9   Seamus Deane and Barre Fitzpatrick, 'Interview with John Hume', *The Crane Bag*, 4, 2 (1980–1).
10   The Sunningdale Agreement (December 1973). Available at: http://cain.ulst.ac.uk/ events/sunningdale/agreement.htm (accessed on 21 June 2017).
11   A letter dated 10 May 1974, from G.W. Harding of the Republic of Ireland Department to the Secretary of State for Northern Ireland, Merlyn Rees, quotes the US Department of State perspective on the John Hume visit to the US.
12   Robert Fisk, *Point of No Return: The Strike Which Broke the British in Ulster* (London: Times Books, 1975).
13   Seamus Heaney, 'Crediting Poetry', Nobel lecture delivered on 7 December 1995. Available   at   http://www.nobelprize.org/nobel_prizes/literature/laureates/1995/ heaney-lecture.html (accessed on 7 June 2017).
14   Brian Faulkner, *Memoirs of a Statesman*, edited by John Houston (London: Weidenfield and Nicolson, 1978), p. 237.
15   Maurice Fitzpatrick, 'An Interview with Seamus Deane', *Journal of Irish Studies*, 22 (2007), pp. 84–92.
16   Edward M. Kennedy Oral History, 'Interview with Edward M. Kennedy (2/27/2006)'.
17   'Ireland in the Atlantic Community', speech by Mr. John Hume, Member of the European Parliament, Airlie House Conference, Waterville, Ireland, Sunday, 23 September 1979.

Chapter 3

1   Paul Bew, *Ireland: The Politics of Enmity 1789–2006* (Oxford: Oxford University Press, 2007), p. 300.
2   Edward M. Kennedy Oral History, 'Interview with Edward M. Kennedy (2/27/2006)'.
3   Joseph Nye, 'Soft Power and Higher Education', *The Internet and the University* (Aspen: Educause, 2004), pp. 11–14. Available at: https://net.educause.edu/ir/library/ pdf/ffp0502s.pdf (accessed on 22 June 2017).

4   Edward M. Kennedy Oral History, 'Interview with Edward M. Kennedy (3/20/2006)', Miller Center; University of Virginia, 20 March 2006. Available at: http://archive. millercenter.org/oralhistory/interview/edward_m_kennedy_3-20-2006 (accessed on 22 June 2017).
5   Ibid.
6   Fitzpatrick, *The Boys of St. Columb's*, p. 159.
7   Edward M. Kennedy Oral History, 'Interview with Edward M. Kennedy (3/20/2006)'.
8   Ibid.
9   Kevin McNamara, *The MacBride Principles: Irish America Strikes Back* (Liverpool: Liverpool University Press, 2009), p. 2.
10   Jimmy Carter, 'Northern Ireland Statement on U.S. Policy', The American Presidency Project, 30 August 1977. Available at: http://www.presidency.ucsb.edu/ws/?pid=8014 (accessed on 22 June 2017).

Chapter 4

1   Office of the Press Secretary, 'Remarks by President Obama and Prime Minister Kenny of Ireland at "Friends of Ireland" Luncheon', The White House, 15 March 2016. Available at: https://obamawhitehouse.archives.gov/the-press-office/2016/03/15/ remarks-president-obama-and-prime-minister-kenny-ireland-friends-ireland (accessed on 22 June 2017).
2   'Atkins unlikely to sway SDLP', *The Irish Times*, 29 June 1979.
3   Seán Donlon, 'NI policy with Haughey in Power', *The Irish Times*, 27 July 2009. Available   at: https://www.irishtimes.com/opinion/ni-policy-with-haughey-in-power-1.707667 (accessed on 22 June 2017).
4   Ibid.
5   Leonard Downie Jr, 'The Donlon Affair', *The Washington Post*, 9 July 1980. Available at: https://www.washingtonpost.com/archive/politics/1980/07/09/the-donlon-affair/0484e63c-7132-4118-a13d-3d5c96b95d8f/?utm_term=.d4e7eb191caa (accessed on 22 June 2017).
6   Seán Donlon, 'Haughey bid to tighten grip on Northern policy derailed', *The Irish Times*, 28 July 2009. Available at: https://www.irishtimes.com/opinion/haughey-bid-to-tighten-grip-on-northern-policy-derailed-1.708214 (accessed on 22 June 2017).
7   Ibid.
8   US Department of State, 'Speaker Calls for New British Initiative on Northern Ireland', *Public Library of US Diplomacy*, 20 April 1979. Available at: https://wikileaks.org/ plusd/cables/1979DUBLIN01793_e.html (accessed on 22 June 2017).
9   James T. Cooper, '"A log-rolling, Irish-American politician, out to raise votes in the United States": Tip O'Neill and the Irish dimension of Anglo-American relations, 1977–1986', *Congress and the Presidency*, 42, 1 (2015), p. 22. Available at: https://radar. brookes.ac.uk/radar/file/c47e04bc-3d86-4286-b5a6-80316d4d119e/1/cooper2015log-rolling.pdf (accessed on 09 June 2017).
10   Seamus Deane, 'Who Began the Killing?', *The New York Review of Books*, 30 May 1974. Available at: http://www.nybooks.com/articles/1974/05/30/who-began-the-killing-1/ (accessed on 08 June 2017).
11   Cooper, 'A log-rolling, Irish-American politician', p. 25.

Chapter 5

1   Tim Pat Coogan, *Ireland in the Twentieth Century* (London: St Martin's Griffin, 2006), p. 542.

2   Irish Press Reporters, 'Taoiseach urges need for solution and lasting peace', *The Irish Press*, 5 May 1981. Available at: http://www.irishnewsarchive.com/ina_wp/wp-content/uploads/2016/05/Irish-Press-1931-1995-Tuesday-May-05-1981.pdf (accessed on 22 June 2017).

3   H.D.S. Greenway, 'Ireland's only hope', *The Boston Globe*, 28 October 1993.

4   Brian Hutton, 'Reagan was urged to pressure Thatcher over hunger strikes', *Irish Examiner*, 9 April 2013. Available at: http://www.irishexaminer.com/world/reagan-was-urged-to-pressure-thatcher-over-hunger-strikes-227789.html (accessed on 4 July 2017).

5   Edward M. Kennedy Oral History, 'Interview with Edward M. Kennedy' (2/27/2006).

6   *Hansard*, 'Death Penalty' HC Deb 13 July 1983, vol. 45 cc 882–986. Available at: http://hansard.millbanksystems.com/commons/1983/jul/13/death-penalty (accessed on 9 June 2017).

7   'Statement by Mr. John Hume, M.E.P. Leader of the Social Democratic and Labour Party, Northern Ireland' (21 September 1981).

8   Edward M. Kennedy Oral History Project, 'Peace and Reconciliation in Northern Ireland', 16 May 2016. See video resource at 1:04:05. Available at https://www.emkinstitute.org/explore-the-institute/public-events-programs/public/ohp-northern-ireland-2016 (accessed on 9 June 2017).

9   Dan Keenan, 'Blair praised in moving speech', *The Irish Times*, 14 February 2005. Available at: https://www.irishtimes.com/news/blair-praised-in-moving-speech-1.414789 (accessed on 22 June 2017).

Chapter 6

1   SDLP, *Towards a New Ireland: Proposals by the Social Democratic and Labour Party* (Belfast: Social Democratic and Labour Party, 1972). Available at: http://cain.ulst.ac.uk/events/crights/sdlp1972.htm (accessed 23 June 2017).

2   'The Way Forward – As I See It', Address by Mr John Hume, MEP, Leader of the SDLP, at St Anne's Cathedral, Belfast, 2 March 1982 / Servite Priory, Benurb, 3 March 1982.

3   Deane and Fitzpatrick, 'Interview with John Hume'.

4   RTÉ Archives, 'Thatcher Rules Out A Unified Ireland', 19 November 1994. Available at: http://www.rte.ie/archives/2014/1118/660538-out-out-out/ (accessed on 9 June 2017).

5   *The Guardian*, 26 November 1984.

6   'The Ins and Outs of Ireland', *The New York Times*, 24 November 1984. Available at: http://www.nytimes.com/1984/11/24/opinion/ins-outs-ireland-diplomatic-reports-full-frank-talks-are-those-that-fail-reach.html?mcubz=2 (accessed on 9 June 2017).

7   Cooper, 'A log-rolling, Irish-American politician', p. 31.

8   Letter from Speaker O'Neill to President Reagan, 13 December 1984.

9   Letter from President Reagan to Speaker O'Neill, 9 January 1985.

10   Margaret Thatcher moved from believing that British Parliament would respond to the wishes of the majority in Northern Ireland to affirming that it would. Article 1 (c) of the Anglo-Irish Agreement provides that 'if in the future a majority of the people of Northern Ireland clearly wish for and formally consent to the establishment of a united Ireland, they [the British and Irish governments] will introduce and support in the respective Parliaments legislation to give effect to that wish': http://cain.ulst.ac.uk/events/aia/aiadoc.htm.

11   Margaret Thatcher Foundation, 'Speech to Joint Houses of Congress', 20 February 1985. Available at: http://www.margaretthatcher.org/document/105968 (accessed on 9 June 2017).

12   Edward M. Kennedy Oral History, 'Interview with Edward M. Kennedy (2/27/2006)'.

13   Ibid.

14   See also, Conor O'Clery, 'Reagan in the White House leaned on Thatcher to reach historic agreement', The Irish Times, 6 November 2015. Available at: https://www.irishtimes.com/news/politics/reagan-in-the-white-house-leaned-on-thatcher-to-reach-historic-agreement-1.2429179 (accessed on 23 June 2017).

15   As of June 2017. See http://www.internationalfundforireland.com/ for more information about the work of the International Fund for Ireland.

16   Andrew J. Wilson, Irish America and the Ulster Conflict (Washington, D.C.: Catholic University of America Press, 1995).

17   Interview with a senior official.

18   Michael Lillis and David Goodall, 'Edging Towards Peace', Dublin Review of Books. Available at: http://www.drb.ie/essays/edging-towards-peace (accessed on 3 July 2017).

19   Edward M. Kennedy Oral History, 'Interview with John Hume', The Miller Center: University of Virginia (29 September 2005). Available at; http://archive.millercenter.org/oralhistory/interview/john_hume (accessed on 9 June 2017).

20   'Hume is now "uncrowned king" of NI, says Paisley', The Irish Times, 29 May 1986.

Chapter 7

1   'Ireland in the Atlantic Community', speech by John Hume, 23 September 1979.

2   Kevin Cullen, 'The long, bloody path to Irish peace', The Boston Globe, 19 April 1998.

3   Edward M. Kennedy Oral History, 'Interview with Edward M. Kennedy (27/2/2006)'.

4   Edward M. Kennedy Oral History, 'Interview with Nancy Soderberg', The Miller Center: University of Virginia, 9 October 2008. Available at http://archive.millercenter.org/oralhistory/interview/nancy_soderberg (accessed on 11 June 2017).

5   In a letter from Hume to Adams. See Routledge, John Hume, p. 221.

6   Paul Hamann, Real Lives: At the Edge of the Union, BBC Television (1985). See also, Lisa O'Carroll, 'The truth behind Real Lives', The Guardian, 12 December 2005. Available at: https://www.theguardian.com/media/2005/dec/12/mondaymediasection.northernireland (accessed on 23 June 2017).

7   Times Wire Services, 'Protestants in Ulster Mark 1689 Victory', Los Angeles Times, 5 April 1988. Available at http://articles.latimes.com/1988-04-05/news/mn-565_1_protestant-march (accessed 11 June 2017).

8   John Major, John Major: The Autobiography (London: HarperCollins, 1999), p. 413.

9   Edward M. Kennedy Oral History, 'Interview with Niall O'Dowd', Miller Center: University of Virginia, 18 November 2010. Available at: http://archive.millercenter. org/oralhistory/interview/niall_odowd (accessed on 11 June 2017).
10   Conor Cruise O'Brien, 'It's time for Mr Hume to go', *The Independent*, 31 March 1994. Available at: http://www.independent.co.uk/voices/its-time-for-mr-hume-to-go-1367169.html (accessed 11 June 2017).
11   *An Phoblacht/Republican News*, 2 June 1979.

Chapter 8

1   Padraig O'Malley, *The Uncivil Wars*, Third Edition (Beacon Press, Boston: Beacon Press), p. 99.
2   Father Seán McManus, 'The Macbride Principles', University of Minnesota: Human Rights Library, December 1997. Available at: http://hrlibrary.umn.edu/links/macbride. html (accessed on 23 June 2017).

Chapter 9

1   'Remarks at a Saint Patrick's Day Ceremony with Prime Minister Albert Reynolds of Ireland and an Exchange with Reporters', The American Presidency Project, 17 March 1993. Available at: http://www.presidency.ucsb.edu/ws/index.php?pid=46348 (accessed on 24 June 2017).
2   'Exchange with Reporters Prior to Discussions with President Mary Robinson of Ireland', The American Presidency Project, 14 May 1993. Available at: http://www. presidency.ucsb.edu/ws/index.php?pid=46562 (accessed on 24 June 2017).
3   'Remarks at a Saint Patrick's Day Ceremony with Prime Minister John Bruton of Ireland and an Exchange with Reporters', The American Presidency Project, 17 March 1995. Available at: http://www.presidency.ucsb.edu/ws/index.php?pid=51115 (accessed on 24 June 2017).
4   Edward M. Kennedy Oral History, 'Interview with Edward M. Kennedy (20/3/2006)', Miller Center: University of Virginia, 20 March 2006. Available at: http://archive. millercenter.org/oralhistory/interview/edward_m_kennedy_3-20-2006 (accessed on 11 June 2017).
5   Edward M. Kennedy Oral History, 'Interview with Niall O'Dowd'.
6   Edward M. Kennedy Oral History, 'Interview with Edward M. Kennedy (20/3/2006)'.
7   Edward M. Kennedy Oral History, 'Interview with George Mitchell', Miller Center: University of Virginia, 6 September 2011. Available at: http://archive.millercenter.org/ oralhistory/interview/george_mitchell (accessed on 11 June 2017).
8   'The President's News Conference with Prime Minister John Major of the United Kingdom in London, England', The American Presidency Project, 29 November 1995. Available at: http://www.presidency.ucsb.edu/ws/?pid=50815 (accessed on 11 June 2017).
9   'Full text of this week's statement by the IRA', *The Independent*, 15 March 1994. Available at: http://www.independent.co.uk/news/uk/full-text-of-this-weeks-statement-by-the-ira-1429130.html (accessed on 24 June 2017).

10   Kevin Cullen, 'Ulster leader, backing IRA, prods British', *The Boston Globe*, 15 March 1994.

11   Eamonn McCann, 'History in the Re-making', *Hot Press*, 21 September 1994. Available at: https://www.hotpress.com/politics/HISTORY-IN-THE-REMAKING/482873.html (accessed on 11 June 2017).

12   Peter S. Canellos, 'Hume renews call for all-Ireland referendum', *The Boston Globe*, 14 March 1996.

13   *Charlie Rose*, PBS, 21 March 1996. Available at: https://charlierose.com/videos/3672 (accessed on 11 June 2017).

14   Deane and Fitzpatrick, 'Interview with John Hume'.

15   'Remarks by the President to the Citizens of Londonderry', *Congressional Record, Proceedings and Debates of the 104th Congress* (Washington: United States Government Printing Office), 104, 25 (30 November 1995), p. 35,515.

16   'Remarks at a Saint Patrick's Day Ceremony with Prime Minister John Bruton of Ireland and an Exchange with Reporters', The American Presidency Project, 15 March 1996. Available at: http://www.presidency.ucsb.edu/ws/index.php?pid=52549 (accessed on 24 June 2017).

17   'The President's News Conference with Prime Minister Tony Blair of the United Kingdom in London', The American Presidency Project, 29 May 1997. Available at: http://www.presidency.ucsb.edu/ws/?pid=54196 (accessed on 11 June 2017).

18   *On The Record*, 'Interview with John Hume', BBC TV, 17 October 1993. Available at: http://www.bbc.co.uk/otr/intext93-94/Hume17.10.93.html (accessed on 11 June 2017).

19   'Remarks by the President on the Northern Ireland Peace Process', The White House, Office of the Press Secretary, 10 April 1998. Available at: https://clinton2.nara.gov/WH/New/html/19980413-11395.html (accessed on 11 June 2017).

20   'Interview with Sean O'Huiginn', Edward M. Kennedy Institute (8 November 2010). Available at: https://www.emkinstitute.org/resources/sean-ohuiginn (accessed on 24 June 2017).

21   Seamus Heaney, 'The Hedgehog and The Fox', *The Irish Times*, 17 October 1998. Available at: http://www.irishtimes.com/news/the-hedgehog-and-the-fox-1.204446 (accessed on 11 June 2017).

22   Hume, 'The Northern Catholic II'.

Epilogue

1   Paul Routledge, *John Hume* (London: HarperCollins, 1997), p. 5.

2   George Orwell, 'Politics and the English Language', 1946. Available at: http://www.orwell.ru/library/essays/politics/english/e_polit (accessed on 22 June 2017).

3   *Towards a United Ireland: A Sinn Féin discussion document* (2016). Available at: https://www.sinnfein.ie/files/2016/Towards-a-United-Ireland.pdf (accessed on 22 June 2017).

4   *Towards a New Ireland: Proposals by the Social Democratic and Labour Party* (1972). Available at: http://cain.ulst.ac.uk/events/crights/sdlp1972.htm (accessed on 22 June 2017).

5   Conor O'Clery, 'How Irish America Came in from the Cold', *The Irish Times*, 20 January 1996.

6   Bette Browne, 'Irish America bids to put second Clinton in the White House', *The Irish Examiner*, 17 March 2015.

7   Office of the Press Secretary, 'Remarks by President Obama and Prime Minister Kenny of Ireland at "Friends of Ireland" Luncheon', The White House, 15 March 2016. Available at: https://obamawhitehouse.archives.gov/the-press-office/2016/03/15/remarks-president-obama-and-prime-minister-kenny-ireland-friends-ireland (accessed on 22 June 2017).

8   Henry McDonald, 'Unionists Condemn Gerry Adam Insult', *The Guardian*, 25 November 2014.

9   Transcript of archival footage used in the documentary, *John Hume in America*.

10   Conor Cruise O'Brien, 'Why John Hume has decided to leave Assembly', *Irish Independent*, 2 September 2000.

11   Paul Bew, *C.S. Parnell* (Dublin: Gill and MacMillan, 1980), p. 129.

12   John Hume, 'The Northern Catholic', *The Irish Times*, 18 May 1964.

13   'Humespeak is not apologising for single transferable speech', *The Irish Times*, 6 November 1999.

INDEX